MOSHE ARENS
STATESMAN AND SCIENTIST
SPEAKS OUT

MOSHE ARENS
STATESMAN AND SCIENTIST
SPEAKS OUT

MERRILL SIMON

With a Foreword by
Senator Daniel K. Inouye

Edited by Judith Featherman, Ed.D.

DEAN BOOKS
MIDDLE ISLAND, NEW YORK 11953

MOSHE ARENS
STATESMAN AND SCIENTIST
SPEAKS OUT

Library of Congress Cataloging in Publication Data

Arens, Moshe.
  Moshe Arens, statesman and scientist speaks out.

  Includes index.
  1. Israel. I. Simon, Merrill. II. Featherman, Judith.
III. Title.
DS102.95.A74 1988   956.94   87-71916
ISBN 0-9619243-0-6

Printed in the United States of America

Dedication

To my son, Melech, his wife, Devorah,
and my grandchildren, Yisroel Meir
and Esther Leah.

To my daughter, Michal, her husband, David,
and my grandchildren, Channah Sarah, Chava Eta,
and the latest addition to the family,
my grandson, Chaim Shalom.

Acknowledgments

I wish to extend my profound gratitude to:

My wife, Amalia, who continues her loving support with understanding and patience, while supporting my efforts in behalf of the Jewish people and the State of Israel.

My secretary, Joan Gannett, for coordinating and preparing materials for this as well as my four previous books.

Dr. Judith Featherman, for her invaluable editing of the questions and answers—an extremely tedious and time consuming job—which she meticulously executed not only with accuracy but meeting all deadlines. I knew of no other person more eminently qualified to undertake this task.

Contents

Foreword

Countries are always in need of leaders—in government, in military service, in business, and, in fact, in all walks of life. Often the question is asked, Are leaders born as leaders or are they developed? I believe it is a little of both, but certainly development and training have great impact on the final product. Usually there is one great influencing factor—or perhaps more—that makes a great leader.

In the case of Moshe Arens, I believe his early childhood experiences in Kaunas, Lithuania played a determining part in the development of his character and his outlook on life. In conversation with me he often noted that his origins were in Lithuania and Latvia. When the Nazi holocaust swept across Europe, 95 percent of the Jews living in Lithuania and Latvia did not survive. Moshe Arens has never forgotten that, and, to this day, he regards Israel as the living testament to the will to survive.

Arens was also tempered by his childhood and early learning experiences in America. Like so many others, his family fled to America and raised their children in the nourishing air of freedom and liberty. The lasting impression of this experience is set in his character as well. His love of freedom and liberty is something Arens has also never forgotten.

Then, like so many others, Arens left America to return to Israel in her hour of greatest need. In 1948, against his family's wishes, he went to Israel and joined the underground Irgun Zvi Leumi. There he came under the command and influence of a man who would be his political and philosophical mentor, Menachem Begin. The elements of his character which are most frequently used to describe him—integrity, ability to handle pressure, coolheaded credibility—were, I believe, forged in the heat of battle at Begin's side.

In the 1950s, Arens returned to America; and it was at this time, I think, that the elements of his intellect and his manner of thinking his way through difficult problems were shaped by his rigorous academic training at the Massachusetts Institute of Technology and the California Institute of Technology. This not only prepared him for a principal role in the development of the Kfir fighter and, as head of Israeli Aircraft Industries, the Lavi, but it also equipped him to appraise clinically events and policies of import to Israel.

With these years of experience and their tempering of mind and spirit, Moshe Arens became the reluctant diplomat. When his old commander, Menachem Begin, at the time the Prime Minister of Israel, asked that he serve on Israel's diplomatic front-line in Washington, Arens took on the task—reluctantly, but with the precision and perseverance that have become his hallmark. During his tenure in Washington, Moshe Arens faced a series of trying moments. Israel was confronted by a sequence of traumatic events: the return of the Sinai, the invasion of Lebanon, and the ensuing tragedy at Shabra and Shatilia in Beirut.

The tragedy in Beirut was a singular event in the relationship between Israel and the United States. Moshe Arens was under tremendous pressure; the accusations against the government he represented were mounting by the hour. The press and public in the United States were calling for the resignation of Prime Minister Begin and his defense minister, Ariel Sharon. In Israel, demands for an independent investigation culminated in the largest protest rally in Israel's history. Israel's former foreign minister, Abba Eban, noted at the time that Israel's ". . . policies, image, character, values, and aspirations [were] less understood and admired . . . than in any other period of her history."

If ever there was a need for a man known for coolheaded credibility, for a trusted leader to step forward, this was such a time. Through it all, Moshe Arens was Israel's spokesman—and champion—in Washington. As the Begin government became increasingly controversial, it was Moshe Arens who expressed Israel's dismay and shock at the killing in Beirut, which he called ". . . an event of unparalleled tragedy." He told Americans, "Since the creation of Israel in 1948, I don't remember one [event] that was itself so terribly painful and the cause of such horror."

It was he who stepped forward to assure the American people that, whatever the truth, in Israel all the facts would come out. He reminded us that Israel is a free and open society, much like that which he had known in his youth in America. With incisive logic and reason he turned away rumor and speculation. And, this man who is not known for giving way to emotion, showed to America a compassion and a depth of understanding few could emulate.

What follows is a book not so much <u>about</u> Moshe Arens as it is a book <u>of</u> Moshe Arens. His is a life deeply etched by experience. And in the pages of this book, in his thoughts and musings about Israel—and about Israel in the world— there is revealed a man whose thinking is the product of experience and reason. We find also a man whose passions center on the supreme and ultimate importance of Israel to the survival of the Jewish people. That, he reminds us, is something we should never forget.

DANIEL K. INOUYE
United States Senator

Editor's Preface

Mine has been a most gratifying experience. Although Mr. Simon makes reference in his introduction to similarities between himself and Mr. Arens in terms of their past experiences, he does not mention other commonalities I feel obliged to share with the reader. Both Merrill Simon and Moshe Arens are blessed with a height of intelligence and a depth of knowledge of the world around us that exceed imagination. Both perceive in a single question and its answer, not only the essence of that question's and answer's focal point but also the global ramifications for Israel, for world Jewry, and for world peace. Although their ideological backgrounds may have been different, both place the continued existence and welfare of the State of Israel before self. At times, it has been challenging to impose the required objectivity in those areas where their positions may differ, but the task has been rewarding. It is my privilege to have come to know, and somewhat understand, these two incredibly great minds.

And mine, too, has been a most clarifying experience. I've known since the year I lived in Israel that, even though I was returning to the same country, the same community, the same job, the same family, and the same friends, my life would be very different. And different it has been. My Jewish heritage, which, previously, I simply took for granted, has become my most prized possession. My Jewish education has come alive, and the focus of my attention is almost exclusively on things Jewish. My goal is to contribute to the survival of the State of Israel and of the Jewish people. My dream is to make *aliyah*. In short, I have become a committed Jew. But if, previously, I had difficulty understanding just why—fathoming the underlying stream and recognizing the somewhat obscured reasons—now I have a much clearer picture. For this clarification, I am grateful to both Mr. Simon and Mr. Arens.

Judith Featherman

Introduction

During the fifty years prior to the establishment of the State of Israel, the Zionist movement and the Jewish Agency in Palestine, which operated as the "shadow" government, were controlled and staffed by Socialist Zionists. These were people who had shed the rigid Orthodox Jewish backgrounds acquired in their youth in Eastern Europe—mainly Russia—and settled in Palestine. They adopted a concept of Jewish emancipation that was a combination of Jewish nationalism and Marxist socialism and created such famous institutions as the Kibbutz, the Moshav, and the Histadrut (General Labor Federation).

Their accomplishments were nothing short of miraculous, given the adverse and impossible conditions under which they had to function—political, economic, and security wise. After the establishment of the State of Israel in May 1948, the Socialist Zionists governed and held the seats of power for twenty-nine years—until May 1977. Up to that date, to the outside world—including world Jewry—it was mainly due to the efforts of the Socialist Zionists that the State of Israel came into being and thrived.

The most famous Zionist and Israeli names came from among those who were Labor (Socialist) Zionists, whether it was from the ranks of the great ideologues such as A. D. Gordon, Berl Katznelson, Y. Ben Zvi, or Chaim Greenberg or from the ranks of the great generals such as Moshe Dayan, Yigal Allon, Yigal Yadin, or Yitzhak Rabin. These are just a few of those who became household names among Jewish communities throughout the world. To most, there was no other Israel but the Israel created in the image of the Labor Zionist movement, and there was no other relevant Zionist activity but theirs.

Billions of dollars were raised in America from within a Jewish community in which the bulk of the people neither worked as laborers nor were ideologically Socialists—certainly not Marxists. In fact, the bulk of the Jewish community tended to be ideologically liberal, and they were, in the main, either professionals or entrepreneurs who believed in and thrived under the American capitalistic free enterprise system. Of course, the really big givers among the Jewish multimillionaires were the great beneficiaries of capitalism who made their money in such uniquely capitalistic endeavors as real estate, commerce, and industry. The Socialist Zionist leaders of Israel, who rejected G-d and the Jewish religion, had little problem raising money from the capitalist Jews in America who were also the main contributors to building the great Jewish religious institutions in America—whether Orthodox, Conservative, or Reform.

The Kibbutz, the Moshav, and the Histadrut had become synonomous with the State of Israel and those individuals at the helm. During the twenty-nine years of statehood, hundreds, if not thousands, of representatives of Labor Israel visited the United States and other Jewish communities throughout the Free World to raise money and spread the message of Israel. They visited Jewish community centers, "Ys," and synagogues of all three denominations to spread the word of the miracles of Israel and to raise money for her institutions, including universities, the Kupat Holim sick fund, and the Histadrut social welfare fund, and for recreational requirements such as swimming pools for Kibbutzim. To the vast majority of American Jewish leadership and committed rank and file, there was no Israel other than Labor Israel.

It was only in May 1977, when the Israeli electorate decided to transfer power to Menachim Began and his Likud Party, that the outside world—especially American Jewry—realized that there was an ideological alternative to the Labor Zionists, their institutions, and their people. Only then did they discover that there actually existed another Israel with another viewpoint on such issues as Judaism, the economy, and the disposition of the territories acquired during the June 1967 war.

Menachem Begin and the Likud party won the election again in 1981. In the election of 1984, there was a virtual split in the electorate, forcing the formation of the National Unity government, led by Labor Israel (Ma'arach) and the other Israel (Likud). These events have made it necesary for the American Jewish community, its leaders, and its friends to become aware of that "other" Israel, as represented by the Likud party. What were its roots, its ideology, its contribution to Zionist activity before and after statehood? Who were and are its leaders? What were and are their goals in contrast to those with which we have been all too familiar?

As an adult, I joined and became active in the Labor Zionist movement in 1960. I became an active participant in national Labor Zionist activities after being elected to the Labor Zionist Central Committee in 1964. I remained as an executive of the Labor Zionist Alliance until 1981. During a period of political inactivity, I had the opportunity to re-evaluate some of my Zionist positions. Presently, I am taking an active role in forming Techya-America, which has recently joined with the Herut party in this country.

I firmly believe it is necessary that the American Jewish community and its leaders become familiar with the roots, the ideology, the accomplishments, and the leaders of that "other" Zionist movement and that "other" Israel. This in no way detracts from the greatness of the "first" but only places their achievements, people, and ideology in proper historical context. The mere fact that the nearly 4 million Jews of Israel are almost equally split on which ideology or path the nation should take for the future, makes our knowledge and awareness of these two powerful political forces even more significant. The "other" nonreligious Zionist movement, of course, was the Revisionist party, physically and ideologically led by Vladimir Jabotinsky.

Having spent much of my adult life reading the works of the great Zionist thinkers, my personal heroes came from the ranks of the Labor Zionist movement. It is difficult not to look back with nostalgia at the development of practical Zionism as espoused by the great Labor Zionist thinkers and implementers. They were the creators of the nation's agricultural development through the Kibbutz and the Moshav movements, and they established the Histadrut, the greatest single labor union in the world, which pioneered the concept of social justice and espoused the dignity of the working men and women of (Palestine and) Israel, while literally creating her basic industries.

However, in order to do justice and to have a clear understanding of past events and all the forces that contributed to the creation and development of the State of Israel, I must admit it is necessary to comprehend the "other" Israel. It is essential, therefore, to understand the role played by Jabotinsky and the Zionist Revisionists. Menachem Begin was a pupil of Jabotinsky and took over his leadership in Palestine after Jabotinsky's death. In the post-State era, Begin was the articulator of Jabotinsky's ideologies; however, today the mantle of ideological heir to Zionist revisionism, as espoused by the *Herut* party (Likud), falls on the shoulders of Moshe Arens.

None of these men—Jabotinsky, Begin, or Arens—have been less dedicated to the unity of the Jewish people, Jewish national development, social justice, or the dignity of the Jews than their Labor Zionist adversaries. They have been no less articulate in presenting the case of Israel and the Jewish people in world forums or before the leaders of the Western nations.

I first met Moshe Arens in the summer of 1977 in his office near Savyon. He was a member of the Knesset and served as chairman of its Defense and Foreign Affairs Committee. I interviewed him for an article for the California-based Anglo-Jewish newspaper, *Israel Today*, for which I functioned as the national political editor. It soon became apparent that there were unusual similarities in our backgrounds. We both had advanced degrees in Engineering—he in aeronautical from M.I.T. and Cal-Tech and I in electronics from Purdue. We both worked as engineers in New Jersey in the mid-fifties—he designing jet engines, after having served in the War of Independence, and I working on semiconductors, after returning from the Korean War. He returned to Israel in 1957 to become a professor at the Technion, while I was teaching at the Newark College of Engineering. In 1962, he joined Israel Aircraft Industries as Vice President of Engineering and remained there until 1971 when he formed an engineering consulting firm. During that period, I, too, was a vice president and corporate officer of an electronics company and left it to form my own consulting firm. At that time, Moshe Arens and I were in the process of forming a partnership, Arens-Simon Inc.—a consulting firm for bringing American high-technology companies to

Israel in order to establish manufacturing and R & D divisions for export to Europe. However, Arens accepted Begin's offer to be Israel's ambassador in Washington, so our partnership never came to fruition. Arens later replaced Ariel Sharon as Israel's Minister of Defense—after the Sabra and Shatilla inquiry—and has since become Minister Without Portfolio in the National Unity government which was formed in 1984.

Arens is a soft-spoken, lucid man with a quick, incisive mind. His confident speech comes from the unique combination of success, experience, and intelligence. I do believe it is essential that Moshe Arens, as a disciple of Jabotinsky and the ideological heir to his brand of Zionism, address issues concerning internal Israel, world Jewry, and Israel's relations with the rest of the world. He has the required intellectual capacity, personal integrity, and deep commitment to the Jewish people. He holds the respect and admiration of his political opponents within the Labor party, as well as comrades within the *Herut* party. He also became known and respected by the American Jewish community during his very successful tenure as Israel's ambassador to Washington.

I chose a question and answer format for this book because it is not possible for me to be objective when it comes to Moshe Arens. I believe in him as a person and as a leader. I support much of what he stands for but, certainly, not all his positions, since my Zionist background differs greatly from his. Therefore, Moshe Arens and I agreed that the question and answer format would be best suited for achieving the objectives of this book, as I did not want to play the role of supporter, apologist, or interpreter of Moshe Arens—only the role of a reporter.

In order to achieve objectivity, I sought the assistance of Dr. Judith Featherman to edit both the questions and the answers. By virtue of her background, education, and experiences, she is eminently qualified. Dr. Featherman comes from the ranks of American Conservative Judaism and is a product of its synagogue schools as well as a graduate of Gratz Hebrew College of Philadelphia. She has been active in synagogue life and in Jewish professional, educational, and cultural organizations. Dr. Featherman holds a B.S. in Education, a M.Ed. in Educational Psychology, and an Ed.D. in Special Education. Additionally, she lived in Israel from August 1984 to July 1985. In terms of Israeli politics, she had no particular political orientation, nor did she previously know Moshe Arens personally.

To implement this book and accurately capture the viewpoints of Arens regarding the vast scope of material required over one hundred hours to prepare and finalize the questions, six trips to Israel for thirty taping sessions exceeding sixty hours of discussion and yielding nearly fifty hours of tape, countless hours of transcription, and the production of five draft copies. Interviewing took place at the home of Arens in Savyon and in his offices in East Jerusalem, Tel Aviv, and the Knesset.

Part One

On Internal Israel

On Internal Israel

Moshe Arens' Overview

In many ways, a new nation is being built in Israel—a Jewish nation "reborn" in its ancient homeland. It is based on the ingathering of the exiles from the four corners of the world and their amalgamation into one society. This is one of Israel's greatest successes—that people from England, Kurdistan, Morocco, Poland, Russia, the United States, and Yemen have created one integrated society. Although today in Israel, we can still differentiate between Ashkenazi and "oriental" Jews, within another twenty or thirty years, because of the intermingling of Jews from different lands, we'll have an even more uniform society and nation.

I am hopeful that we can bring Soviet Jewry here. That will mean an influx of hundreds of thousands of Jews from the Soviet Union who've kept their Jewishness and longing for Israel alive over fifty to seventy years of Bolshevik rule. I am hopeful, too, that large numbers of Jews from the Western world—especially the United States—will come to Israel. They have a great contribution to make because they bring with them all the attributes, all the accumulated knowledge, and all the norms and standards that exist in the Western world today. In ten or twenty years, therefore, I foresee Israel with a much larger Jewish population that would include large-scale immigration from the East and the West.

Israel is a unique event in the history of man. We will continue to be imbued with the feeling that we are doing something very special here and that we will, therefore, continue to attract Jews from all over the world. Every Jew living today and every Jew born in the future is really a survivor of the Holocaust. They would not be alive, or born, if Hitler had had his way. We have a special obligation to assure the defeat of Hitler, to assure the existence of the Jewish people, and to assure that the message of the Jewish people will continue to come out of Zion. That can only be achieved here in Israel.

It is essential that we bring about a much greater level of integration of the Arab population into Israel's society so that they feel they are equal partners in the building of this country. In this area, we still have a long way to go, but I'm

3

convinced we're going to go all the way—to apply our Western standards and values to the large, ethnic minority that lives among us.

There are already signs of Westernization— Israelization—of our Arab population. Today, many of Israel's Arabs take pride in the fact that they are Israeli Arabs. In time, many of the Arabs in Judea and Samaria will also feel that way and will want to be a part of Israeli society. They will take part in the upbuilding of Israel, carry the full burden of Israeli citizenship, and be ready to defend Israel against aggression from surrounding Arab countries. It is the real key to peace in the area.

I am convinced that, in time, we will have peace, but Israel must remain strong enough to win and to deter war. Even though we are very inferior in numbers, we can continue to maintain the capability of winning and deterring wars by making up in quality for the quantity we lack.

Militarily, we must continue to read the impact of technology on the battlefield so that we are always ahead of others in applying that technology to the battlefield. Today, Israel already produces some of the most advanced weapon systems in the world. And this is only the beginning. We have the basic capability, the motivation, and, unfortunately, the operational experience to design and develop the technology-intensive weapon systems required to maintain Israel's qualitative military superiority.

Israel must be part of the Western world—not only in terms of values but also in terms of her economic system. The Israeli gross national product (GNP) per capita right now is a little above one-third of what it is in the United States. It's very difficult to explain the discrepancy. It's not explained by our allocation to defense—which might reduce our full potential by 10 or 15 percent, but certainly not by 50 or 60 percent. The reason is that our overall economic system is inefficient—what I call a Bolshevik economy. It's like having a factory with good workers but poor management—a factory that is running in the red because the management simply doesn't know how to use the capable workers it has. We must do away with government and labor union involvement in business and allow freedom for private enterprise.

The Israeli population is highly skilled. Obviously, that means that Israel's economy will be based more and more on high-technology, skill-intensive activities in industry as well as in services. Although the future directions of technological endeavors are difficult to predict, Israel will always be at the forefront—a leader in research, as well as in translating research into industrial products and services. We shall develop and produce high-technology products not only for our own small home market but also for much larger markets in the most advanced countries in the world. Although these markets are quite distant from us and market penetration may be difficult, we shall continue to be successful in those pursuits. The recent free-trade agreement between Israel and the United States will be beneficial. And we shall continue to encourage established American companies to come to Israel and produce here. In that way, they have access to a very talented pool of manpower, and we are relieved of the concern about marketing.

In terms of the number of people who practice their religion, Israel is a secular country—even more so than most Western countries. What does characterize Israel as compared to other Western countries, however, is that those who are religious also participate in politics in the form of religious parties. Because of the coalition system that we have, it is these religious parties that frequently are in a position to make demands that the party forming the government must meet. This explains the intensity of conflict that exists between the secular and the religious and why many in the secular population in Israel feel that the religious are dictating their way of life. As we move closer to an executive, two-party system, we will find that the religious, while at liberty to practice their religion free from infringement, will not have that kind of political power and will not, therefore, have the leverage to impose their will upon the entire population of Israel.

It is fortunate that we live in an age when a country's human resources are more important than her resources under the ground. The quality of population in Israel is among the highest in the world. In terms of native talents, skills, and motivation, there is no country in the world that can match Israel's human resources. This will be the basis for Israel's becoming a very strong country economically, a very affluent country, and a country with a very high standard of living.

Israel should enter the twenty-first century economically, militarily, and technically stronger and better equipped to handle the problems facing her than at any time in her short history.

Merrill Simon's Overview

The significant differences between the two major parties in Israel's National Unity government—Labor *(Ma'arach)* and Likud *(Herut)*—appear to cluster in three areas: the approach to accepted religious practice as it relates to Orthodox, Conservative, and Reform Judaism; the approach to peace with Israel's Arab neighbors as it relates to settlement in and relinquishing of the administered territories; and the approach to Israel's economy as it relates to private and collective activity. In terms of religious practice, Likud remains sympathetic toward the needs and wants of Orthodox Judaism, while Labor supports the acceptance and legalization of Conservative and Reform Judaism in Israel.

Regarding their attitude toward settlement in Judea and Samaria and the relinquishing of land in future peace agreements, Likud favors massive expansion—increased quantity and scope—of settlements and a halt to territorial concessions. Labor, on the other hand, favors containment of further settlement in Judea and Samaria and has indicated willingness to negotiate some territory for future peace. My personal assessment of this situation is that these differences may be more tactical than substantive.

While both Likud and Labor support a mixed economy for Israel, they differ on which sector of the economy deserves priority. The Likud believes that the private entrepreneurial sector should be emphasized; Labor is traditionally on the side of the collective sector. Both agree that Israel's economic well-being should rely on high-technology industries with short to medium production. Both understand that Israel cannot afford the traditional smokestack industries and cannot compete in world markets with high-volume consumer products.

Aliyah (Jewish immigration) to Israel has fallen considerably in the last decade and currently is only keeping pace with the number of citizens who are leaving the country. Now, any growth in population is the result of the discrepancy between births and deaths in a given year. The key to Israel's future economic growth lies in her ability to attract large numbers of Jewish immigrants from all parts of the world. They will provide the skilled, semiskilled, and unskilled labor that is so essential for fueling an expanding economy.

For Israel to succeed in reaching her economic growth potential and meeting the challenges of the future, an influx of Western immigrants is essential. We know that most of the Western immigration now is comprised predominantly of young professional Orthodox Jews who have sufficient ideological motivation to move to a land where economic sacrifice is required. These people generally settle in Jerusalem, Judea, Samaria, or the Golan Heights. They represent the most successful *aliyah* in the past ten years. They bring high-technology skills with them and generally find their place in the private sector.

In pre-State Israel, and in the State's early years, the Kibbutz and Moshav were the major attractions for *aliyah* and, as a result, absorbed the most immmigrants. Now, the conditions for expanding the Kibbutz and Moshav movements no longer exist. There is no longer any organizational structure for the absorption into Israeli society of nonreligious, ideological, middle-class professionals. Most middle-income families from the West cannot afford the move to Israel and certainly cannot withstand the necessary economic sacrifices. Many are willing to give up a lot, but few can cope with the discrepancy that they encounter. In other words, *aliyah*, except for a chosen few, is much too costly and is beyond the means of the vast majority of young, middle-income Western Jews.

Labor's failure to create urban collectives based on high- tech industries, which could attract ideologically motivated Western youth of varying religious commitments, has created a vacuum that must be filled. Such collectives, based on an individual industry, could be established in urban, suburban, or rural settings. These collectives would encourage the settlement of Judea and Samaria, the Galilee, and the Negev, as people would be encouraged to settle within commuting distance of Israel's four major cities—Haifa, Beersheva, Jerusalem, and Tel Aviv—in order to avail themselves of the facilities, services, and cultural activities that urban centers have to offer. This activity, in concert with the private entrepreneurial endeavors supported by Likud, would assure Israel's future economic growth.

ECONOMY

What do you see as the role of government in the economy in Israel?

Certainly far less than its current role! One of the things that characterizes the Israeli economy at the present time and has, in effect, since Israel came into existence, is the very extensive and overbearing role of the Israeli government in the economy. As a matter of fact, the Israeli government intervenes massively, almost brutally, in all the day-to-day affairs in the marketplace. It owns a large part of the business enterprises. It sets prices, wages, and the foreign-exchange rate. It even sets the prices of stocks on the stock exchange, on occasion. In Israel, 30 percent of the civilian work force is on the public payroll in one way or another. So all these things will have to be tackled. The Israeli economy in future years, I'm sure, will begin to look more like Western economies, with a much smaller government role. The Israeli government will restrict itself to the role of policeman, making sure the rules of the game are being followed, but will not be participating actively in business itself.

The founding fathers of the State of Israel were Socialist Zionists who believed that Israel had to centrally plan her economy and that the society had to be egalitarian. Given that you believe Israel's future development is in technology-intensive products, how do you reconcile the narrow wage differential among scientists, engineers, and technicians that presently exists? Do you believe Israel can meet her technology growth targets and still maintain this egalitarian approach? What kind of salary differentials do you envision?

The Socialist ideology that was adhered to by many of Israel's founding fathers—certainly the people from the Labor party—was an ideology based on the assumption, quite current in the early part of the twentieth century, that central planning would lead to efficiency in the overall economic system: in other words, government bureaucrats would make good managers of the overall economic system. There are very few people around who believe that today. I suppose there was a time, even in the United States, when maybe not Socialists but "new dealers" felt that the government had a great deal to contribute to steering and directing the economy. Based on what we've seen in various countries throughout the world, especially since World War II, the general conclusion is that the less government interferes, the better the economy runs. That is not to say that there is no task for the government in economic affairs but, clearly, today it is generally agreed that it should be limited.

Israel's economic problems are in a large measure a result of the fact that the Israeli economy was built on massive government interference. And we can add to that the interference of the Histadrut, which, while not officially a government agency, is almost a para-government establishment—a labor union that is Israel's biggest business organization. All of that has contributed to reducing the efficiency of the Israeli economy.

The reduction of the efficiency of the Israeli economy has meant that the government has had trouble collecting in revenue what it expends. It expends far too much, but it needs those monies in order to cover the costs of its very large-scale operation. In its attempts to collect revenues to cover its expenditures, or as large a percentage of its expenditures as possible, it has established a very high tax rate. That is the main reason for what you call the egalitarian wage structure. It's not so much that an engineer doesn't make more than a technician or a laborer. But when we impose the tax structure on the salary structure, we find the engineer doesn't make very much more than people considerably further down in the labor grade.

The net result—very small wage differentials and, therefore, very little incentive for productivity or for exerting oneself at work—is a very negative element in the present Israeli economy. We must rectify this before the economy can really take off. This can only be achieved by reducing the taxes that are collected, reducing the tax rates, and giving the people a higher share of the income they obtain by working harder or by working more. And that can only be attained by the government's reducing its involvement in the Israeli economy.

The income tax rate in Israel is one of the highest in the Western world. Since it is an accepted axiom that high taxes reduce worker initiative and incentive, what do you believe the tax rate or structure should be in order to stimulate productivity, improve the work ethic of labor, and attract technologists to this country from the Western world, especially the United States?

Everyone who has looked at the Israeli economy—whether they are Israelis or people from abroad like George Shultz, who has taken a real interest in our economy—has said "reduce taxes." If there is such a thing as a Laffer Curve— some point at which increasing the tax rates actually reduces tax revenues, then Israel is certainly beyond that point. There is sufficient reason to assume that if the government were to reduce tax rates, actual tax revenues would eventually increase. I firmly believe that by increasing incentives, we would increase productivity; by increasing productivity, we would actually get more tax revenues at lower tax rates.

The problem has been, and continues to be, that the Israeli government has a large budget deficit. In other words, it spends considerably more than it collects in revenues and is able to raise in loans. We have rectified that a little bit with the recent economic program the government has undertaken; however, it still represents a problem. Right now, the immediate effect of reducing tax rates is to increase that budget deficit, and the immediate effect of that is to decrease government revenues. This has been the "Catch 22" of Israeli economic policy.

Everybody knows that we've already decreased tax rates. Yet there's concern that if we decrease them significantly again, we will increase the government budget deficit and perhaps return the country into another inflationary spiral. Sooner or later, we must reduce tax rates; it's clear that the only way we can reduce tax rates is to decrease government expenditure. This again means decreasing government involvement in the economy.

What do you see as the role of Histadrut in the Israeli economy?

Well, that's really the second layer. Today everyone is aware that the Israeli government's role in the economy is excessive and that most of our economic problems stem from this over-involvement. People are far more hesitant to discuss another matter of very similar nature—the involvement of the Histadrut Labor Federation in the economy.

Most people know that the Labor Federation in Israel is not a trade union in the conventional Western sense. It's an octopus which, in addition to dealing with the interests of the working people organized in the trade union, runs agricultural enterprises, industries, banks, insurance companies, and trading corporations. It controls approximately 15 to 20 percent of the GNP. That, in my view, does not have a positive effect on the Israeli economy or on the efficiency of the Israeli economic system. It will be very important in the future for the Histadrut to reduce sharply its involvement in business enterprises and assume the conventional role of a labor union dedicated to protecting the rights and the working conditions of its members.

Was Ben Gurion correct during the latter period of his tenure as Prime Minister when he claimed, publicly, that the Histadrut's power had to be bridled because it was a shadow government within a government?

Yes. The power that is vested today in the Histadrut is gigantic. As I've indicated, the companies it owns produce close to one-fourth of the GNP. It owns one of the biggest banks, insurance companies, and construction companies in Israel. You name it, and they're in it. In many of the sectors of the Israeli economy, not only does the labor union own companies, but frequently it has a monopoly position in that sector—a concentration of power that, in my view, is excessive.

I don't know that the labor union has misused that power. In all fairness, it should be remembered that in the recent economic program, when salaried workers were called on to make very large sacrifices—when we eroded people's wages by 25 to 30 percent—the labor union and the leadership of the labor union acted very responsibly in cooperating and carrying out that program. It could not have been done without them. However, it is not healthy for a democratic country to have such a tremendous concentration of power and resources in the hands of the labor union.

The trend throughout the Western world is toward weaker labor unions with dwindling memberships. Israel is unique in that the Histadrut, the Labor Federation, not only represents the workers, but it is an employer as well. What do you see to be the trend in Israel in this regard?

I do not doubt that eventually the labor union is going to get out of the business of being in business. Certainly, my colleagues from the Labor party in the government will not agree with me. They'll probably fight this trend; however, there's no doubt that this is the trend. It's becoming clear—even to them. The Labor Federation is not a good business manager, and businesses run and owned by it are not being run well. In the final analysis, it's the people who work in these companies who pay the cost. This is not good for Israel and the Israeli economy, nor is it good for the Israeli worker.

Traditionally, labor unions take an adversarial role against management. Only in Israel, where the Histadrut owns so much industry, does it take an adversarial role against labor. Do you see these roles continuing?

If the Histadrut gets out of the business of being in business, as they should and eventually will, then that incongruous role of the Labor Federation acting as an employer and finding itself in conflict with the laborers will, of course, disappear from the Israeli scene.

It exists at this very moment in Israel. Solel Boneh, the largest contractor in Israel, which is owned by the Labor Federation, is in deep economic trouble. It may have to lay off a significant number of its employees. It is in dire conflict with the employees, who are threatening the Labor Federation and the secretary of the labor union because they fear inadequate compensation when fired. There is a clash between employer and employee, although the employer is actually the employee's representative.

What do you believe the role of the Histadrut should be in the future, given that government employment is decreasing, basic industries are dwindling, and manufacturing is moving toward advanced technologies with a higher percentage of technically educated personnel?

There is a very important role for the labor unions to play. When we implement all of the economic reforms currently in process and arrive at that point when the Israeli economy begins to resemble Western economies, then we will have many businesses that will run efficiently and return a profit. The traditional classic question of the division of that profit between owners of the companies and their workers will arise. This is the classic role that the labor union has to play.

Since the formation of the State of Israel, it has been government policy to maintain zero unemployment of employables. Do you believe that this policy should be continued?

It certainly should be an objective of the Israeli government and Israeli society not to have a high level of unemployment. That's the goal of any modern, or certainly Western, society—to keep unemployment at as low a level as possible. I doubt that it's possible to get it down to zero. There's a fractional level of unemployment in any economy in which people are free to move from one job to another or in which businesses close down, fail, or go bankrupt forcing people to move on to other jobs. The question is whether the society is ready to use any and all means to keep unemployment at a "zero" level.

In Israel's case, for a long period—even at the present time—the government has been ready to use "any and all means." What does "any and all means" mean? It means we have what we in Israel call "hidden unemployment." It means we have people "working" in companies who are really not working there but are getting a salary—people who go to work in the morning and come home in the evening, but don't do anything productive in the middle. There's an Israeli expression for that called "eight zero four." They go to work at eight, do zero work, and come home at four.

This policy is ruinous to Israel's economy. It means that we have a lot of businesses which, in effect, are not profitable and are not earning their way. How do they exist? How do salaries get paid? It's the Israeli taxpayer who makes up the difference. This is one of the major reasons why we have this horrific tax structure.

It's a closed loop. With this kind of a policy, the government has to have excessive tax rates. Excessive tax rates mean that people don't have an incentive to work, and if people don't have an incentive to work, the national product in the country is lower than it should be. The national product being lower than it should be means that tax revenues are lower than they might be, even at existing tax rates, which means the government has to raise tax rates more. And so it goes. This is how we got to where we are right now.

There's no substitute for a reasonably free economy where firms survive by virtue of being profitable, being able to stand on their own two feet, and having people who work for them really work and produce a value that is equivalent to the salary they are being paid (or, maybe, a little bit more to make up for taxes and for profits to the owners of the company). We don't have a section of the population that is unemployable—that doesn't have the talents or the skills required in this latter part of the twentieth century to produce something that is saleable. Since we do have a very talented and skilled population, there's no reason why there should be unemployment. All we need is a system that will employ them in an efficient manner.

Do you believe the size of the Israeli government work force should be reduced? If so, how do you suggest it be reduced?

We have at the present time 400,000 people on the public payroll in Israel, which represents 30 percent of the civilian work force. By any Western standard, that's far too much. To the best of my knowledge, there is no other example of that among Western countries whose economies are reasonably competitive and in reasonably good shape.

There's no doubt that 30 percent is too much of a burden for the productive sector to carry. On the average, it means we have to deduct 30 percent of people's salaries in taxes just to pay the wages of those 30 percent who are government-employed. It's the beginning of our impossible tax structure and another indication of the brutal government involvement in the economy, which is an outgrowth of government bureaucrats who spend their time trying to regulate the economy and conduct government services. I have no doubt that we must reduce the number of people employed in the public sector.

If you believe the number of people employed by the Israeli government must be reduced, how do you suggest the ensuing unemployment be handled?

There may be many disadvantages to Israel's being a small country, but one of the advantages is that our markets are unlimited. The market for Israeli firms is not just Israel; in fact, it isn't even primarily Israel. The markets for Israeli firms are in the Western world—first, and foremost, in the United States. These are unlimited markets.

We don't have the problem of finding sufficient markets for our products; therefore, we don't have the problem of being able to find sufficient jobs for our highly skilled population. If we had an efficient economy—good, competitive firms established in an economy working primarily for export, there would be no limit to the markets that Israel could gain. We would be limited only by the number of people we have living in Israel. Inherently, therefore, there should be no problem in transferring people from the public sector into the business sector where they would be working for export, rather than working for the government bureaucracy.

Do you believe the Israeli government should sell its ownership in existing enterprises? If so, why?

The Israeli government should sell its ownership in most of the government enterprises because it has no business being in business. We see time and again that the government is not a good manager and cannot run businesses economically. Neither is the Histadrut a good manager, which we see time and again, also. We see it in these very days of problems at Solel Boneh, the big contracting firm owned by the Histadrut, and in Bank Hapolaim, the bank that is owned by the Labor Federation. We see it, too, in companies like the Israeli shipyards owned by the government. You don't have to search very far for the reasons. The business of the government is to create a proper business climate—to see that business will be good—not to be in business.

What do you see as the role of the private sector in the Israeli economy?

At the present time, it's far smaller than it should be. Since we have so large a share of the economy controlled by the government and the Histadrut Labor Federation, there isn't very much left over for the private sector. Over and above the government and Labor Federation ownership of businesses in various sectors of the Israeli economy, we've got intervention in the marketplace, which makes it difficult for the private sector to operate in a conventional and efficient manner. The private sector will assume an increased share in the Israeli economy as a result of the cutbacks that I expect will take place in government intervention in the marketplace, government ownership of various parts of the Israeli economy, and in the Labor Federation's involvement in the economy.

Do you believe that Israeli government workers should have the right to strike?

No, I don't. Among the many areas in which we're badly in need of reform is industrial relations within the public sector. Not only do we have 30 percent of our work force employed in the public sector, but we have, also, a situation that, to my knowledge, doesn't exist in most Western countries—certainly not in the United States. The public sector in Israel has rights and privileges that, in my view, it should not have. If someone doesn't want to work in the public sector because the pay is not good enough or the conditions are not right, then employment in the business sector should be an alternative. This is not the way it is in Israel. Here, if you don't like the conditions under which you work in the public sector, you strike.

In Israel, the labor union is very strong. Even the specific unions in each and every ministry in the government—and every ministry has its own union representation and union committee—have such a strong position that they, in effect, dictate how ministries are going to be run. They don't restrict their demands to working conditions or salaries, which in my view is not legitimate, but they insist they should have the right to make appointments, to decide who's going to be promoted, and to determine who's going to run the various branches of the ministry. They get that power from the right to strike.

Government workers who strike are not making demands upon a businessman or an owner of a plant, who, if pushed too far, will simply close down the plant, thereby restraining their demands because they are aware of that eventuality. Rather, they are making their demands of politicians who can be pushed endlessly—eventually to print more money. This is an illegitimate aspect of labor-management relations. If we look upon the employees of a government ministry as laborers and the top people in the ministry as managers, what we have going on here is a political game in which the people of the country finally are the losers.

The right to strike—the right to use various weapons that labor unions use in the Western world—is perfectly proper in the business world. There is a conflict of interest there as to how the profits should be divided between the person(s) who owns the company and the people who work in the company. Under such conditions, the labor union should have the weapons, the influence, and the means to engage successfully in that conflict. A government, however, is not a profit center; there are no profits to be divided. There are no profits, period. When, as a government employee, you make demands for increased wages, you are, in effect, telling the government to print more money. That is what's been happening in Israel.

What is your attitude toward strikes in Israel that impact directly on fundamental services, such as electricity, water, basic foods, air transportation, mass transportation, communications, and hospitals?

Most essential services in Israel are owned by the government or nationalized in one way or another. In dealing with an essential service, whether as a civil servant working in the Ministry of Defense or as an employee of the electric corporation in the country, the right to strike provides the ability to cause insufferable harm to the entire population of Israel. This is simply an illegitimate weapon.

For decades, the Israeli economy operated with relative stability, even with inflation higher than in nations of the Western world, through a system of linkage —linking wages and savings to some index such as the cost-of-living index, the U.S. dollar, or a building index. In this way, the citizens of Israel could deal successfully with inflation without worrying about an erosion in their real wages or savings. There now is much criticism from economists and the U.S. administration that the linkage is a major cause of the inflation and must be neutralized. How do you propose to delink and still maintain integrity in wages and savings, or isn't it necessary?

It is true that for many years when Israelis were asked how they could get along with such high rates of inflation, they would answer, very smugly, that they had found the solution to that problem by indexing everything—indexing wages and indexing savings. But you will find few Israelis who will give you that answer today, after having experienced months of hyperinflation before the inflationary spiral was stopped. A former finance minister, Mr. Modai, once said that the man who invented indexing should be given a Nobel prize and then should be taken out and shot. People are not very enthusiastic about indexing in Israel anymore, because it is now realized by most that indexing is what engineers call positive feedback.

In effect, it feeds instability into the system. As costs go up wages go up because they're indexed. As wages go up, the Israeli currency has to be devalued. As the Israeli currency is devalued, wages must go up, and so on down the line. Indexing creates a spiral which cannot be controlled. The solution to this basic problem is to keep prices from rising, then there would be no need for indexing. It has become clear that indexing is a way of making sure that things will continue in an unstable manner. It's basically a destabilizing effect in the economy.

The basic interpretation of inflation is that it is a government method of cheating the people. It also creates, within the society, an understanding by the people that since they are being cheated by the government, they, in turn, in order to protect themselves, should look for ways to cheat the government. Debilitating moral or ethical values are created because of this whole problem of inflation. What level of inflation do you think is acceptable in a country like Israel?

I don't know that any level of inflation is acceptable. I suppose, as a norm, we would all like to have zero inflation and to see things stable. We would like to see market forces adjust prices, meaning that sometimes they would go up and sometimes they would go down. It shouldn't be a one-way street where everything just keeps rising at an increasing pace.

We have lived in Israel with 100 percent inflation, 130 percent inflation, and, at the time, we thought it was liveable—that we could manage it. In retrospect, we know it wasn't. We were just on a roller-coaster ride that was taking us to economic collapse. Although still high, inflation is down now to about 20 or 25 percent on an annual basis. That's still too high. In part, the answer to your question lies in the experience of other Western countries which, when reaching double-digit inflation, found it insufferable and in need of control. That's equally true in Israel. Single-digit inflation is something most Western countries do live with, and we should be able to also.

There are several billions of dollars secretly held by private Israeli citizens which could be put back into the system. What do you think should be done to attract this capital for utilization in the technological development of the nation?

Israel's problem is not lack of capital. It's common knowledge that wherever there is money to be made, there is not a shortage of capital. There is sufficient money in the world; there is sufficient money in Israel; and there is sufficient money outside of Israel that would be ready to come to Israel, if the perception existed that there was a good chance of making money in an Israeli investment.

In the past, Israel has gone through periods during which significant investments of considerable money have been made. The fact that we have not had that level of investment in recent years is a reflection that people outside and inside Israel believed that investing in her or in her industry just was not good business. This was in large measure the result of our hyperinflation. Most people in business abroad couldn't understand how they could make money in an inflationary environment. They didn't understand how they could even operate in that kind of situation, and they didn't want the headache of trying. So they simply shied away from investments in Israel.

Israeli investors are no different than American investors who look at the possibility of investing in Israel. If investments in Israel are not attractive, they're not attractive to Israeli investors just as they are not attractive to American investors. This is something we are in the process of trying to change. The fact that we have brought inflation down dramatically is the first step, and a very important one, in improving the economic climate in Israel. We must continue to create conditions in which investors, Israeli or foreign, will understand that there are some important resources in Israel—the human resources—and believe that there is a good chance that their investments will pay off.

There have been estimates that as much as 50 percent of Israel's economic activity comes from the underground, dubbed the "black economy." How can the Israeli government control inflation in the long term and raise equitably sufficient taxes with so much economic activity taking place outside the legal system?

First of all, I don't know if those numbers are correct, and I don't think anybody else knows. I suppose in every country in the world today people talk about the "black economy" as opposed to the "white" or the "official economy," but nobody can put a finger on just how large it is.

What is the "black economy?" Presumably, it's money that's been made without taxes having been paid on the profit. As a result, people are circumspect or careful about how they use that money, so they don't get caught and have to pay the taxes or have to go to court for not having paid the taxes. Considering the fact that Israel has had, over the years, consistently, the highest tax rates in the world, it is reasonable to assume that there is a significant percentage of such money floating around the country. By the way, it may not be in the country anymore.

This is not the crucial question when we ask where Israel's economy is going and how we can develop it. If the business climate in Israel were to be good—if people who have money, regardless of where it came from, "white" or "black," were to think that there's money to be made in Israel—then money would be invested here. Even if we were to assume that a significant percentage of Israeli money is in the underground economy and, therefore, cannot be invested in Israel, there's lots more money in the world that will flow into Israel when the business climate is appropriate.

Inherently, Israel has some tremendous advantages in this era of technological revolution, when the human resources are more important than other resources. If we could only put our economic house in order, with the talents and the skills that exist in Israel, there would be no shortage of funds that would stream into the country for investment.

Given the size of the "black economy" within Israel and the high levels of inflation that have existed and may exist in the future, how can the society be prevented from deteriorating to that of a nation of "cheaters?"

This gets back to the question of laws that are unenforceable. Clearly, the high tax rates that we have are very difficult to enforce, certainly as far as the entire population is concerned. Which is the worst aspect of this kind of situation where the government tries to impose such a heavy tax burden? Is it the fact that it cannot be enforced, and, as a result, we've pushed a number of people into the underground economy? Or is it that money in the country becomes unavailable for normal channels of investment? To my mind, the worst part is that it creates this very unhealthy economic structure that inhibits growth, that causes inflation, and that makes it impossible for people to earn a living—to get a return on their efforts that is commensurate with what they know is available in the Western world. All that must be changed.

Do you believe there should be a moratorium, for a limited period, on the penalty for possession of dollars, so that huge amounts of hidden dollars could be placed back into Israel's banking institutions to be used for investments in the nation's growth and to help reduce taxes?

I am not certain whether making special allowances for people who have broken the law in the past by not paying taxes, or by taking money out of the country illegally, is a wise thing to do. As I've indicated previously, Israel's basic problem is the economic structure of the country. If we fix that, I don't think there is going to be any shortage of money. So even though we may have people who have smuggled their money out of the country or have their money somewhere here in the "black economy," we are not going to have a shortage of investment capital—not if we make the appropriate reforms in the Israeli economic structure.

A former finance minister by the name of Aridor was forced to resign because he talked about dollarization. More recently, however, there has been much talk in Israel suggesting that the solution to the problem of the Israeli local currency is some form of dollarization. What is your definition of dollarization, and what is your attitude toward it?

Dollarization is just a term which, in effect, implies a stable exchange rate. If the intention of dollarization is that the Israeli exchange rate be totally inflexible—the rate of exchange of the Israeli shekel to the U.S. dollar never fluctuate—then I believe most economists would say it's not reasonable, because economic circumstances change.

We believe the Israeli economy will become much more efficient than it is at the present time. When it does, there will be no reason for the rate of exchange to remain exactly the same. As a matter of fact, it would not be good for either of the two countries for the rate of exchange to remain fixed. In the past, the fixation with dollarization was simply the result of the hyperinflation we were experiencing. People wanted, and rightfully so, to see some stabilization in the value of Israeli currency; so, tying it for a given period of time to the dollar seemed advisable.

The new Israeli shekel was issued August 1985. The rate of exchange between it and the dollar was set at one and a half Israeli shekels to the dollar—where it remained for a period of nine months. In a way, that was dollarization. More importantly, it was a sign that we had licked inflation. Since then, the Israeli shekel has been allowed to float from the dollar and has been tied to a basket of Western European currencies—continuing to reflect control of inflation and economic stability.

What do you see as the role of the banking system in the Israeli economy?

The role of the banking system in Israel essentially should not be different from the role of the banking system in other Western economies. But banking in Israel is being carried out in an entirely different manner than in Western economies. The scandals we had recently about the manipulation of the prices of bank shares on the Israeli stock exchange probably could not happen in the United States, nor in any other Western country. It's an indication that the banks in Israel have operated, and possibly still do, as a cartel. No effective measures have been taken to prevent that.

The banks in Israel also operate in various spheres from which they are prohibited in other Western countries. They are stockbrokers. They have investment firms. They manage business enterprises. They do all sorts of things they really should not be doing, if we want to preclude conficts of interest; and I think we must. At least that's what I would like to see. The banks must be decartelized and limited to the kinds of operations that banks normally carry out in the United States.

What do you see as the role of the stock market in the economy of Israel?

The stock market in Israel should be fulfilling the very same function that it performs in other countries, namely, providing a convenient marketplace where people can invest money in the country's businesses. The Israeli stock exchange has not really served that purpose in past years, and I don't think it serves that purpose at the present time. It does not operate according to the rules and regulations of stock exchanges in the United States or Western Europe.

The investor in Israel who has looked at the Israeli stock market as an appropriate market for investments, in general, has not found his investment as secure as he would expect it to be in other stock markets. He is not provided the kind of information that is available in other countries in order to be able to make rational decisions as to where to place that investment. In Israel, there is not the kind of regulation of companies that are listed on the stock exchange as there is in other countries. As long as there is no regulation that will satisfy the customer and no information provided that will make for rational decisions, the Israeli stock market will not be able to fulfill its proper function.

What do you see as the role of Kibbutzim and Moshavim in the economy of Israel?

It is a positive role; it has been in the past and, hopefully, it will continue to be in the future. I believe Kibbutzim and Moshavim will be able to maintain themselves and their present percentage of agricultural and industrial activities in Israel. This will be all to the good, because Kibbutzim and Moshavim have shown that they're capable, within their organizational framework, of carrying out economic activities efficiently—in many cases, more efficiently than some of the more conventional economic frameworks for agricultural and industry. So, over and above the contribution Kibbutzim and Moshavim have made to Israeli society, they have made, and I hope will continue to make, this contribution to Israel's economy.

MILITARY

Should the Israeli military be restructured in the future, with a higher percentage of highly trained and well-paid professionals, or should the present size of the reserves be maintained?

Israel, being a small country with a relatively small population and potential, has a small regular, or standing, army. She is faced, potentially, with a very large enemy armed force. The worst case scenario is a coalition, in effect, of all the

Arab countries facing Israel and attacking her. It's not just a nightmare. It's happened in the past, and it cannot be excluded from happening in the future. There's no doubt that an army based on reserves is a solution to that problem. It involves many nonconventional methods to build a reserve force that's capable of being mobilized and taking the field ready to fight within a matter of twenty-four or forty-eight hours. But Israel's done it before, and she will have to continue to be ready to do it again.

Just as an indication of the problems we face and the way we go about solving them, consider the force ratios at the present time. The Syrian standing army is an army of half a million men under arms. The Israeli regular army—standing army—is far smaller. We can attain the size of the Syrian army only when we mobilize our reserves. Although we can't possibly maintain a standing regular army that would match the quantity of the Syrian standing army, our quality is far, far better.

Our system is based upon relying on the regular army to absorb the initial shock of a surprise attack—as happened in the Yom Kippur War—then counting on the reserve army, which means, in effect, that the entire population of Israel is mobilized, armed, and takes to the field within a matter of hours. I believe that this system will continue to be the basic strategy regarding the force structure in Israel.

You mentioned forty-eight hours as the period it takes to mobilize the Israeli reserve military. In the past, it was indicated that the time required to obtain full strength was seventy-two hours. Has it recently been reduced to forty-eight?

There really isn't a single number. The Yom Kippur War is a good example. Mobilization time ranges from twenty or twenty-four hours up to seventy-two hours, but there will be people taking the battlefield within a matter of twenty-four hours.

Should the role of women in the Israel Defense Forces (IDF) be expanded and, if so, to what extent?

It is being expanded. I don't believe there is another country in the world where there is compulsory service for women. Here women serve on active duty for two years and then serve in the reserves until the age of twenty-four. Men serve in the reserves until the age of fifty-four.

Because there is such a strain on our manpower, we've been finding, especially during the last two years, additional roles for effective use of women in the IDF.

In the past, many of the women in the IDF complained that too many of them were serving as clerks and making tea and coffee for the officers in the various military units. Essentially, their complaint was that they weren't doing anything very useful.

Even today, we'll find women in the IDF performing those functions they considered mundane; however, I know that the vast majority of women who serve today are doing very useful work—work that requires brain power, for example, in intelligence, including operations of various electronic equipment. Women can perform those tasks just as well as men. Today women in the IDF are serving as instructors for active combat, instructors for tank crews, and instructors for maintenance crews, while providing much of the maintenance in the air force. A large percentage of the maintenance work on ordinance and aircraft systems is being done by women. Many Israelis are surprised when they visit installations and see to just what extent female soldiers are participating. And it's growing all the time.

Should women be utlized in an active combat role?

Although they learn during their basic training some of the skills that are required for active combat, such as how to shoot a weapon, women in the IDF are not used in active combat at the present time. The Israeli army did use women in active combat during the War of Independence. But there was no choice then; everybody who could hold a gun, man or woman, had to be utilized.

While there were no complaints about their performance, we would use women in active combat roles today only in cases of dire emergency, as existed during the War of Independence. We didn't use women soldiers to fight in Lebanon, because we didn't want to see our women falling prisoners. Neither do we want to see our women seriously injured or killed on the battlefield. Although it is not a law of the land that women not be utilized for combat roles, it is a reflection of national will.

In the future, what should be the sizes of the Israeli army, navy, and air force relative to each other, as a percentage of the total? Where should future emphasis lie?

The emphasis must be on using a combination of very advanced weaponry and nonconventional tactics. Basically, our strategy must be a strategy devoted to deterrence, despite the fact that Israel has won every war in the past and would, undoubtedly, win any future wars if, G-d forbid, we have to engage in them. We have been ready to pay, and have paid, the price for these victories. The price is a very heavy one, and we don't want to have to pay that price again, so, of course, the preferred scenario is one where we deter aggression.

Deterring aggression requires presenting the potential aggressors with a problem—the perception that they have no way of foretelling the course or the outcome of the war. If they have no way of assessing the degree of damage that may be inflicted upon them in the very short and immediate period after they start the aggression, it is likely to bring them to the conclusion that they're better off just not trying. The only way to achieve this is with very advanced weaponry that's been developed primarily by us. With such weaponry, we can utilize the element of surprise. Israeli-developed weaponry—unknown to the enemy— provides us with a military capability that the aggressor will not be able to gauge and, thus, respond to.

That is why there must be a tremendous accent put on local development of new weaponry. This requires spending a great deal of money to achieve this. We are in the missile age—on land, on sea, and in the air. But these missiles must be utilized with Command Control Communications and Intelligence (C3I). This enables us to use the weaponry and the troops that we have in a very efficient manner and to develop tactics that have the potential of causing surprises, thus throwing the aggressor into total disequilibrium within a very short period of time. This is where the money has got to be placed.

Emphasis doesn't necessarily or easily fall into the conventional categories of navy, air force, and army. As far as tactics are concerned, and as far as weapon systems are concerned, it will mean combined operations—in other words, building up the capability in all three dimensions almost simultaneously. If it's not in all three dimensions, then it must be in two dimensions—in the air and on the ground. This is the direction in which the IDF is moving now and in which I pushed for development while I was Minister of Defense. It must continue to develop this way in the future.

People claim that one of the lessons learned during the American military action against Libya in the Gulf of Sidra is that ships are undefendable from the air. Should Israel, therefore, be rethinking the role of her navy and the kind of ships she'll be producing and incorporating into the navy in the future?

I don't see why that should be one of the conclusions drawn from the Sidra affair, since no American ship was hit during that incident. Nonetheless, ships, especially large ships, are vulnerable. They are vulnerable to aircraft, even more so to missiles fired from long range—from other ships, from the shore, or from aircraft that keep themselves at a considerable distance. This is a fact, and I don't think the events of the Sidra incident threw any new light on that situation. Recent fighting between the British navy and the Argentinians in the Falkland Islands, however, made it clear that today's technology makes large ships very vulnerable.

Should Israel place greater emphasis on developing unmanned vehicles?

Missiles are unmanned vehicles, and Israel is already placing great emphasis in that area. There are a number of missiles Israel has developed that have achieved a measure of fame. The first one which became famous was the Gabriel sea-to-sea missile. It was the first sea-to-sea missile developed in the Western world. At the present time, Israel is also close to the top of the list when it comes to marine missile technology. Likewise, Israel has earned a very high reputation for herself in air missilery; in fact, in some areas of air missilery, Israel is recognized as the leader.

As you know, Israel has built a good reputation for herself in the development of mini remotely piloted vehicles (RPVs). Although many Western countries have talked about them during the past ten years, Israel is the first Western country to have developed, successfully used, and shown the capability of mini RPVs. The U.S. Navy has acquired mini RPVs developed by Israel.

What I'm saying should be clear: much weaponry that moves over distances at significant speeds does not have to include a man. For example, it does not have to be an airplane. There's a great deal that can be done automatically or directed from a distance. I'm sure we'll see a lot more of that in the future.

Can you expand a little bit on the RPV and its role in the future?

The RPV is just what it says—a vehicle which is piloted from a distance. It doesn't have a man sitting in it; instead, it contains a lot of electronics. The smaller it is, the better. That's why we've gone to mini RPVs. The RPV provides the opportunity to sense the battlefield at a distance without having to have a man fly over it.

Because it is hardly discernable and very difficult to hit, sensing the battlefield in a vehicle so small frequently provides real-time intelligence. This is the dream of every battlefield commander: to know what's going on over the hill and exactly what is facing him. The RPV can also provide the commander with sorely needed information on his own troops. After all, winning battles means getting there "first with the most." In order to do that, it is necessary to know, in real time, just exactly what is going on in the battlefield. Most battlefield problems can be traced back to the lack of knowledge or insufficient intelligence. The RPV and the mini RPV have shown themselves to be instruments that can provide the kind of intelligence that's needed in real time.

Mini RPVs, of course, can do many other things. They can engage in electronic warfare. Since we can place a little missile, or demolition charges of various sorts, on the mini RPV, they can actually be used to hit targets. But the real change that the mini RPV brings about in the battlefield is the ability to provide efficient combined operations.

In the past, if ground forces needed information, it had to be obtained by air. We had the lengthy problem of transmitting the requirement from the ground-forces commander up the various echelons to the air force; having the air force send out an airplane to take pictures which would then have to be developed; then transmitting the information back to the ground commander. Often, by the time he received the information, it was no longer relevant. A mini RPV provides the possibility of immediately putting into the hands of the division commander on the ground the equivalent of what the forward artillery observers may have provided in the past. Now, when the commander wants to know what's going on ten miles down stream or over the hill, he can launch a mini RPV and, within minutes, receive real-time information. Then he can make the right decision.

In 1956 and 1982, Israel fought preventive wars. In 1967, Israel fought a preemptive war. In 1970, Israel fought an attrition war, and in 1973, as well as in 1948, Israel absorbed a first strike. Given her present borders and the size of her Jewish population relative to that of her enemies, should Israel ever again absorb a first strike or fight an attrition war, or should she be prepared to launch a preemptive strike, like the Iraqi raid and/or a preventive war?

The possibility of Israel's making a preemptive strike in the future cannot, and should not, be ruled out. Israel is a very small country. Her present borders are only tens of miles from her population centers. Some people would like to see us concede territories so as to bring our borders right into our population centers. If there were to be renewed aggression against Israel, a scenario could emerge in which we are suddenly faced with the certainty that we are about to be attacked. Under those circumstances, if we knew that absorbing the first strike would weaken our ability to defend ourselves and place into question our winning the war, then the only reasonable choice would be to take the initiative.

I know we faced that dilemma on the eve of the Yom Kippur War—the question of whether or not to strike first in order to assure ourselves of winning the war with a minimum of casualties. These are very difficult choices. Golda Meir, Prime Minister at that time, was faced with that choice. There was certain knowledge that we were about to be attacked. She was urged by some of the people in the military to strike first, to disrupt the impending attack. She decided not to do so, because she thought it would be difficult to prove that Arab aggression was imminent, and she did not want to present the world with an image of Israel as an aggressor. That's a luxury I'm not sure we can always afford.

Many people have had second thoughts about the strategy that Mrs. Meir used on the eve of the Yom Kippur War. That was a terrible war for Israel. An entire high school class was decimated during the first forty-eight hours. In retrospect, if a preventive strike by Israel in the hours before the Arabs launched their attack would have softened the blow and would have saved lives, then a preemptive strike would have been the right decision. It is my opinion that it would have saved many lives. In any case, we might very well be faced with that kind of situation in the future, and I don't believe Israel can afford to rule out the use of a preemptive strike.

What about Israel's undertaking a preventive war as she did in the Sinai Campaign in 1956?

The preventive war tactic really isn't that different from the preemptive strike tactic. There's a common denominator between the '56 Sinai Campaign and the '82 Campaign in Lebanon. Both of these wars were wars initiated by Israel in order to provide the kind of physical security for her citizens that I believe a government is obligated to provide.

In the 1956 Sinai Campaign, then Prime Minister, David Ben Gurion, who also served simultaneously as Minister of Defense, undertook that kind of initiative. Terrorist action, primarily from the Egyptian-controlled Gaza Strip, went on unrelentlessly, terrorizing Israel's civilian population. The terrorists penetrated right into the heartland of Israel. They operated especially in the Negev in the South but came all the way up to Yahud (which is only a couple of hundred yards from where we sit right now in Savyon). Israelis were killed by terrorists operating out of the Gaza Strip. After trying various other measures, Ben Gurion decided to put an end to it by launching an attack on Egypt.

He had tried retaliatory actions by sending army commando units into the Gaza Strip, by attempting to locate the centers of terrorist training and headquarters in Gaza, and by striking at Egyptian installations on a sporadic basis. After doing all that, he came to the conclusion that it didn't provide the answer—it didn't put an end to terrorism. Therefore, he sent the army in and conducted a war—what you call a preventive war—that was very successful. It put an end to terrorism conducted from bases in the Gaza Strip.

We almost had a replay of that with Lebanon in 1982. Of course, there were some differences. We had years of terrorist activity originating in Lebanon against the civilian population in the northern part of Israel. We attempted to use all kinds of retaliatory measures to try to put an end to that. This included shelling with artillery, using the Israeli air force to bomb terrorist targets in Lebanon, incursions of Israeli army units, and the Litani Campaign, which, in a way, was a mini-war that actually provided an Israeli army presence in the border area of southern Lebanon. With all that effort, the job didn't get done.

Finally, in June 1982, Israel went to war. The idea was to go into Lebanon in an attempt to put an end to the danger that faced the civilians living in the northern part of the country. It's really too soon to say definitively whether or not the objective was achieved. We've now had over five years of peace in the Galilee, and there's reason to believe that that will continue.

In answer to your question then, if Israel were to be faced again with a problem of terrorism emanating from a neighboring country across the border— making life unbearable for Israeli civilians in towns and villages close to that border—I have no doubt that the Israeli government would take whatever preventive military action considered necessary in order to provide the security and safety that the government owes its people.

In the future, what kind of war should Israel attempt to fight—one in which there should be maximum destruction of enemy troops and equipment, but not look to conquer territory, or one in which territory is also conquered?

Israel's defense posture must be based on a maximum effort to deter war. We are capable of winning any future wars in the Middle East, and we are ready to pay the price of such victories. We don't want to pay that price because we pay it in the lives of our young men. We must think of ways that will deter the Arabs from initiating war against us.

Nevertheless, if a war does break out—and that could be interpreted as meaning that our deterrent posture has not succeeded—then even the conduct of that war must, in large measure, be determined by our desire to deter any future wars. So if a war does break out, it's going to have deterrent implications for any future wars, and that means that the consequences of that war on the people who started it will be very harsh.

Given the growing disparity between the combined Arab forces and Israeli forces—numbers of weapon systems and men under arms, should Israel attempt to develop and utilize weapon systems that destroy masses of men, or should she look toward concentrating only on the destruction of their weapon systems?

Unfortunately, in warfare men are an integral part of weapon systems, and they form an integral part of the defensive and offensive capabilities of the different armies. There is no way of fighting a war without killing people, as brutal as that may sound. There is no way of fighting a war without having systems that are directed at the destruction not only of machines but also of the people who operate the machines. That includes people in air forces and armed forces as well as ground troops. The Arab armies have a large number of commando battalions that are specifically trained to carry out important missions.

In many ways, the importance of the ground soldier has increased in recent years, because modern technology puts into the hands of the ground soldier weapons of very high accuracy that have great capability of destruction. A man can hold in his hand a system that is capable of directing a high volume of very accurate fire at very considerable distances. The one advantage the individual soldier has is that he's difficult to locate—he's a target that's difficult to acquire and, therefore, not easy to direct weaponry against. This increased importance of the ground soldier has emphasized the need to contend with him as a weapon system.

Given the introduction into the region of mass-destruct weapon systems delivered by ballistic missiles, what should be Israel's response?

The problem of ballistic missiles in the area is certainly a serious problem for Israel. Since the establishment of the Israeli air force in 1948, Israel has proven that she is capable of dealing very effectively with an aerial threat from neighboring Arab countries. In all the wars since 1956, Israel has enjoyed almost total control of the skies. It is important to remember that in the fighting in Lebanon, where the Israeli air force faced the Syrian air force, the air combat results were eighty-six to zero. That's some indication of the superiority that the Israeli air force has attained and the kind of security that the Israeli air force provides Israel's civilian population from the danger of aerial attacks. It doesn't mean the possibility of an aerial attack doesn't exist, but the Israeli air force has shown that it can obtain dominance of the skies in the Middle East, whenever needed.

We can't, however, dominate the skies against ballistic missiles. With the present level of technology, ballistic missiles cannot be shot down. There is no air combat engagement; a button is pushed. Until recently, the surface-to-surface missiles that were in the hands of the Arab armies were of no particular concern. The surface-to-surface missiles in the hands of the Syrians were not very accurate missiles. Their guidance was not very good; therefore, they did not pose a threat to military targets inside Israel. However, even without great accuracy, they were clearly of concern when it came to the danger of civilian targets being attacked— cities being bombed. For that, great accuracy is not necessary.

Recently, the Syrians have acquired from the Soviets, the SS21, which is a much more accurate missile—a missile which has a pretty good guidance system. These surface-to-surface missiles do pose a threat that we must be concerned about. Of course, we are giving serious thought to various methods of dealing with that threat, and I believe we will be successful in that effort.

Beginning with the War of Attrition (1968-70) and continuing on to the Yom Kippur War (1973), the aerial superiority that the Israeli air force had attained was significantly impaired by surface-to-air missiles—a new system on the battlefield that definitely moved the balance in the duel between aircraft and ground-based, antiaircraft weapons. Russian surface-to-air missiles used by the Egyptians during the Yom Kippur War turned out to be very effective. They reduced the ability of the Israeli air force to fulfill its mission—to provide the ground forces with the support it was scheduled to provide. It was a problem that we addressed. During the war in Lebanon, when we had to deal again with Russian-made, surface-to-air missiles, this time operated by the Syrians, we proved that it was a problem we had solved. The Israeli air force showed its ability to wipe out the surface-to-air missile installations, without sustaining a single loss in aircraft.

To what degree in the future should Israel become self-sufficient in military weapon systems, and at what level is it today?

Certainly for a small country, a very high percentage of the weaponry Israel uses is from her own resources. I don't think Israel has to aim for self-sufficiency to the point where we will make every nut and bolt and every piece of hardware we intend to use from our own resources. There's no need for that kind of self-sufficiency. We receive a lot of support from our good friend, the United States. We're two countries that are essentially in a state of alliance. We acquire much of our weaponry in the United States, and under these circumstances, there's really no need to reinvent the wheel and try to develop something here that we can purchase for less abroad.

Israel develops all major weapon platforms—sea, air, and ground. We develop and produce missile boats for our navy. We also develop and produce aircraft, although we don't develop all our aircraft. The Israeli air force uses Skyhawks, Phantoms (F4s), F15s, and F16s—all aircraft that we acquired from the United States. But it also uses the Kfir, and it will use the Lavi planes developed in Israel. We develop tanks, but, again, we have not developed all the tanks that we have in our inventory. We've got British-made Centurian tanks and American-made M60s; we also have the Israeli-developed and -produced Merkava. So in all areas of major weapon platforms, we use our ability to develop what we need.

In addition to major weapon platforms, we develop and produce a vast array of electronics, as well as a variety of missiles and RPVs. Our strategy must concentrate on those specific and limited areas in which we feel that our own developed weapon systems will enable us to arrive at that deterrent posture we talked about previously. These are also the areas in which we have the ability to develop weapon systems that are better and more unique than available anywhere else in the world.

What should be the size of Israel's military budget as expressed in percentage of her GNP?

You might think that that would depend only on the threat that we are facing, but in actual fact, it depends to some extent, also, on the assistance we get from the United States. In other words, Israel's limited economic potential will almost invariably lead us to a defense budget that, in a conventional view, is too small. It involves quite significant risks.

The Arab armies and their inventory of weaponry is larger than the combined armies and weapons inventory of NATO. This has become much more so the case here in the past few years, as the Iraqi Army has expanded almost exponentially during its fighting with Iran. That struggle, of course, keeps the Iraqi Army occupied, so it doesn't have to be a source of great concern to Israel—right now. However, we can predict with a reasonable degree of certainty that when, and if, that Iraqi-Iranian War winds down, Israel will have to consider the contingency of the very massive Iraqi Army—almost three times the size of what it used to be—being a potential aggressor, since the Iraqis have taken part in wars against Israel in the past.

Israel has limited economic potential, and if we base our military spending solely on our own resources, we're going to have a defense budget that involves risks that a country, ordinarily, should not take upon herself. However, with American assistance, we are in a position to limit some of these risks.

With the kind of participation that we've had in the past from the U.S. Military Assistance Program, Israel can maintain a defense budget, exclusive of American assistance, that will range from 20 to 25 percent of her GNP—still a very high percentage. This is more than four times that of the United States and five or six times that of any other Western democracy. It represents a very heavy burden on the Israeli economy, even considering U.S. assistance.

Do you believe that beyond the Lavi aircraft, the Merkava tank, and the Reshef missile boat that Israel should undertake the next generation of weapons platforms, given the huge cost involved and the drain in resources, or should Israel not develop future platforms and just buy from the United States or Western Europe?

Generally, I attach a great deal of importance to the development of weapon systems in Israel by Israelis. Israel has a comparative advantage in the area of weapon systems because weapon systems require two things that Israel has. One is brain-power skills. We have those skills in abundance in Israel and at a cost lower than is generally the case in other advanced countries. Secondly, but unfortunately for us, we have a great deal of combat experience. It's these two components that are required to be successful in developing weapon systems, and Israel has been successful in doing that. There is economic justification in pursuing these activities.

Israel should continue in the future to use that comparative advantage for her own benefit, primarily in war, but also in her industry and economy. The fact is that the products of our aerospace industry are the foremost export products of the Israeli economy. There is no reason why Israel should be restrictive in the systems that she develops. There's no reason why Israel should not want to develop the overall system—the aircraft, the combat vehicle, or the missile boat—and want to restrict herself to developing only certain components of these overall systems. Maximum leverage in all directions comes from control of the overall system, especially in terms of the combat potential and the deterrent effect the system may have on the battlefield.

Based on our experience, the maximum potential in the export business also comes from control of the overall system. By selling the overall system, we can sell a multitude of subsystems; however, by selling subsystems, we can't sell a multitide of other subsystems or the overall system itself. It is the nature of large weapon systems, such as aircraft, main battle tanks, and missile boats to have very long lifespans. Modern-day fighter aircraft have a longevity of twenty, thirty, and sometimes even forty years. We have the Phantom, which has been flying for over thirty years, still flying very successfully in the Israeli air force and other air forces as well. We are now talking about upgrading it and continuing it in service in the Israeli air force. I'm sure the Lavi will have similar longevity. We will be working on upgrading the Lavi and various versions of it for at least another twenty or thirty years. The same is true for the Merkava. Today, we already have a number of models of the Merkava, and we will continue with improvements on new models. The same is true of missile boats. So Israel will be busy in the platform business—aircraft, tanks, and navy boats—for many, many years.

Somewhere along the path, of course, the question arises whether the time has come to develop a new platform. Right now, that's really a very premature question when it comes to fighter aircraft, because we are just in the stages of developing the next generation of fighter aircraft. I don't think anybody can tell whether twenty years from now we will want to develop the next generation, because we don't know what the position of fighter aircraft will be twenty or thirty years from now. If we decide to develop a new fighter aircraft twenty years from now, we will be looking at the battlefield forty years from now. Whether fighter aircraft will play as important a position on the battlefield forty years from now, we don't know.

Do you think the United States will continue to finance the Lavi through the production of 300 planes despite the objections of the U.S. Secretary of Defense, Casper Weinberger, and, if so, why?

The United States provides military assistance to Israel, but it is recognized in the United States—certainly in Washington—that the decision as to how that assistance is to be used is Israel's. It is the Israeli government that carries the responsiblity for the security and the defense of Israel; therefore, it is the Israeli government that has to decide whether Israel will buy helicopters, tanks, and F16s, or whether she will manufacture the Lavi.

The Israeli government's decision is that developing and manufacturing the Lavi aircraft is the best use of the total funds that we have available which, of course, is the sum of what Israeli taxpayers provide and what the United States provides Israel. Once that decision was reached in Israel, the U.S. government could not presume to tell Israel to use the funds in a different manner. After all, the United States does not carry on her shoulders the responsibility for Israel's security. The United States certainly can provide advice; she can ask for explanations as to what our thinking is; she can ask why we are spending our defense money the way we do. But, in the final analysis, it's our decision, and our decision is to make the Lavi.

Strategic Defense Initiative, commonly referred to as "Star Wars," has become a focus of debate in America. Now that the Reagan administration has invited Israel to participate in this program, some discussion has developed as to the wisdom of Israel's participating. What do you see as the asset of Israel's participation in "Star Wars?"

We've had some discussion here, but there's really no significant debate. The vast majority of people involved in the decision making, and the public as well, are in favor of Israel's participation for two reasons. Israel sees herself as a member of the Free World, of which the United States is the leader. In many ways, our fortunes are dependent on the fortunes of the Free World and on the ability of the United States to lead the Free World in it's confrontation with the Communist world. Whatever Israel can do to assist the United States in a strategic initiative, whose purpose it is to strengthen the hand of the Free World against communism, Israel should want to do.

It would be of great strategic value to Israel to strengthen the United States' position, or the West's position, vis-á-vis the East's. That's very important to Israel. The Strategic Defense Initiative, or "Star Wars," is a very advanced technological effort. Even though Israel is a small country, she has considerable expertise in those areas and the ability, therefore, to make a contribution.

Additionally, as in any high-technology development effort, there are spin-offs—advantages that remain after the job has been done. I'm sure that would be the case here. Israeli participation in this program could lead to further development and advancement of Israel's industry, especially of her high-technology industry.

Terrorism

How do you think terrorism against Israel should be dealt with when it occurs outside of Israel, and how should it be dealt with when it occurs within Israel?

The question really is a more general and universal one—how should terrorism be dealt with? How should the United States deal with terrorism outside her borders, and how should she deal with it within her borders? There is no different answer when the question is asked of Israel, the United States, France, or any Western country whose citizens or carriers are the targets of terrorism.

We have reached a consensus in the Western world—a consensus that Israel and the United States subscribe to. It is that terrorism must be fought essentially without any reservations—that there must not be surrender to terrorist blackmail and that in those cases where terrorist bases, or individual terrorists, can be located and identified, pre-emptive action should be taken against them in order to prevent their carrying out terrorist acts. That is the general philosophy regarding fighting terrorism that I believe in and that we in Israel practice. I understand that the United States believes in and now practices the same philosophy. This still leaves us, of course, with certain problems and special individual cases that we must deal with depending on the unique circumstances.

Do you think we are gaining ground on control of terrorist activity occurring within Israel, and do we have better control of terrorism against Israelis outside of Israel? Is the world gaining ground on terrorism?

We have had a drop in the level of terrorist activity in Israel during the last year. That gain is the result of the work of our security services and the Israel Defense Forces, and also the result of the more stringent attitude that King Hussein has taken against the Palestinian Liberation Organization (PLO) in Jordan itself.

As far as the world is concerned, a great blow against terrorism was struck recently when the U.S. Air Force and Navy attacked bases in Libya. This was a blow against state support of terrorism, which is the most dangerous of all. In one way or another, most terrorist activity is state supported. Terrorists would never be able to achieve the level of activity they have without support from states like Iran, Iraq, Libya, Syria, and, in some cases, the Soviet Union and South Yemen. The attack against terrorist bases in Libya has had a great effect. We can see that the Syrians have become a great deal more hesitant—at least in terms of their pronouncements in support of terrorism. They now claim they are not engaged in terrorism. A number of states that supported terrorism in the past are rethinking their roles for the future.

What is your opinion of the General Security Service (GSS) incident regarding the cover-up of the deaths of the two Palestinian terrorists who hijacked an Israeli bus? What impact do you think it will have on the Israeli political scene and on Israeli security in the future?

It looks like the security services are guilty of some mistakes in this particular incident—probably both on the scene and thereafter. In terms of what has been referred to as a "cover-up," it's almost impossible for security services engaged in a war against terrorism to have a perfect batting average and not, on occasion, make a mistake. But, certainly, lessons must be learned from mistakes and corrective measures must be taken.

We are now in the process of finding out exactly what happened and taking the necessary corrective measures. It's somewhat of a trauma because Israel has never had a public investigation or police investigation of the activities of the security services. I doubt that it's ever been done in any other democratic country. We know of the Senate Inquiry Committee on the Central Intelligence Agency (CIA) in the seventies led by the late Senator Frank Church, who was, by the way, not only one of the outstanding people in the U. S. Senate at the time but also a great friend of Israel. Today, most people are of the opinion that that investigation, although carried on, I'm sure, with the best of intentions, did a great deal of damage to the CIA and effected its ability to function. It took years thereafter to repair some of that damage.

Similarly in Israel, any public or police investigation of the security services is going to do damage to the ability of that group, which is still engaged in the battle against terrorism. Damage has already been done by the great exposure that has been given to the GSS and to senior officials in that agency. Whatever investigation needed to be carried out—and I do believe one needed to be carried out—should have been done in a more informal and cautious manner.

In retrospect, what is your opinion of Yitzhak Rabin's release of over 1,000 Palestinian terrorists in 1984? What effect has it had on terrorist activity during the last few years?

The decision to release those terrorists has to be weighed in terms of the pluses and minuses as they were at the time the decision was made. The plus was that we managed to return three Israeli soldiers who had fallen into captivity during Israel's operation in Lebanon. We have a long tradition of not abandoning the wounded and the dead on the field of battle and, certainly, people who are taken as prisoners of war. From the time they were taken prisoners, we engaged in very active efforts to effect their return.

On the negative side, there were two concerns: (1) that some of the terrorists who would be released might return to terrorist activities, and, therefore, this arrangement might be directly responsible for people being killed by terrorist action at some future time and (2) that the arrangement might be taken as a signal by the terrorists that Israel was abandoning her very firm policy in dealing with terrorism—her policy of not giving in to terrorist blackmail—and, therefore, from then on it would be easy to get Israel to surrender to terrorist demands when hostages were taken.

When we examine the plus side of that situation, we did have three prisoners of war returned. On the thought-to-be negative side, there have been very few instances of released terrorists being apprehended for engaging in terrorist activity again—no more than three or four. Also, it is clear to the terrorist organizations that Israel has not abandoned her policy of firmness in dealing with them. We have had terrorist incidents since, and we have had Israeli actions and responses to terrorist activities since. It is clear throughout the world, particularly to the terrorists, that, if anything, Israel's attitude toward dealing with terrorism and attempts at blackmail is firmer than it ever was before. Under these conditions, I view the terrorist release as more positive than negative.

Do you think the death penalty should be applied to terrorists who have murdered someone within Israel?

Absolutely. I have no qualifications about that at all. It is a major mistake on the part of Israel that the death penalty is not imposed. There is no doubt in my mind that some of the people—those who have murdered Israelis in cold blood—deserve the death penalty. Their acts are inhuman. We've had the case of two Israeli teachers—a man and a woman—who were taken off the road and killed in cold blood. We've had the case of an Israeli soldier whose grave was dug right before his eyes before he was choked to death. These are beastly acts carried out by people who deserve no mercy at all.

As we know from our experience, many of these people feel, since the death penalty is not applied, that they have a good chance of getting out alive, at some future date, through an exchange for people who have been taken as hostages. Therefore, by not imposing the death penalty, the present system indirectly serves as an encouragement to further terrorist acts.

What do you think should happen to Israeli soldiers who have disobeyed orders and have killed terrorists?

The Israel Defense Forces has a code of military law, which contains codes of procedures and penalties. Anyone who disobeys the law or is suspected of breaking the law is investigated, and, if that investigation shows justification, is put on trial. The same would be true if someone had killed a terrorist prisoner—he would be in violation of Israeli law.

Do you believe world terrorism, in general, is supported by the Soviet Union? Is there evidence of Soviet support of terrorism against Israel?

There is no doubt that the Soviet Union supports terrorism. During Israel's operation in Lebanon, we captured many documents that proved that terrorists had been undergoing terrorist training in the Soviet Union from Soviet instructors. Almost all of the arms in the hands of the terrorists who were captured in Lebanon were of Soviet manufacture and, clearly, were sold by the Soviets, either directly or indirectly, to the terrorist organizations. There's incontrovertible evidence that the Soviet Union has supported terrorism against Israel. It is a fair guess that Soviet support of terrorism is not limited to the PLO, or other Palestinian terrorist organizations, and is probably extended to terrorist organizations throughout the world.

POLITICS

What kind of parliamentary system do you prefer for Israel—proportional or direct representational?

I prefer direct representational on condition that we have a presidential system of government, but I don't prefer direct representational in the parliamentary system of government. The reason for that is that, in addition to wanting a government to be basically democratic in its nature and representative of the wishes of the people elected, we would like the government, also, to be responsive to the wishes of the people who elect it. Additionally, we want governments to be stable. This is particularly important for Israel. We don't want a government that will fall every few months, with all the problems that could arise and all the difficulties that would then be involved in constituting a new government.

The parliamentary system, combined with the direct election of representatives to the legislature, could conceivably make for a very unstable government. The executive-type system that exists in the United States produces a stable government. The chief executive is elected for a four-year term, and the legislature cannot remove him in the intervening period, barring some very exceptional circumstances, like impeachment. That level of stability, which can be provided only by the executive system, is essential for Israel. The direct election of representatives makes for independent legislatures, which is all to the good, so long as they don't have the power to bring down the government.

Are you in favor of the system of two legislative bodies, as in the British Parliament and the American Congress?

I really see no advantage to establishing a second legislature in Israel to work together with the Knesset. It would probably be cumbersome and increase the difficulties and complications of the legislative process without contributing anything.

In your opinion, what should be the blocking vote—the minimum vote required before a party can be represented in the Knesset?

Currently it is 1 percent, but I would go all the way to 5 percent. The number depends on the objectives. If we want to keep the lunatic fringe out, the higher we make it, the better our chances for success. One percent is really a very small number, and, in effect, it means we're opening the door for the lunatic fringes to be represented in the Knesset. If a party can get only 1 percent of the support of the population, there's a fair chance that it's out on the lunatic fringe. We've had examples, like Kahane, in the Israeli Knesset. We should raise the percentage and, thus, remove these very small splinter groups from the legislature.

If we want to reduce the number of parties so as to decrease the probability that a small party will have undue power because it is needed to put a coalition together then, again, the higher the blocking percentage, the greater the chance for success. If we decrease the number of parties in the legislature, it would make for a more stable government.

I believe, however, we should not muzzle political opinion in Israel; we must not create a situation in which a constituency that is significant in the Israeli political spectrum doesn't have the chance to speak out in the Israeli legislature (Knesset). Looking at both of these views, 5 percent seems like the right number.

Why, then, before the '84 election, did you suggest to Peres a 2¹/₂ percent blocking vote?

I didn't suggest 2¹/₂ percent to Peres. I suggested to him, before the '81 election, not before the '84 election, that we have a higher blocking percentage. I told him that Likud was ready to discuss it with him and come to some agreement. We couldn't get Labor to agree, and when 2¹/₂ percent was voted down, we introduced 2 percent. We still couldn't get a majority, but my view was and is that any increase is for the good. If somebody said to me 1¹/₂ percent or nothing, I would say that 1¹/₂ percent is okay, because 1¹/₂ percent is better than 1 percent; however, my view has always been that 4 percent or 5 percent is probably the best.

Do you think a non-Zionist or an anti-Zionist political party should be allowed to be a member of the Israeli Coalition government?

That's a matter of definition. Agudat Israel is a non-Zionist party; some people would even consider it an anti-Zionist party. They declare themselves to be a non-Zionist party, and they are members of the present coalition. They were members of the previous coalition, also, and I see nothing wrong with that. They're a perfectly legitimate party in Israel. They certainly would like to see the State of Israel safe, sound, and prosperous, so there's really no conflct of basic motivations and goals with them.

But if we go beyond that and start looking at parties that are dedicated to the destruction of the State of Israel—that are anti-Zionist in that sense—then not only do I think they shouldn't be in the coalition, but I also believe they shouldn't be in the Knesset.

Do you believe that party jumping among members of the Knesset should be eliminated by law?

Absolutely. The Israeli form of government, particularly the Israeli system of elections, is entirely different from the one that exists in the United States. We have a parliamentary system of government and our elections are by "PR"—proportional representation. What does that mean? It means that when people vote in the elections for the Israeli Knesset, they do not vote for individuals; they vote for a party.

The party presents an ordinal list of names to its voters, and, depending upon the number of votes the party gets, the percentage of that list who will become Knesset members is determined. When people are asked to vote for a party, the Knesset candidates appear on a party list as representatives of that party. The candidates, in effect, do not get votes on a personal basis but, rather, collect party votes. I believe it is totally illegitimate for a person elected in such a manner to move from one party to another, while maintaining his seat in the Knesset.

It is quite possible, and certainly legitimate, for a person who has been elected on one party ticket to change his mind and say that he doesn't belong to that party anymore or that he can't represent that party anymore. He simply has to remember that he was elected on that party list and resign his seat in the Knesset, while simultaneously leaving the party. He does not have the right to take the seat which he did not earn on a personal basis and turn it over to another party.

In your opinion, is there a role for religious parties within the political system in Israel?

Yes, simply on empirical grounds. There are religious parties in Israel that have been here since Israel was established. I'm sure there are many religious people in Israel who don't vote for religious parties—who don't feel the need to be represented politically by a religious party. Clearly, however, some in the religious community in Israel feel that they want political representation. In the present Israeli Parliament, we probably have twelve (10 percent) members representing religious parties. That's far higher than any blocking percentage we would want to introduce. If that many people feel that they want political representation, there's no way of denying it to them.

In your opinion should parties whose platforms are in opposition to the democratic system be abolished by law, for example, the Communist party, Rabbi Kahane's Koch party?

Parties that are subversive should not be permitted to operate and should not be permitted to run for the Knesset. By subversive, I mean pledged to the destruction of the State of Israel—the State of Israel as we know it today. I don't believe we should give such parties the opportunity to make their voices heard in the Israeli legislature.

Currently, there are examples of such parties. The Communist party is one that is basically subversive, although it seems to behave in a reasonably tame manner. Another example is the party calling itself the Progressive Party for Peace, Matti Peled's party. The Progressive Party for Peace and the Communist party brag about their support of the PLO—their support of a terrorist organization that is dedicated to the destruction of the State of Israel. They shouldn't be represented in the Israeli legislature. Many people would agree that Kahane's Koch party also is one that is basically subversive.

What is your attitude toward the present role of the president in Israel? Are you in favor of expanding the powers of the president?

In the present system, he has the powers that he should have, but if we were to go to an executive system, it would be an entirely different presidency. In that case, I think he ought to be elected directly, rather than by the Knesset, which is the way he's elected right now.

What is your attitude toward the autonomy of Israel's cabinet members?

We've got to look at the whole system as one package—the behavior of legislators, the role that the prime minister plays in Israeli party politics, and the degree of autonomy that the members of the cabinet have. It is all a reflection of the kind of system we have—parliamentary with proportional representation—in which the cabinet members do not serve at the pleasure of the prime minister. It is unlike the situation in the United States where cabinet members do serve at the pleasure of the president.

In Israel, cabinet members are representatives of political factions in the government, which makes the cabinet, in effect, a mini parliament. It's not that the prime minister listens to the opinions of cabinet members and then decides what he wants to do. Decisions are brought to the cabinet for a vote. In the Israeli cabinet, decisions are made by majority vote. They can be, and frequently are, made against the wishes of the prime minister. That, inevitably, gives cabinet members a very large degree of autonomy. As a matter of fact, it's difficult to visualize them in the present system without having that level of autonomy.

Are you in favor of extending the period between elections in Israel from four years to six years?

No. During Israel's thirty-seven years of existence, we've had eleven elections. In our system we can have, and frequently have had, elections before the four years are up. And we've had changes of government without elections. So, as long as our system remains what it is, it really wouldn't be meaningful to extend the time between elections, which is actually only the maximum time.

What is your attitude toward the privileges taken by the Knesset members?

I don't know what privileges you're referring to. If you're referring to salary, they're really not very privileged. Knesset members make only about $800 or $1,000 a month.

The whole issue is something that surprises me. Just recently, I spoke with a newspaperman about it. People talk about the importance of safeguarding democracy in Israel. Some speak of the dangers to democracy. I don't really think there are any significant dangers to democracy here—except for the spate of criticism constantly leveled at Israel's elected representatives by Israel's newspapers.

Often I see articles in the Israeli newspapers that lambaste and make fun of Israeli legislators and cabinet members. They really are not intended to build respect for the people who are elected by the Israeli public. I don't think you see anything like that in the United States; at least, I never saw it. U.S. senators make about $65,000 or $70,000 a year. They probably could make a lot more money in business in the United States, but it's a reasonable salary. It's a fabulous salary compared to what Israeli legislators make. Yet, I have never seen articles in the U.S. press referring to the fabulous salaries senators make. In the Israeli press, however, we see it all the time. They say that Israeli legislators are living high-off-the-hog, while everybody else is suffering. Breeding that kind of disrespect for legislators, members of the cabinet, and for the prime minister is not good for democracy.

What is your attitude toward limiting the number of Israeli cabinet members by law?

We generally do run cabinets that are too large, so there might be something to be said for establishing, legislatively, some kind of constraint. The prime minister, when forming the cabinet, could then use that as a crutch in order to keep the cabinet from getting too large.

The reason the cabinet gets so large, of course, is because of coalition building. It's not because the prime minister wants such a large cabinet but, rather, because that's usually what it takes in order to get the cabinet to function with all the coalition members. They all want what they consider their appropriate share, which is usually completely disproportionate to their representation. We've had cases where Knesset factions having two members have had two seats in the cabinet. It happened to the Independent Liberal party some years ago. We've had, more recently, Knesset factions with one member being represented in the cabinet. So it might be a good idea to provide some kind of constraint. Of course, before I'd vote for it, I'd want to think very carefully about whether that kind of constraint might, under certain circumstances, make it impossible to form a coalition government, even though that would not be the purpose of such legislation.

You've been described as a hawk in a gray suit. What are your reactions to that?

I belong to the Likud, which is a party that evolved from the Zionist movement originally founded by Jabotinsky. I was a member of Betar, the youth organization that was founded by Jabotinsky, and I've always felt that Jabotinsky's role in the Zionist movement differentiated him from all the other Zionist leaders. What differentiated his movement from the other Zionist movements was political realism. In other words, when he looked at problems, he didn't look at them from an idealized point of view.

Jabotinsky was an idealist, but he was not an idealizer who looked at the world through rose-colored glasses. Rather, he looked at things very realistically. There are a number of cases, now a part of history, in which, in retrospect, we can see that he was a man who saw things far more realistically than anybody else. One was the danger facing European Jewry prior to World War II, after Hitler's rise to power. He was very explicit in pointing out the danger. He called for the evacuation of the European Jewish community from Europe to what was then Palestine. Unfortunately, his voice was not heeded.

Additionally, he was far more realistic than the rest of the Zionist leadership in understanding, very early, that the British would not live up to the mandate that had been entrusted to them by the League of Nations—that they had no intention of furthering the establishment of a Jewish state in Palestine. He realized it would take military action directed against them by an underground movement in order to force them either to live up to the mandate or to leave the country so that a Jewish state could be established.

Jabotinsky was far more realistic than others in the Zionist movement in realizing the depth and the fundamental nature of the Jewish-Arab conflict in the area. Again, he did not idealize the conflict. He understood that there was a conflict between two people over the same piece of territory.

I belong to that school of realism. I like to think that my views are neither hawkish nor dovish but, simply, realistic. At least, I make an attempt to size up the dangers that face us in a realistic manner.

SCIENCE AND TECHNOLOGY

Although Israel does not even rank among the top 100 countries of the world in either area or population, she has the world's sixteenth largest scientific community. She has, as well, both the highest per-capita scientific activity and the highest percentage of scientists and engineers of any country in the world. However, given the number of unsolved problems that Israel has identified, do you think that her scientists should engage in—(a) pure research for the sake of research, which has no apparent problem-solving value for Israel or any other country, or (b) pure research which currently has no problem-solving value for Israel, but which would be of value to other countries?

It's difficult to tell scientists anywhere what they should or should not do. Generally, they end up doing what they like to do, and this is true for Israeli scientists. We can look at the distribution of scientific activities and ask ourselves if it is appropriate or if it is the best possible distribution. But there really isn't too much we can do about it.

The government can change the distribution to some extent by setting up a system of incentives—encouraging applied research by supplying more funds for applied as opposed to pure research, if it chooses to move the distribution in that direction. From an economic perspective, as we all know, pure research has its fallout. It's just that it's not predictable. It's only known after the fact. But the contributions of pure research to eventual industrial applications is significant everywhere, including Israel.

On the whole, the distribution of scientific activity in Israel, at the present time, is really quite good. It has changed over the years. There was a time, perhaps twenty years ago, when most Israeli scientists worked on pure research. That, by the way, also reflected the system of incentives as they existed at the time. The government was spending very little research and development money on applied research. Industry was not developed. There was hardly any product development going on at the time, so Israel's scientific community worked either for international academic recognition, which required pure research and the publication of results, or on pure research supported by funds that were contributed by governmental agencies abroad, mainly the United States.

More recently, however, Israel's scientific community has developed greatly, and, today, the government is spending large sums of money on applied research. Very rapidly, a high-technology industrial base is developing in Israel, and it is attracting scientists. It is moving people from pure research toward applied research and product development. At the present time, the distribution of activity of Israel's scientific community is quite good and appropriate to Israel's current economic situation.

Should the Israeli government direct the scientific research effort of the country through the establishment of a national science foundation?

We already have the equivalent of a national science foundation. It's called the National Committee for Research and Development. Directing scientific research is really not possible and, perhaps, not even desirable. What the government should do is provide some degree of guidance, mainly through systems of incentives, and then leave the rest up to the scientists. If the government feels that the distribution of scientific activity is not what it wishes it to be, then, rather than tell the scientists to do something else, it should allocate more funds in directions it considers to be more important.

Today, the Israeli government spends considerable funds on research and development. As a matter of fact, Israel is very close to the top of the list of countries whose governments spend a high percentage of their GNP on research and development. And you can see the results of it. A good part of the Israeli scientific community is working on government-sponsored research, first and foremost, of course, on defense. The Ministry of Trade and Industry is also spending considerable sums, providing matching funds to Israeli industries that are engaged in product development. So the Israeli government is providing direction for the scientific community here and, as a result, is bringing about the kind of activity that we need at the present time.

Should Israel be pursuing research and development in the field of genetic engineering, and if you think so, why?

I'm neither a genetic engineer nor a molecular biologist, but as far as I know, genetic engineering is a field of the future. It is already providing the basis for industrial products that could be important to any country's economy. Since this is a growing industrial field, I believe it is a good field for Israel to be involved in. We already have the beginnings here. We have good relevant manpower in this area: physicians, molecular biologists, pharmacologists. In fact, we have, on a per-capita basis, a significant amount of genetic engineering going on in Israel. I'm sure that in five or ten years there will be a number of Israeli companies active and successful in genetic engineering.

Do you foresee the Israeli aircraft industry undertaking a major mission, beyond the production of the Lavi?

Yes, because the Israeli aircraft industry is the largest industry in Israel today. It has a concentration of very high quality, very experienced scientists, engineers, technicians, test pilots, and other professionals from all the various diciplines involved in developing and manufacturing aircraft and missiles. It's the area in which Israel has a comparative advantage, more so than in any other area—a comparative advantage that is based on both our abilities in skill-intensive, high-technology activities, as well as the operational experience that we and our defense forces have gained over the years. Israel is unique in that sense and probably has an advantage over the most advanced countries in the world.

There's no reason to suppose that after having completed one project that will be the end of it. In aerospace engineering, we build one project on the previous one, and we just keep going. It makes good economic sense to keep going. I'm sure that, just as after the Kfir came the Lavi, after the Lavi will come something else. Whether it will be an airplane or a missile, it's too early to tell. I'm sure, too, that just as with the Kfir, where there were a number of growth versions of the airplane, the original version of the Lavi will be just that, the original version; after that will come many growth versions of the airplane.

Do you foresee Israel stretching the Lavi, making a larger type of plane out of it?

Yes, I do. We've got enough emperical evidence to know that airplanes just grow. They start out as relatively small and light, then we keep adding things to them and increasing the envelope of flight performance, continually asking for better performance in various regions.

Presently, the size of the Lavi is midway between two concepts that people examined at the time it was designed. The airplane size is really determined by the airplane's engines, and there was talk about building an airplane around the General Electric 404 engine—an engine with 16,000 pounds thrust. I was in favor of building the airplane around the Pratt & Whitney F100 engine, which has 24,000 pounds thrust, mainly because it's an engine that's available. It's currently utilized in the Israeli air force. It powers the F15 and the F16. The Lavi's configuration finally was built around the Pratt & Whitney 1120 engine, an engine with 20,000 pounds thrust. An airplane built around such an engine is adequate; it has the space and weight required to include the systems that a modern airplane needs.

One thing, and maybe the most important, that differentiates the Lavi from other airplanes, like the F15 and F16, is that it is more advanced in its systems. There is a connection between the level of advanced technology in an airplane and the size of the airplane. We wanted to be more advanced in the systems in the Lavi, so the airplane, of course, had to be big enough to accommodate these systems. The 1120 engine was developed for the Lavi. It was developed on the basis of the F100, but it's a different engine. Using the new 1120 rather than the F100, however, required additional costs and time.

The decision was made to upgrade the F4 Phantom using the F100 engine. Does that close out the possibility of making a larger Lavi?

No. The upgraded F4 Phantom will be using the 1120 engine, the same engine that's in the Lavi. I foresee growth versions of the Lavi also being based on the 1120 engine. I don't see the F100 ever being used in the Lavi.

In an airplane, when we say bigger, it generally means heavier. The plane really doesn't get to be significantly bigger in terms of its geometric dimensions. Usually what happens in airplane development programs is that the engine grows; in other words, the engine manufacturer manages to increase the thrust of the engine. That same engine, more or less in the same envelope, then permits the airplane to become heavier. The 1120 is just at the beginning of its life cycle. I'm sure that it will start at 20,000 pounds, but I won't be at all surprised if it eventually grows to 24,000.

Development costs for products utilizing new technologies are very high. Do you think that Israel should invest in her local industries for such production, or should she pursue joint ventures with foreign high-tech firms?

We've got to be very pragmatic in addressing that question. We want to do what's best for the Israeli economy. Under certain circumstances, full utilization of any specific advantage we have means doing it all ourselves and getting the total benefit from it, without sharing it with anybody else. From a commercial angle, we'll share the benefits, of course, with all the people who acquire the product and get the benefit of the acquisition.

In many other cases, a combined venture is useful. Marketing and market entry is a very important aspect of the success or failure of the development of any industrial product. Since the market for Israeli high-technology products is, first and foremost, the United States, clearly a joint venture with an American company that is well established in the American market short cuts many, if not all, of the problems connected with marketing.

We can look at the Lavi as an example. The Lavi, in many ways, is an Israeli-American airplane; and it makes good economic sense. There are many American systems in the Lavi; for example, Pratt & Whitney makes the engine, and Grumman makes the wing. Lear Siegler, Garrett, and Hughes also participate. This not only takes advantage of capability that already exists, but it also could conceivably open the American market to us in future years for this airplane or some versions of it. This would have been quite impossible had there not been this kind of American participation.

INDUSTRY

What do you believe will be the optimum size of future industrial enterprises in Israel?

I'm not sure how to define optimum under our circumstances. My guess is that Israeli industries in the future will cover the entire gamut from very small enterprises employing no more than a few tens of employees to very large enterprises that essentially will be multinational corporations with their headquarters in Israel. Perhaps these large corporations will draw much of their manpower and management from Israel, but, in effect, they will be established all over the world.

If I were to project the emphasis of the development of Israeli industry in future years, it could be in the area of larger enterprises, since we don't yet have these multinational corporations. We have lots of small companies, and we do have some larger enterprises that have a few branches in countries outside of Israel. But I believe in the future that we will be moving more in the direction of very large multinational companies headquartered in Israel.

Where do you believe new industrial enterprises should be located within Israel in the future?

Everyone's desire, and quite correctly so, is to get away from that very dense concentration that we have on the coastal strip from Ashkelon to Nahariyya. There are many people there, and much of Israel's industry is there. It's a very vulnerable area, and it creates environmental problems. Generally, the movement must be primarily eastward and, to some extent, southward. So, I foresee that much of Israel's future industrial development will be in Judea, Samaria, and the Negev.

If that's your conclusion, then wouldn't the future industrial enterprises, by the very nature of that comment, tend to be smaller type individual entities because of the sparsity of the population?

There has already been significant movement of population to Judea and Samaria, and I believe there will be more. Population and industry go together; population will follow industry. Israel is a very tiny country, so living in Tel Aviv and working in a plant in Samaria is no problem. In some cases, it's only a twenty-minute drive; if it's deeper into Samaria, it may be a forty-minute drive.

But if the trend in Israel is toward high technology—robotics, automation, computerization—wouldn't, then, there tend to be movement toward smaller, individual enterprises?

I don't think so. For most of Israel's high-technology industry, the market is America. I don't see how very small companies are really going to penetrate that market. It's going to require large companies. It may be that special marketing organizations will be established to serve smaller companies which, on their own, can't take on the marketing job. But, in general, it's going to have to be large companies.

What may occur here, as well as in other parts of the world, is the development of a cottage industry—people working in their homes on computer terminals. We'll have companies that will be able to employ members of Kibbutzim and Moshavim without their having to leave their homes. Religious girls, who tend not to work in factories with other people, will be able to work at home on computer terminals. But these girls, as well as the other women and men who will work on terminals in their homes, will probably be working for very large companies.

Do you believe the Israeli industry should concentrate its efforts on developing systems or subsystems, for example, work stations or computers?

I don't believe that we should set ourselves objectives of one sort in lieu of the other. In Israel, we have the abilities to develop in both directions, and we really shouldn't choose between them. Israeli industry must and will do both.

For which markets should Israeli industry be encouraged to develop products—Third World, Western Europe (Common Market), or the United States?

Our comparative advantage is in the area of skill-intensive activities—what we call today high technology. So we have to look for those areas that are markets for high-technology products. Those generally are in the more advanced countries of the world—the countries with the higher standards of living. That means, first and foremost, the United States. The second largest high-technology market in the Western world is Japan; after Japan, it's Western Europe. We've had serious penetration of the American market, and I believe that will continue to grow. Israel has not yet had any serious penetration of the Japanese market; we've had some penetration of the Western European market, and I believe that, too, will grow.

What should be the Israeli government's financial involvement in assisting local industries and/or desirable foreign companies to develop products in Israel for export markets?

Generally, I'm not a believer of government involvement in business. The Israeli government at the present time is, and for many years has been, overinvolved in the country's economy. I believe there is a role for the government to play in encouraging industry to develop in certain directions that it feels are important for the country. But beyond government-provided incentives, financial obligations must be those of private investors and entrepreneurs.

Is it desirable for Israeli companies to establish manufacturing facilities in foreign countries?

There's no universal answer. That's a question that has to be addressed by the particular company that's facing that situation. Generally, I'd say that if a particular company were trying to penetrate a certain market, or trying to service a certain market, or if certain other conditions prevailed, it may be a useful and productive thing to do.

Given the fact that these companies receive so much government benefit— incentives—is it good for Israel if they actually set up these branches in foreign countries for the purpose of manufacturing?

Again, there's no general answer to that question. If I were asked that question about a particular situation, I would want to know: Is it good for the company? Will it increase the sales of the company? Will it increase the business that the company does in Israel or employment by the company in Israel? If the answer to all of those is positive, I'd say, "Why not? Do it!" If, on the other hand, it would detract from the company's activity in Israel, reduce the employment by the company in Israel, or turn the company into a non-Israeli company—a foreign company—that is beginning to move the center of gravity of its activity from Israel to another country, I'd say, "No."

How do you see Israeli industry meeting its personnel requirements in the coming decades? Will there be sufficient scientific, engineering, technical, and skilled labor? Will it be home-grown or aliyah?

The basic situation, and a very favorable one at that, is that the Israeli population is very talented. Given the process of skill acquisition, Israeli industry will be able to find, in Israel, a very sizable population with the skills and the capabilities that a skill-intensive, high-technology industry needs. So, if there is further industrial development, if there is a growing demand for that kind of activity, we will find more and more of Israel's population studying subjects related to technology—at the level of technicians, at the level of engineering assistants, at the level of engineers, and at levels for people with higher academic qualifications.

If the demand should be even larger than that, then Israel, of course, has the advantage of being a country of immigration. It is a country of *aliyah*. As the demand grows, I'm sure that it will give rise to increasing *aliyah* from countries where people also have obtained the necessary qualifications.

What can be done with the displaced labor force as obsolete industries in Israel are phased out?

We're facing that problem to some extent at the present time, and what we're saying is that we need to retrain them. We haven't done it yet, so I don't think anyone here is really in the position to say just how easy or how difficult that task is. We'll learn more about it in coming years. I'm sure there must be some segments of the working population—those who for many, many years have worked in activities that didn't require any special skills—for whom retraining in highly skilled activities will be very difficult, and in some cases, probably impossible. But when we talk about younger people, or people who are engaged, for example, in the teaching profession, then in this day of the computer, the required retraining can be accomplished more easily.

What should be the method of phasing out obsolete industries, for example, ATA, the textile factory. This is going to come up in the future.

The best method is to let them phase themselves out. Let the people who manage them simply come to the conclusion that, in the current business climate, there's really no room for them, and there's no money to be made.

When we examine the finances, we find that the Israeli government support, per employee, is much more costly when trying to keep a com-

pany (such as ATA) open than it is if the workers were put on unemploy-
ment insurance for long periods of time. Do you believe in this method of
artificially maintaining these factories?

No, I don't. I've been involved in the long series of discussions we've had
about ATA and have been opposed to the continuing government intervention and
support for what is a private industry. My view has been and remains that if it
cannot support itself, then it has to be shut down.

Of course, financial cost to the government cannot be the only consideration.
It's correct that frequently, as in the case of ATA, government support to keep a
factory open costs more financially than the unemployment pay the government
would have to provide were the factory to close. But those two alternatives really
are not the same. In other words, a man who works is not the same as a man who
is unemployed. So in terms of human values, generally, we consider it to be a
better situation and perhaps worth some additional government expenditure when
we can keep a man working, rather than having him unemployed. On the whole,
however, the government should not be in that business.

The government's business is not business. If a company cannot stand on its
own feet, then I think the natural course must be allowed to develop, except in
those unusual circumstances when it is obvious that, with temporary assistance to
tide it over, a company can succeed in the end.

By Western standards, the number of people employed by the government
in Israel is out of proportion to that employed by industry. What should be
done to scale down the size of the government work force?

There are 400,000 Israelis on the public payroll working in governmental
services. This represents 30 percent of the work force of this country. That's a
staggering percentage! According to *The Wall Street Journal*, it's 11 percent in the
United States. When Israelis first hear that 30 percent of the population are
government employees, they don't react. But when they're told that this translates
to an average 30 percent deduction from everyone's pay in order to cover those
salaries, they are shocked.

Part of the explanation is that Israel is a country in the process of being
developed and gathering immigrants, so there's more of a role for the government
in various spheres of life in Israel than there is in other countries. There's no
excuse, however, and no justification for such a staggering number of government
employees. Economically, it's an insufferable situation.

There must be some transfer of people from the public payroll, and it must
come mainly from the government's ceasing to provide certain services that
governments in other Western countries do not provide. For example, a fair

number of the people on the public payroll in Israel work in hospitals—in government hospitals. These include doctors and nurses as well as many other people who provide a variety of related services. We should have a reduction in hospitals run and owned by the government.

In addition to providing services that governments in other Western countries do not provide, the Israeli government also provides services that are traditionally provided by governments in Western countries. However, these offices are over-populated, utilizing too many people.

Another reason for excessive government employment, and a reason that must likewise be addressed, has to do with labor relations in the public sector in Israel. People who work for the government of Israel—who work for the public sector—strike. They engage in all the various practices that workers in the private sector do when they have a conflict of interest with their bosses. They use the very same methods that are used by workers who are fighting for a larger share of the profits of the company. Well, when somebody works for the public sector, it's not a matter of getting money from the profits of the company; it's a matter of getting money from the taxpayer. For example, people who work for the Electric Corporation in Israel, which is a public service, are ready to shut down the electricity in the country so they can get themselves higher pay. That, I believe, must change. It's a very unhealthy situation.

Because of the tremendous power that the labor union has acquired, especially in the public sector among the people who work for the government, the public sector has just continuously been enlarged—in terms of both the numbers of people working and the working conditions. There has been no restraint on that movement in the public sector. In the private business sector, the workers themselves understand that if the owners were to meet their demands continuously, the business could go bankrupt and that would be the end of their employment opportunity. People who work in the public sector and the trade union leaders in the public sector have no fear of that. They know that they can get the government either to print more money or to go to the United States and borrow more money so as to improve their working conditions. That must be changed.

What is your attitude toward products developed by local research and development which are then manufactured outside Israel?

There may be a justification for that occasionally. Generally, of course, we like to exploit the results of R & D in Israel all the way—right to the product. We want to market the product and get the full benefit of that initial investment of Israeli skills and capital for the Israeli economy. Although there may have been a few cases of Israeli products being developed in Israel then being manufactured abroad, that is not the direction we want to go in.

What kinds of joint industrial ventures with foreign firms should be encouraged?

Whatever is good for Israel. The entrepreneurs and the people involved in the businesses know what is good for Israel. If it's good for their business in Israel, it's probably good for Israel. I don't believe the government knows.

Generally, our past experience has shown that the involvement of foreign companies in partnerships with Israeli companies is good for the Israeli companies and is good for Israel because it widens the base. It creates a certain amount of synergy. It often assists in gaining access to foreign markets. When an Israeli company involved in high technology goes into a joint venture or partnership with an American company, frequently the American company provides certain marketing skills and a place in the American market that didn't exist for the Israeli product prior to that joint venture.

As you know, the Law for Encouragement of Capital Investment in Israel, which was passed in '77, brought several large foreign companies to Israel, among them Lambda, which is now expanding another 50,000 square feet, National Semiconductor, and Intel. I gather from your attitude that you're not in favor of such involvement of the government?

I'm not in favor of that kind of overinvolvement. I believe it's quite possible that some of these companies, like Intel and National Semiconductor, in setting up their manufacturing facilities in Israel, reaped more benefits at the expense of the Israeli taxpayer than they should have.

As I pointed out before, the major benefit we have to offer anyone from abroad who sets up a business in high technology in Israel, is Israeli manpower—Israeli talent and skill. I don't think that we have to add to that all kinds of financial inducements at the expense of the Israeli taxpayer, which, in turn, burdens the Israeli government budget. The root of Israel's economic problems today is the tremendous government budget deficit—the tremendous government expenditures that are not met by equivalent revenues. The incentives we have paid to people to set up plants in Israel over the years are included in those government expenditures.

I've asked that a study be made as to just how effective the Law for Encouragement of Capital Investment in Israel has been. My guess is that it's really not that effective. Intel and National Semiconductor perhaps stand out because they're very good companies, very advanced companies; but I doubt that anyone has really been able to put a price on what it is worth to Israel to have these companies here. That law has provided the taxpayers' money to hundreds, if not thousands, of people who, I'm sure, have done very well in terms of their own financial interests. I doubt whether it's really been very instrumental in advancing the Israeli economy.

Do you believe the Israeli laws that exist today are satisfactory for the establishment of the kind of high-technology companies that are going to be required for the next few decades?

As I said, I'm a little critical of the present Law for Encouragement of Capital Investments in Israel, and I believe it ought to be changed. The change should be in the direction of reducing Israeli government expenditures when it comes to setting up businesses in Israel. What needs to be rectified is perhaps not so much in the realm of that which can be fixed by changing the law, but rather the environmental conditions for people who establish businesses in Israel. The tremendous bureaucracy they have to deal with has to be streamlined. Reducing the government's involvement in the economy will cut down the necessary contact between businessmen and the government's bureaucracy, especially in the area of the basic infrastructure that business requires, whether it's telephones, or telex, or roads, or anything else it takes in the modern economy to make a business work. For example, people who invest in Israel frequently find that they must wait nine months to get a telephone. Well, it's pretty hard to run a business, especially if you want to sell in the international marketplace, if you don't have a telephone.

Israel is looked upon by the government planners as an alternative to Ireland as a place to manufacture for the Common Market, because Ireland has been very successful in attracting high-technology industry and basic industries to support manufacture-for-export to the European Common Market. That was the basis upon which the Law for Encouragement of Capital Investment in Israel was enacted. Do you think that concept is still sound?

Israel may have something in common with Ireland in the sense that both countries have access to the European market. Other than that, Israel is very different from Ireland. Today, Israel has an advantage over Ireland—access to the American market, especially now that the free-trade agreement has been signed. Ireland does not have the pool of skilled people that Israel has to offer. Basically, Israel is probably looking for different types of industries than Ireland is looking for. I don't really think that we have to provide the kind of financial incentives that Ireland provides. The incentive that we provide is the people of Israel.

Do you see Israel staking out a unique position with regard to American firms coming here and setting up high-technology enterprises, other than the original position—as an alternative to Ireland?

Israel provides some very unique advantages to people who are interested in high-technology industries, namely, her human resources. Without undue modesty, I believe they're hardly equaled anywhere else in the world. I'm sure there are places in the United States where there are concentrations of people with talents and skills in high technology, but for a country as a whole, there are probably few in the world that can equal Israel's capability.

What proportion of Israel's industrial efforts should be directed toward military industries?

It should be a significant number. First of all, because of our unique defense needs, it is important that a large part of our requirement for weapon systems be developed and manufactured locally. It is in this direction that we will find a solution to providing a deterrent to renewed warfare in the area. We must have weaponry at our disposal that Arab countries don't know about or are not acquainted with.

Additionally, for economic reasons, it makes good sense for Israel to develop her aerospace industry because we should work in areas in which we have a comparative advantage. And we have a comparative advantage in high-technology areas. In addition, we have an advantage by virtue of the large amount of military operational experience we have acquired over the years because of the wars we've had to fight. So in many areas of aerospace systems, we have a distinct advantage over most industries in most countries in the world. Of course, we would like to exploit that advantage.

What percentage of Israel's industrial output today is oriented toward the military?

I'm not sure of the percentage, but part of the answer to your question is the fact that Israel Aircraft Industries is the largest company in Israel and also the largest exporter in Israel. The second largest company in Israel is Israel Military Industries, and it is also the second largest exporter. If we add to that companies like Elbit and Tadiran, we'll find that the aerospace industries in Israel represent a very significant segment of Israeli industry and even a more significant segment of industrial exports from Israel.

Do you foresee military industries growing as a percentage of the total Israeli industry?

As a percentage, it probably will not grow. We're now at the point where some of the basic technological infrastructure that has been built in Israel will be used more and more for industries that direct their efforts toward commercial products and toward selling in the civilian marketplace.

What percentage of Israel's military needs is Israel now satisfying, and what percentage is she importing? Do you think those percentages will change later?

In 1978, when the size of our budget and our defense needs were much smaller, the percentages were 50-50. At that time, we were already producing major platforms—missile boats, tanks, and aircraft. Today, with a substantially larger budget and far greater defense needs, Israel is meeting more than 50 percent of her military requirements.

I believe there will be an additional increase as the Lavi goes into production, because the Lavi will constitute a greater proportion of the Israeli air force's inventory of weaponry than did the Kfir. Additionally, Israel's upgrading of the Phantom will contribute to the increase in the percentage.

What do you envision in the next ten to twenty years—will Israel, on her own, ever be able to meet 75 or 80 percent of her defense needs?

It's not likely, and not even really desirable, because we don't want to make everything. I'm sure it is not worthwhile making everything. We want to acquire those items from the United States that are better and/or less expensive.

Actually, the Lavi is a very good example. I talk about the Lavi as being likely to increase the percentage of Israeli-made weaponry in the inventory, but I'm not even sure that's accurate. A good part of the Lavi is made, or has been developed, in the United States. I believe that a good part of it will be manufactured in the United States as part of the overall Lavi manufacturing program. In developing the Lavi, people took a business view of things when they determined what to make in Israel and what to buy in the United States. Of course, they found that it made good sense to buy a significant part of the airplane, or have certain systems developed, in the United States.

AGRICULTURE

Today, Israel has the second lowest percentage of population working in agriculture—approximately 3.5 percent. In the United States, the percentage presently is 2.4 percent. Israel's total export of agricultural products, mainly citrus, is not increasing because of entry into the European Economic Community (EEC) of countries like Portugal and Spain, whose citrus products are extremely competitive with those of Israel. Do you foresee a drop in the percentage of population engaged in agricultural pursuits?

The trend whereby a smaller and smaller percentage of the population is engaged in agricultural activity is one that reflects the increasing productivity of the agricultural sector. It is a trend that's very noticeable in Israel because there has been so much progress as a result of our agricultural research. That trend should continue. It's a trend that's inevitable and, in many ways, healthy. It's good for the world and, as a result, good for Israel that a smaller and smaller percentage of the population can grow the food that is required for the population of the world. We in Israel don't want to fight that trend. We want to continue to make our contributions to increasing productivity in agriculture. We want to continue with agricultural research because we have shown ourselves to be good at that activity.

Israeli agricultural exports today are not just in the area of citrus. We export vegetables and flowers to Europe and that's on an increasing curve.

Given the fact that Israel presently utilizes 99 percent of her available water resources, including sewage, and almost all of her land resources, do you believe she can continue to increase her agricultural production? If so, how?

Probably not, although I wouldn't want to put an ultimate limit on the level of agricultural production. It might still increase some, but I don't believe it's going to go up a great deal. Israel is one of those countries in the world where the supply of water is very short. We've done a very good job in utilizing our limited water resources. We serve as an example to many other countries. Perhaps we have done a better job than anyone else, our circumstances —living in this part of the world where water is so short—have forced us to do a good job. It's just a reality we have to live with.

How do you see the revitalization of Israel's agricultural sector taking place, given that the traditional agricultural products have peaked because of market limitations, and land and water resources are already fully utilized?

First of all, I don't know that revitalization is the right word, because the Israeli agricultural sector is a very vital sector—a productive sector, an exporter. It has been rated highly by people around the world. It ranks among the highest in level of technology used in agriculture and in level of productivity. Israel has been, and will continue to be, among the world leaders in agricultural research. So, whatever revolution takes place in agriculture in the world, and I suppose a revolution is taking place now through genetic engineering, we will find Israel in the forefront.

Do you believe that Israel should make financial and manpower investments in genetic engineering to attempt to restructure her agriculture toward growing and producing industrial agricultural products?

I'm enchanted by genetic engineering. It seems to hold tremendous promise in many areas, not just agriculture. We are just at the beginning of that technology. It hasn't progressed as fast as some people anticipated it would, but there is considerable activity in genetic engineering in Israel. We have many people with talents and skills in the life sciences. Israel will be in the forefront of all aspects of genetic engineering.

Do you believe that air freight costs can be reduced sufficiently in the future for Israel to shift her agricultural exports from Western Europe to places like Latin America, North America, or even Southeast Asia?

Air freight rates are decreasing and will continue to go down because we are in a position to increase efficiency in air transport. But whether, in the foreseeable future, we will get to the point where we can justify flying Israeli agricultural exports to South America, or perhaps someday to Southeast Asia, I don't really know.

Do you foresee large-scale expansion in arid farming, growing such crops as jute and cotton with very little water?

I've talked to people from the cotton lobby. Almost all Israel's cotton is grown with irrigation. Perhaps there are some strains that can be grown without water, but we haven't found them yet.

What role should the Israeli government take in assisting in the research and development of industrial agricultural products?

The Israeli government is taking a significant role in agricultural research at the Agricultural Research Station. It's a government-funded institute that has been doing an outstanding job.

Given that Israel must encourage an eastward and southward population shift from the densely populated coastal strip from Nahariyya to Ashqelon, and given Israel's lack of water and arable land resources for establishing the traditional agriculturally based settlements, what kinds of settlements do you envision for the future?

First of all, the Israeli economy has been moving, and will continue to move, toward an increasingly higher level of industrialization. The reduced number of people who will be working in agriculture is part of that structural change in the occupational cross-section of Israel's population. That means that more and more of the people who will live in the Golan, Judea, Negev, or Samaria will be working in industry rather than agriculture.

We see an example of that change in Samaria today. Most of the settlements in Samaria are not agricultural. They are settlements—even suburbs—of people who work in industry. Some of that industry is in Samaria, and some of that industry is in the established population centers of Israel.

Do you foresee the urbanization of Kibbutzim and Moshavim and their reliance on technology-intensive products for their livelihood?

Some of that is inevitable—urbanization. There are quite a few Kibbutzim and Moshavim that once were out in the wilds but today are essentially the suburbs of Israel's cities. As the level of urbanization grows, it's going to encompass areas that up to now have not been considered urban or even suburban.

Technology-intensive products are found mostly in the area of industry, and Kibbutzim have been moving in that direction. Again, that trend away from agriculture—that decrease in the number of people who work in agricultural activity—means that more people will work in other areas, the first and foremost of which is industry. Although originally Kibbutzim were established with the aim of working primarily in agriculture—some of them with the aim of working solely in agriculture, we hardly find a Kibbutz today that is not also working in industry. Currently, many Kibbutzim employ more people in industry than they do in farming. That's just a sign of a trend that will continue.

EDUCATION

What is your position on establishing special education for Israel's gifted children?

We want to provide the opportunity for talented and gifted children to develop fully their natural abilities, so long as it is not done at the expense of children at other ability levels and so long as it doesn't lead to a separation between the gifted and ungifted, the talented and untalented. Without infringing on these principles, we can, and do, provide such opportunities for very gifted children within the normal school program, including extracurricular activities in various spheres, and in special areas of interest.

Should religious education be offered in the non-religious schools, and, if so, how much?

The answer to that depends on the definition of religious education. Among the Jewish people, religion and nationality are really very directly intertwined, and it's difficult to separate the two. Israel, until the fifties, had what was called a trend system of education. There were religious schools, general schools, and labor schools. Labor schools were the ultimate, presumably, in secular education. They were almost antireligious in their tenor; however, they had a very heavy content of Bible studies, which apparently fell under the category of history or national Jewish education.

But the Bible is the Bible, and it is the very foundation of the Jewish religion. Studies connected with Jewish history—with the Bible and with Jewish tradition—must be an integral part of the Jewish educational system. Here in Israel, they are, and I'm sure they will continue to be.

Do you believe that Israeli youth groups should have the official sanction to operate within or from the schools?

Yes. The youth groups in Israel have, in the past, performed a very important service to the country. They have provided an additional educational framework—over and above that of the schools. Much of Israeli life and the Israeli ethic is internalized as the result of what children have experienced in the youth groups. We should continue that.

Should a high school education be free, or should fees be established on a graduated scale?

We've had both. We had fees on a graduated scale for many, many years. People from the Western countries, especially the United States, considered that situation as unnatural and not really very attractive. Then we went through a period when we had free high school education—we did away with all fees.

Now we are in the process of restoring fees for all those parents who can afford it. That, of course, is an indication of the present state of the Israeli economy. We would like to have free high school education, and even beyond that, we would like to have free college education in Israel, but we can't afford it right now. If we can't afford it, those who have the ability to pay must share the cost of education. Those who don't have the ability to pay should get the education at the expense of the State.

It's a seemingly very acceptable and convincing system. The reason we deviated from it earlier is that, when possible, we like to avoid all the procedures connected with establishing whether or not people have the financial means to pay for their children's education. Universal free education just does away with all that. It provides free education for people who can't afford it as well as for people who can afford it, but at the taxpayers' expense, of course. Israel can't afford that, at least not at the present time. As the Israeli economy develops during future years, I don't doubt that we will return to universal free high school education. Eventually, we may get to the point where we will have free university education, as well.

Do you think the private high schools, such as those of the Yeshivah system, should be supported by the government?

There's room for government support of educational endeavors that are positive in nature. There are many institutions—not private in the commercial sense but, rather, the result of the initiative of private groups or groups connected with various movements, including religious—which deserve government support. There's justification for sharing in the cost of the effort they undertake.

Where do you think the emphasis should be placed in the high school curriculum—humanities, science, or religion?

We really want to emphasize all areas, and not any one to the exclusion of the others. However, if we talk about shifting emphasis, we probably do want to shift in the direction of science. Science and technology in this day and age, including the use of computers, are making an increasing impact on our lives. With all the reservations we have about our ability to predict the future, we know that our children will have to be much more conversant with computers than we are; we want to prepare them for that in the schools.

How does the percentage of Jewish students attending universities in Israel compare to the percentage of Jewish students attending universities in America?

Presently, it's a much smaller percentage in Israel than in the United States. When I came to Israel in 1948, many of the young Israelis I met had not finished high school and had no intention of finishing; they saw no need. As a matter of fact, to this day in many of the Kibbutzim where they have high schools, they do not prepare their students for matriculation exams, which are essential in Israel if you want a college education. They feel that it's really not important, and they prefer to have their children stay on the farm and become farmers, rather than go to study at a university.

The way that Israel's young people and their parents look upon advanced education has changed over the years. There was a time when our young people felt that the right thing to do was to get a minimum of education and then go out to work, join the army, or go into a settlement—do something "useful" with their time, rather than spend it going to college. Much of that has changed, and, today, more and more Israelis feel that an advanced education is an essential part of the preparation that is needed for life—even for life on a Kibbutz.

But we haven't caught up to the United States yet. We still have a far smaller percentage of our young people studying at universities. Part of the reason for that, of course, is the army service. Israelis who go to college don't start, usually, until the age of twenty-two. If they've signed up for additional periods of time in the service, they don't start until the age of twenty-four. If beginning a college education is postponed until that age level, it means postponing it altogether for some people. After army service, many women get married and start raising a family. They don't have the chance to go to college that they would have had if they could have started after high school. Some boys don't feel like going back to school after they've spent four or five years in the army. From year to year, however, the percentage of Israeli young people going to colleges and universities is increasing, and I'm sure it will continue to increase.

What is your attitude toward the Israeli government's provision of differential support for university students, depending upon their field of study, such as agriculture, engineering, science, humanities?

Let's discuss, first, how much government support we provide to university education generally. The Israeli government today provides very extensive support. As a matter of fact, some 60 to 70 percent of the budgets of Israeli universities are provided for by the government. A good bit of the rest is covered by contributions that come from abroad, and a very small fraction is provided by tuition fees. That means that the people who do the studying or their parents pay a tiny fraction of the cost of these studies.

During the present economic crisis, it has become clear to everyone that we really can't afford to maintain our present level of government support. Even though Israeli universities have very high standards and the cost of education is very significant, tuition fees are very low. They're a few hundred dollars a year. Right now, we're in the process of getting away from the high level of government support and raising the tuition fees. Although we're having those who can afford it pay for their education, we are providing scholarships to people who have the talent and the need for this education but who can't afford it.

Should the Israeli government discriminate in its support for university education—provide more support in those areas that seemingly are more important to the country than others? The answer is yes. To some extent, this is even taking place at the present time. Israeli government support is almost universal, and Israeli university students pay the same small tuition fee, regardless of what they study. Since a liberal arts education costs much less than a technological education or than a medical education, people who study engineering or science are, at least implicitly, getting more support than those who study liberal arts. But I think the Israeli government could and should move even more firmly in the direction of providing greater encouragement for those who study in the areas that we know are important for the country.

How independent from government interference should the unversities be, given that so much of their budgets are financed by the government?

They should be very independent, and they are very independent. The government really has almost nothing to say about how the universities are run.

Should the university system be expanded to other areas, such as Judea and Samaria, and, if so, what kind of university should it be?

Although we have people who live in Judea and Samaria today attending Israeli universities, we do not have an Israeli university or branch of one located either in Judea or in Samaria. We do have quite a number of Arab universities located there, however, they don't enjoy Israeli government support. They are funded by other agencies.

The question of whether we should have a campus in Judea or Samaria— something very desirable in terms of settlement in these areas—gives rise to the question of how many universities we should have in Israel altogether. There are some people who think we already have one too many, and others say we have two too many. We have, for a small country like Israel, a fairly large number of very high-quality academic institutions.

Should we now start investing money in building a campus in Judea or in Samaria? No. We don't have the resources for it. With the present economic crisis, we're faced with a very large foreign debt. We've got a current deficit in our trade balance. The government can't balance its budget, and the difference between the government's budget and the government's income from taxation and other sources is covered by the printing of money or by borrowing money abroad.

The situation is almost like that in an individual household. When you're facing a big debt and can't balance your books at the end of the month, you don't undertake additional expenditures. You wait until you are managing your debt so that at the end of the month there is something left over after you've covered all your current expenditures. When we get to that point, and I believe we will in the not-too-distant future, that will be the time to undertake large-scale investments in Israel. Those large-scale investments should surely include building a campus, perhaps a branch of one of the Israeli universities, in one of the cities or in one of the settlements in Judea or Samaria.

Should the university system be expanded to home study through the use of computer terminals?

Definitely yes. In general, I'm sure that computer terminals will revolutionize not only studies but work habits as well. This is of special significance for Israel because there are many unique segments of our population that will benefit directly from the home use of computer terminals for study. The aging population of Kibbutzim and Moshavim, who today are no longer required or able to carry the typically heavy workload, never had the opportunity for advanced study through all their years of physical labor required to build the State of Israel. For the religious community, computer terminals allow religious girls, as well as married religious women, the opportunity for advanced study within the confines of their homes. Additionally, home use of computer terminals will allow those settled in sparsely populated areas and in areas where there are no nearby Israel universities to participate in advanced study.

Should the research institute system be expanded, and, if so, must it be attached to existing universities? For example, would an independent research institute be appropriate in Carmiel to serve the Galilee region and in Ariel to serve Judea and Samaria?

Israel is so small that there's really no justification for locating research institutes in particular areas just to serve those areas. We must remember that in research institutes, we're always dealing with a critical mass, so as opposed to fragmentation with a large number of small institutes, there are advantages to having a small number of larger institutes—the synergism and all the good things that come from having the critical mass. We don't want to multiply research institutes all over Israel, not because it is not important, but because we want to concentrate sufficient doses in particular places.

Should the universities be allowed to do research for foreign governments, and, if so, under what conditions?

They should be, and they are. Foreign-government support for research in Israel is of benefit to Israel, because research has its fallouts and leaves behind a store of knowledge. If we can get somebody else to fund it, or to fund part of it, then we're that much further ahead.

Should the state provide financial support to the Yeshivah system for post-high-school education? If so, should it be at the same level as university support?

Yeshivah post-high-school education is like college education in a very specific area. It is deserving of support, no less so than college education generally in Israel. We talked before about favoring certain areas of education that are important to the country's economy. That principle would apply in this case as well, even though Yeshivah education, with all the importance we attach to it, is not the most critical thing in terms of the economic needs of the country at the present time.

INFRASTRUCTURE

Transportation

What kind of mass transportation system should be developed in Israel, if any?

There are two mass transportation systems in Israel today. We have a good system of interurban and urban buses. We also have a rather primitive railroad that runs primarily between Haifa and Tel Aviv and, occasionally, between Tel Aviv and Jerusalem. In parallel, we have a rapidly increasing number of private automobiles on the country's roads, and that, as in all countries, causes congestion, noise, and pollution.

We need a good mass transportation system so that some of the cars will come off the road, and we will have better environmental conditions in the country. To date, we have not been successful in that regard. The trend here, as in most other Western countries, is for people to get into their own private cars. They prefer private transport over any alternatives in mass transportation that we can offer.

We've had, and still have, a very high level of subsidy for bus transportation in Israel. High as it is, it has not been able to pull cars off the road. People still prefer to use private vehicles. The conclusion is that, at the present time, we in Israel are not rich enough to provide the quality of mass transportation that will convince people they are better off traveling by subway, rail, or bus, rather than by private cars.

Israel has one of the highest highway death-and-accident rates per capita per mile of any country in the world. What measures should be taken? Should the highway system be expanded?

There's certainly room for expanding and improving the highway system. If we haven't been doing it as intensively as we should in the past few years, it is because of the economic crisis and because we have been working so hard trying to cut down on government expenditures. But, eventually, considering this inevitable trend toward private automobile transportation in the country, the infrastructure of roads, overpasses, and traffic lights must keep pace with the number of cars on the road.

There is a perception that the highway accident rate in Israel is so high because of insufficient driver training, poor driving skills, and poor maintenance of vehicles due to the high cost of repairs. Do you believe the government should intercede and place stricter control over inspection of automobiles and ensure better driver training?

The requirements for driver training are probably more stringent in Israel than they are in the United States. In Israel, driving lessons from an authorized driving school are required in order to get a license. You can't get a license by having one of your parents teach you how to drive. Sometimes I wonder if this is justified because I never went to a driving school when I got my license, and I know many other people who never had to go through driving school. But that's the way it is in Israel.

We also have very strict regulations about tests for automobiles. They have to be tested on an annual basis to make sure that they're in adequate mechanical shape. As far as rules and regulations are concerned, we may have more than is necessary, certainly not less. If we have an undue accident rate, it's not because we have insufficient rules when it comes to driving instruction or testing cars.

Do you believe the Israeli government should curb the number of automobiles imported each year?

It's very difficult to do that here, even with the high degree of government involvement in the economy. We have learned that when people want to buy automobiles, there is almost no way for the government to stop them from doing so. The taxes people pay for automobiles in Israel are the highest in the world—purchase taxes and custom duties. People from other Western countries sometimes are astounded at what the cost of a car is in Israel. You might think that when the cost of a car here is three or four times what it is in the United States, people wouldn't buy cars. But the fact is that they do.

Some people are surprised that in Israel money is made available for people to buy cars. Some employers pay their employees special allowances for the use of their cars, or special allowances for purchasing cars. These costs are then passed on to the government and to the customers. In the final analysis, we find that the government is paying a good part of the cost of purchasing and running cars in

Israel. So, our experience has indicated that we are not going to be successful by trying to establish arbitrary or bureaucratic barriers to the import of cars into the country. It can't be done.

Do you believe the development of Elat would be enhanced by extending the railroad to Elat?

No question about it. The development of Elat and the development of the Negev, as a whole, would be enhanced by providing an increased level of transportation into the area.

Prior to Camp David and the return of Sinai, the Israeli government approved plans to build a major seaport at Yamit to relieve the congestion that would exist at the ports of Haifa and Ashdod. What do you believe must be done in order to serve Israel's port needs in the coming decades?

I don't consider myself an expert on Israel's ports, but from what I have learned as a member of the government, the two locations at Haifa and Ashdod probably will be adequate to cover Israel's shipping needs in the foreseeable future. Additional investments will have to be made, and the ports in both Haifa and Ashdod will have to be expanded and deepened as well. That's in the planning stage at the present time.

The international airport at Lod is obsolete. It has been estimated that it will not be able to handle the anticipated tourist level of the next decade. When and where should the new international airport be built?

I don't agree that our airport is obsolete. It is handling the traffic at the present time quite adequately, and I believe that most people who use the airport would come to that conclusion. There is room for some improvement in the facilities at the airport for processing passengers, ingoing and outgoing, in order to cut down the time people have to spend standing in line. But it probably compares favorably with most of the big airports in the world. I don't think we're anywhere near saturation at Ben Gurion Airport.

The more immediate need for expanding airport facilities is in the Elat area. We had an excellent airport a few miles from Elat—an air base built by the Israeli air force. It is just across the border established since the evacuation of the Sinai, lying totally unused. As a result, it cannot service Elat anymore—not without Egyptian compliance. If Israel were allowed to use that tremendous facility, then we could have our commerical aircraft land and take off from there. But, in the absence of Egyptian approval to use that air base, we will have to build a new airport in the Elat area in the coming years.

Given El Al's past problems, do you see it continuing to grow—purchasing more airplanes and adding more routes?

It should. I see no reason why El Al shouldn't be one of the most successful airlines in the world. We have the best pilots and mechanics. We don't pay any more for our aircraft and fuel than Pan American, Air France, or KLM. So, there is no reason why El Al should not be a very successful airline. It was for a period of time and then, in effect, it went into bankruptcy. It's another example of mismanagement by government. Many of El Al's problems are the direct result of the fact that the company is owned by the government.

There are terrible labor relations. The labor unions ask for exorbitant conditions, which are totally out of line with the company's ability to pay for them, but they do so in the expectation that the government will make up the difference. Here we have a clear demonstration of how, in a government-owned company, the labor union is not at all concerned about the profitability of the company—it simply depends on politicians to make up the difference, even when the company is pushed into bankruptcy as a result of labor union demands. El Al is a prime example of a company that should be sold to private investors. Once in the hands of the private sector, I have no doubt that it would become a very successful company.

What routes do you think El Al should add?

El Al should be flying all over the world. It certainly should be flying into all areas where there are large concentrations of Jewish people who are naturally attracted to coming to Israel. If we talk about the United States, in addition to New York, it should include Boston, Chicago, Los Angeles, Miami, and Philadelphia. Add to that cities in Canada, South America, and, certainly, Western Europe.

How large should El Al get before it would be advisable that there be a second Israeli airline handling scheduled international passenger and freight flights?

I don't know that we need a second Israeli airline. What we do need is competition. El Al should be competing against other airlines, whether they're Israeli or foreign.

In the past, I believe, you were in favor of establishing a second Israeli airline. Is that not correct?

No, I was never in favor of establishing a second Israeli airline. We've always had an internal airline—Arkia. It was my opinion that Israel was too small a country to allow an internal airline to operate profitably. But, since Arkia already existed, I believed it should be given a chance to fly international routes as well. That's still my opinion.

Do you foresee the establishment of a scheduled helicopter service between Israel's main cities and industrial areas to facilitate travel for businessmen?

Israel is a very small country, and it's not at all clear how essential it is to have helicopter travel or that there would be sufficient demand to pay the cost of such service. Today, it's a forty-five-minute drive from Tel Aviv to Jerusalem. That's going to be hard to beat by helicopter.

Along what line do you see the expansion of Israel's merchant fleet? What type of merchant ships should Israel purchase in the future?

We have a big shipping company, Zim, half of which is owned by the government. That's probably half the problem of Zim—that the government has so large an ownership. It's one of the largest shipping companies in the world, and it should have the ability to be profitable. Considering the skills and talents we have in this country, we should be able to do a good job at running an international shipping company.

Should Israel attempt to expand her shipbuilding facilities to build smaller merchant vessels?

We don't appear to have any competitive advantage when it comes to building ships. We were very successful in building missile boats; there we had a comparative advantage because we had developed very specific naval technology that was not available in other places in the world. For a while, then, the Israeli shipyards that built these missile boats were very profitable. We can continue to be success-ful if we continue to make investments in developing naval technology—ships and the various systems that go on naval boats. But I don't know that we have any specific advantage when competing with Japan, Norway, or Korea in building merchant ships. If we don't have such an advantage, then we should not spend our resources on that.

Communications

Recent experience has shown that mail from the United States can take up to six weeks before delivery. What do you believe can or should be done to improve the quality of mail distribution within Israel?

I don't know where that mail spent its time—whether it was in the United States or Israel or on a ship going from the United States to Israel. We are in the process of a revolution when it comes to communications of all sorts, including facsimile transmission. In the next few years, these problems will be almost behind us.

Given the fact that Israel is a nation that must continue to expand her exports, her communication with the outside world must be maintained with ease and speed. Yet, the reality is that the telephone system in Israel appears to be deteriorating rather than improving. What do you believe is the solution to this problem?

The solution lies in taking the telephone business out of the government's hands. That is the answer to many of our economic problems; it's true in this case, as well.

Israel is a major exporter of modern, advanced technology telephone systems. Why is it that these products have not been utilized to modernize Israel's archaic telephone system?

It's because the Israeli government, which owns the telephone company, is such a poor manager—an archaic manager. If we let the government manage the telephones, the airlines, or any other such systems, it's going to do a poor job. It's got to be taken out of government hands.

A factory established recently in Atarot was partially financed by the Israeli government as encouragement to establish it there. It was also financed by foreign capital and utilized U.S.-developed technology. Yet, it took six months from the time the company began its operations until it received a telephone. Even then, the service was less than adequate for a commercial operation. How do you account for this?

It's not the only case; I've heard of many similar cases. Provision of telephone communications in this country is simply not consistent with a modern, industrialized economy. It's out of step with the times.

How important is it for Israel to have the most modern telecommunications systems—on a par with Western Europe and the United States?

Israel not only should be but must be one of the most advanced industrial countries in the world—an exporter of high-technology products. And, if she's going to be that, it must have an up-to-date communication system to service that economy. If we cannot put that kind of communication system in place, then we are going to be in serious trouble.

How long will it be before every business that needs a phone line, and every family that wants one will be able to have one? It seems that since 1960, every cabinet minister responsible has declared that within five years every family wanting a phone would have one. When do you think this will come?

Some of our cabinet members who have served as Minister of Communication, once seeing what they were up against, threw up their hands and did not make any promises as to what they were going to do.

We have made a change recently in forming a telephone company called Bezek. It is still a government-owned company, but it's not part of the communications ministry. The assumption is that operating as a company, although government-owned, we are going to be able to increase the efficiency of our telephone system. Only time will tell. My view is that it has to be taken out of government hands altogether.

Modern telecommunications systems, such as facsimile transmission from overseas and computers speaking to each other over the telephone, pres-

ently are required to operate a modern business. Why doesn't Israel possess this capability at this time?

We already have most of that technology. More importantly, we have the people who know how to develop and manufacture such modern telecommunications systems and know how to deal with all aspects of such high-technology systems. We simply have to prepare ourselves in such a manner that we can utilize our capabilities, rather than have the knowledgeable people go off to other countries and apply that knowledge there.

Energy

What kind of power generation units should be built to meet Israel's future power needs?

What we are building at the present time are dual-purpose power plants that can use either oil or coal—a decision made during the height of the energy crisis. At that time, there was fear that oil prices would continue to go up, or even that Israel might find herself in a position where she would not be able to purchase oil, considering that the major oil producers are Arab countries. All this was after we had turned over the oil we had to the Egyptians.

The situation is changing at the present time, although I doubt that anyone is very confident that we will not face energy crises in the future as well. It would make a great deal of sense to build nuclear power plants in Israel, but that's become a lot more difficult since we turned the Sinai over to the Egyptians. Israel is a very small country. If we take environmental conditions into consideration, as we must, it is very difficult to find appropriate locations for nuclear power plants. Although there's much talk about such power plants, nothing definitive has been done. My projection is that we will continue with dual-purpose plants.

Do you believe Israel should utilize nuclear energy for power generation or continue with the use of fossil fuels?

I was a great believer in building nuclear power plants while the Sinai was under Israeli control. That was an almost ideal location for them. I put forth the idea, before the Israeli-Egyptian Peace Treaty, that we could establish, in the Sinai, Israeli-Egyptian nuclear power plants that would serve both countries and, thus, be an area for cooperation between us. But that idea was never taken up by the Egyptians at the time, and I've not sensed any enthusiasm on their part since then.

If you believe Israel should utilize nuclear energy for power generation, should she build her own nuclear reactor as Professor Yuval Ne'eman proposes?

We have considerable technology in the area of nuclear engineering. We have two nuclear engineering schools in Israel—Technion and Ben Gurion University—and two nuclear research reactors. We have very good nuclear physics departments at our universities and at the Weizmann Institute. If we were to build a nuclear reactor, we would want to give it a significant Israeli component. But that would depend on the circumstances—whether the contractor would be American or perhaps French—and whether it would make economic sense to introduce a significant Israeli content into such a power plant.

Do you believe the Mediterranean-Dead Sea Canal project will, or should, ever be revitalized?

Not for a while, in any case. Fighting inflation and trying to create an economic climate that will encourage investment preclude very large-scale commitments to that program for which, after all, there are other alternatives. It is basically an energy-generating program, and we are building conventional power plants in order to provide for Israel's energy needs. Under any circumstances, the Mediterranean-Dead Sea program would add a relatively small increment to Israel's energy inventory. It may be that in time we'll find it is economical to provide that additional increment by a hydroelectric project rather than build more conventional power plants. I don't think it is one of the most important or urgent things on Israel's agenda at the present time.

RELIGION

What do you believe should be the status in Israel of the Conservative and Reform movements? Should Conservative and Reform rabbis have a legal status in Israel?

First, we must ask what is the status of these rabbis in Israel at the present time? It's a nonstatus. The entire Jewish religious establishment in Israel is Orthodox. Historically, that's all we've ever had in Israel.

Until very recently, all of the Jews in Israel who were religious and participated in religious functions of one sort or another, did it on an Orthodox basis, regardless of whether they were very observant or not. When it came to the religious aspects of their lives—whether it was being circumcized, being buried, or being married or divorced—it was done through the Orthodox religious establishment; nobody ever had any second thoughts about it. Those people who were irreligious perhaps didn't get married through a religious ceremony or were not particularly concerned whether they were buried with a religious ceremony. That was the extent of their deviation from, or their protest against, the religious establishment.

What we've had in the past few years is a very small segment of the Israeli religious population protesting because they want to participate in religious practices associated with the Reform movement, or the Conservative movement, and not with those of the Orthodox movement. Clearly, that constitutes something of a problem, the major source of which is that we're dealing with such a tiny part of the Israeli population.

There are certain similarities between the Jewish community in Israel and the Jewish community in the United States, but one of the dissimilarities is that the American Jewish community is divided among the Reform, the Conservative, and the Orthodox. Although that division in America may not be equal, each movement has significant magnitude. In Israel, the division is totally skewed— probably 99 percent are Orthodox, and, perhaps, 1 percent is split between Reform and Conservative. People certainly should have the right to practice Judaism according to their own views. If they want to do it according to the practices of the Conservative or Reform movement, they should have the opportunity to do that. But full implementation of that principle here is, to some extent, dependent on there being more people in Israel who want to be Reform or Conservative Jews. This is why it is in very large measure a function of the size of the *aliyah* that will come from the United States.

If there were to be significant *aliyah* from the United States, which would mean that a significant number of people coming into Israel would be Conservative or Reform Jews, then I'm sure the problem would get solved in very short order. Presently, although the problem has emotional overtones and many people in the United States are concerned about it, to most Israelis it's a theoretical problem, not a real one, because it effects so very few Israelis.

Then if an adequate number of Conservative Jews were to make aliyah, *you would foresee legal status being given to a Conservative rabbi?*

There's no question about it, and the same thing would apply for Reform Jews. No question about it.

Given, then, that a sufficient number of Conservative and Reform Jews did come on aliyah, *would you be in favor of legal status being given to Conservative and Reform rabbis?*

Yes, and I think that would happen. It would be right that it would happen. If we're going to give people an equal opportunity to practice Judaism as they see fit, then, since the Orthodox rabbis have legal status, in time we'd have to give legal status to Conservative and Reform rabbis.

We have a religious problem in Israel at the present time with the Ethiopian Jews. The rabbinate has decided that they must go through some kind of pseudo-conversion process in order to make them 100 percent Jews. The Ethiopians are sure they are Jews according to the Orthodox provisions and don't want to do it. If there were two or five Ethiopian Jews in Israel, I don't suppose they would even have made a problem of it; however, it's a problem because there are about 20,000 Ethiopian Jews in Israel. It's a very painful situation for the Ethiopians, and I'm very concerned that we've run into that kind of problem.

We've brought here these Jewish people who have been separated from the mainstream of Jewish life for 2,000 or 3,000 years and yet were able to maintain themselves over that long period as Jews. And now that they're here, we're telling them that they're not really 100 percent Jews and that they must do something more before we can fully accept them. That's incongruous. I'm not an expert in the religious law, but I rebel against what's happening. There are 20,000 Ethiopian Jews here, and Israelis recognize them as Jews, otherwise they wouldn't be here in the first place. So we're going through a little pain and torture, but I'm sure the problem's going to be solved.

What is your position on the issue of "Who is a Jew?"

That goes back to the question of Reform and Conservative Judaism. Israel is a Jewish state. That was its purpose. That was the aim of the Zionist movement—establishing a Jewish state to serve as a home and a haven for Jews from throughout the world. As a result, it raised the question as to who is a Jew, and that question must be answered.

Perhaps in other cases, it wouldn't be necessary, nor would it even be desirable, to define people and to say exactly who they are. Let each person say what he wants to be. But in the case of Israel, a Jewish state established to be a home and a haven for Jews from throughout the world, we have no choice but to provide an answer to the question, "Who is a Jew?"

At the present time, the answer to that question must be the answer of the Halacha—the answer of the Jewish religion. After 2,000 years of exile during which we've remained Jewish because of Halacha and because of the Jewish religion, we're not suddenly going to come up with some new answer.

Everything would be very simple if the Jewish religious establishment throughout the world were all Orthodox. The Orthodox would provide the answer, and we would all accept it, whether we were religious or not. But there are other Jewish religious establishments, like the Conservative and the Reform movements; so the question, of course, arises. It appears quite prominently because it involves the marriage ritual and various other practices about which rabbis must provide answers. As long as the vast majority of people who are religious in Israel are Orthodox, we have no choice but to follow the Orthodox rules and regulations.

If there were the potential to have a significant number of people make *aliyah* from the United States, and if it were to become clear to Israel that the answer to the question "Who is a Jew?" would have a direct bearing on the size of that *aliyah* to Israel, then I think we would respond differently. Under such circumstances, the guiding principle—the dominant motivation—would be the degree to which we would want *aliyah* of Jews from the United States. If it were available, and we wanted it, we would have to take into account the sensitivities of those members of the American Jewish community who belong to Conservative or Reform congregations. Otherwise we would be blocking *aliyah* from the United States. But right now, that's only a hypothetical situation for Israelis.

For thousands of years, the religious definition of a Jew, as defined by Halachic Judaism, has been that a Jew is one whose mother was a Jew. Recently, the Reform movement has decided to recognize a Jew as one whose father is a Jew. The question now becomes, how do you reconcile these two different beliefs—one that defines a Jew by the mother and one that defines by the father?

Most religious Jews will tell you that religious law does not require interpretation or explanation. That's the law. That's the way it's been for 3,000 years, and that's the way it has to continue to be. At the present time, and until a significant number of Reform and/or Conservative Jews make *aliyah* to Israel, the definition of a Jew must be that of Halachic law.

What is your attitude toward the imposition of Halacha on marriage, divorce, public transport, Sabbath laws, and dietary laws?

There's no getting away from the fact that the role of religion in Israel, in Israeli law, and in the Israeli government is far greater than it is in any other Western society. This is because there is a very close interrelationship between the

State of Israel and the Jewish religion, much more so than there is between any other Western country and the religion that's practiced by the majority population of that country. Whether they're Jews by religion, or Jews by nationality, here they're really both.

That's the reason why religion has a significant role in Israel and in Israeli law. That's the reason why the religious establishment has a legal position in Israel and why certain aspects of life are, in effect, relegated to its supervision or control. That's probably not going to change. It's not possible to talk in Israel of a "separation of church and state" (in this case "synagogue and state"). We can't really have such a separation; the two are just too closely intertwined.

What is your attitude toward the operation on the Sabbath of vital industries; for example, where there is equipment that cannot be unattended like computers, power stations, chemical processes? Perhaps you would even like to comment on El Al Sabbath flights?

No, I wouldn't like to comment on El Al Sabbath flights! Regarding facilities that have to be run on a twenty-four-hour-a-day, seven-day-a-week basis, I think that is well established in Israel: they run. It is beyond dispute, as I think it should be. For example, the electric company runs constantly.

To obtain a divorce in Israel presently requires appearing before two courts, civil and religious, which has created a perception of inequality based on whether one of the spouses started proceedings in a civil court or a religious court. Do you agree that such a system is correct and should be continued in present form?

Let me start by telling you I really don't know the details. Fortunately, I have never had to appear before either a religious or civil court on such matters. I know that there is a whole realm of personal matters that are dealt with in Israel by religious courts. What does that mean? It means that such matters are dealt with, by Jews, in rabbinical courts; by Moslems, in Moslem courts; and by Christians, under Christian religious jurisdiction. That reflects not only the existing state of law in Israel but probably also the desire of a significant number of Israel's population—Jews, Moslems, and Christians. In that itself, there may be nothing wrong.

I don't think that is something that calls for a change or represents a problem for most of the people living in Israel. I am not aware of the fact that people have to appear before civil and religious courts, as well—I think it's only one. If it's an issue that falls into the jurisdiction of the religious courts, then you appear before religious courts.

Do you believe a woman who has received a non-Orthodox divorce decree in the Diaspora should be allowed to marry in Israel?

I'm not in a position to give you that kind of a verdict. Clearly, everything in Israel must be done according to the laws of Israel. Personal matters here are handled by religious courts. That means personal matters that relate to people who are Jewish are handled by Jewish religious courts or rabbinical courts. Personal matters having to do with people who are Moslem are handled by Moselm courts, and so on.

There's something of a paradox in Israel because most of the Jewish population here is not religious. Israel, in many ways, is a very secular state in terms of the attitude of her population. But the part of the Jewish population in Israel that is religious is Orthodox—probably 99.5 percent. And the rabbinical court—the entire religious establishment in Israel—is Orthodox. This is why, and I think rightfully so, in the rabbinical establishment in Israel, there is no representation for other than the Orthodox segment.

That creates something of a problem for Jews who come from abroad who have been married or divorced by rabbis belonging to the Conservative or Reform movement. But it is not an insurmountable problem. It may turn out to be a big problem to an individual; I appreciate that, and I don't in any way belittle it. I've been in Israel for many years. I've never yet, among people I know—and I do have a very large circle of friends and acquaintances—come up against anyone who has had a serious problem of that nature that couldn't be solved.

Do you believe that the present law in Israel, which disallows a marriage of a Halachicly divorced woman to a Cohen, should be rescinded?

It's one way or the other. If personal matters, like marriage and divorce, are handled by religious authorities, then they have to be handled according to religious law, and neither I nor you are in a position to change that religious law. Perhaps the Chief Rabbinate in Israel can make some changes. Only they would have the authority to do that.

What do you think should be the role of the Chief Rabbi in Israel?

At the present time, there are two Chief Rabbis, not one. I believe we should have only one Chief Rabbi because we're one Jewish people: one Jewish people—one Chief Rabbi.

What's your position on the "pork" issue? How are you going to vote on the bill before the Knesset prohibiting the marketing of pork in Israel?

I already voted. The first time around, I voted for it, against my better judgment and my conscience. I voted in support of the party that sponsored it. They forced me to vote for it!

At the present time, with a National Unity government that could break up at any moment (although I don't think it's going to), both Labor and Likud are continuously seeking potential partners for a narrow-based government they would try to put together to make sure there would be no defections one way or the other. As a result, the leverage of the religious parties is greater today than it was before. You would think that the opposite would be true, because in the National Unity government (Labor and Likud) religious parties can join the government or they can elect not to be in the government—it's up to them. There's no reason why we have to make any special side payments to them. But because everybody's continuously running in fear or in anticipation of the situation that would develop if the National Unity government should break up, the leverage of the religious parties has increased.

The Likud, of course, wants to stay on the good side of its potential coalition partners. As a result, certain agreements were made with the religious parties during the coalition negotiations. So there are certain commitments, now, that all Likud Knesset members—and I'm one of them—are being called on to meet.

Basically, in answer to your question, I don't believe the government should interfere with the lives of the citizens of the country—that it should tell them what they can and cannot eat and what they can or cannot do. People should be free to make their choices, and that goes for the food they eat and the liquid they drink.

During a debate that I had on the radio in the United States recently with Meir Kahane, he spoke about the establishment of a theocracy in Israel, not unlike that which the Agudah would desire. What is your reaction to this feeling among a certain percentage of Orthodox Jews in Israel about establishing a theocracy—a government run by the rabbinate?

I'm dead set against it. Although I recognize a role for the religious establishment in Israeli life—and I think there always will be such a role, I certainly do not feel that that role should be an imposition on the people who live in the country. People should be free to eat whatever they like, to go to the beach whenever they like, and to drive their cars whenever they like. No one has a right to restrain people from doing what they like. Not only am I strongly opposed to a theocracy, but also I believe that we have to make sure that people who are religious cannot impose their views on people who are not religious. We're in the process now of trying to assure that.

What should Israel's attitude be toward the Netura Karta residing in Mea Shearim?

On a general level, it should be the same as our attitude is toward anyone who lives in Israel as a citizen. We have a particular problem with members of the Netura Karta community because at least some of them insist that they don't recognize either the State of Israel or her laws. I don't think the problems are terribly serious, but, now and then, we see them getting out in the streets and throwing stones at cars. The government must enforce the laws and put a stop to that. At times, they've indicated they prefer being under Jordanian rule. Of course, they can easily exercise that option by crossing the Jordan.

What are your positions on the issues of organ transplants, artificial insemination, human genetic engineering, and autopsy?

I have little knowledge in those areas, so I'm not prepared to comment at length; however, organ transplants, autopsies, and probably even artificial insemination are performed in Israel. They may not be done only for research purposes, but if an autopsy is required to determine the cause of death, then it is done. If an organ transplant is needed to save a life, it, too, is done. There's a certain fringe of the Orthodox who try to stop such practices, but they have not. I have a son who is a doctor, and since the subject comes up in discussion, I'm aware of what's going on.

When it comes to matters related to organ transplants, skin banks, and autopsies, the situation in Israel is not such that it presents a real impediment to proper medical practice or to the advancement of proper medical practice. Some people get upset about it, but we're not in a situation where medicine can't be properly practiced in Israel by Western standards. The level of medical practice here is very good.

Considering the conservative nature of the Orthodox viewpoint regarding

abortion, in contrast to the apparent increased awareness of women's rights here, is legalized abortion an issue?

At the present time, in accordance with Halachic law, abortion is illegal in Israel, so legalized abortion is not really an issue here. Again, there is that very close interrelationship among the Jewish religion, the Jewish people, and the State of Israel. Considering that, along with the long-time emphasis on the family among Jews, as well as recent developments in birth control, I doubt that legalized abortion will ever become an issue here.

As you know, there are three Jewish elementary school systems in Israel. There are the secular schools for general studies in which the Bible is taught as history; the Dati schools, the official government-sponsored religious schools; and the Yeshivah system, sponsored by the Agudah, often referred to as the blacks. What is your attitude toward the government's support of these three separate Jewish elementary school systems?

Again, it's a reflection of the larger role that religion plays in Israel than in any other country in the world. It's been that way for years. If anything, there has been a reduction of one system because we once had a Socialist educational system that we don't have anymore. The one new thing that's come along in recent years is the Yeshivot Hesder, but there's been no major change.

Is it true that there's a movement toward greater religious education in Israel?

There's movement in both directions. Some people are moving toward greater religious identification, and, by the same token, many people who came from religious homes are not religious anymore. Just what the net movement is, I don't know.

The fact is, however, that we have a significant number of Israeli parents who want their children to attend schools that have a substantial religious content. Again, it represents the very large role that religion plays in the life of Israel and the very strong interrelationship between religion and Jewish nationhood. These are just facts. If so many parents want their children to get a religious education, then the State must provide for it and must give assistance to it. If it were a small segment of the population, we might say it's their problem. Let them use their own funds to establish the kind of schools they would like to have for their children. But it's not a small segment in the spectrum of parents. It's a very significant number, and I believe the government has an obligation here.

What is your position regarding the fact that religious girls and Yeshivah boys are not required to perform military service? Do you believe that they should be required to perform some other national service instead?

First of all, some religious girls do go into the army, and many of them do national service. There are some, of course, who don't. Israeli law provides for the fact that a girl can be exempt from military service on grounds of religion. If the girl presents herself at the draft board and explains that her religious mode of life and beliefs are such that she cannot be inducted into the army, then, if she's sufficiently convincing, she may get an exemption. It is a matter of not forcing someone who feels that strongly about her religious beliefs and their conflict with army service to go into the army.

In a similar fashion, that's true for some of the men who get an exemption if they are Yeshivah students. In some cases, it's a postponement, not an exemption, until they finish their studies. In other cases, Yeshivah studies, in effect, are continuous and endless—students devote their lives to study. When they make a claim that army service will represent an interruption in, and an infringement on, that devotion because they feel they must learn on a continuous basis, they do get an exemption from army service.

There are, however, many students in Yeshivot who do their army service. And there are the Yeshivot Hesder, Yeshivot-organized in such a manner that their students go into the army and do their service. By the way, they turn out to be very good soldiers.

Do you feel that those religious girls and Yeshivah boys who are exempt from army service should be required to perform some other national service instead?

Some religious girls who don't go into the army do national service but of another sort—shnat sherut. I'm all for that, but it doesn't provide the full answer to the question. We can't expect that an option to perform an alternate service will bring about a situation wherein everyone will serve in the army or do national service of another sort. One reason is the conscientious objection that is brought forth by some of the girls who say their religious beliefs and practices do not permit them to serve in the army because they must stay at home. Perhaps, in the future, we might respond to such an explanation by indicating that they can do national service while remaining at home because we can install a computer terminal for them to work on.

The Yeshivah boys who insist they cannot do army service are saying, in effect, that they must study the *Gemorrah* and the commentaries day in and day out—every hour of the day. Their objection to joining the army is not the fact that they would have to tote a rifle; they're not conscientious objectors in that sense.

Their objection is to the fact that their mode of life, which involves continuous study from morning until night for every day of the week, would be interrupted by their going into the army. The same would be true if we said to them that instead of going into the army, we would like them to do some other national service. So alternative service wouldn't quite provide the answer to all the people involved.

What is your attitude toward the Yeshivot Hesder?

That is a very good institution. It clearly provides the opportunity for Yeshivah students who are part of that system to devote themselves to learning—as they would like to—and serve in the Israeli army. As I said before, they have turned out to be very good soldiers. Battalion or regimental commanders who have students from the Yeshivot Hesder serving with them invariably say that they are among the best soldiers they have.

Do you believe the government should finance, support, promote, and/or publicly encourage dual track institutions of higher learning for Yeshivah students, such as the Jerusalem College of Technology for young men and the Jerusalem College for Women, where there are both general studies and religious studies?

The Israeli government provides a very large measure of support for all education in Israel. On a per-capita basis, or as a proportion of the budget, the government's support for education in Israel is larger than in most, if not all, places in the world. That's good. It's probably the best investment the Israeli government has made.

The implication of the question here is that these two institutions are really catering to what we call the black Yeshivot—the ones who have traditionally studied only the *Gemorrah*. Now, in these two institutions, we are providing an opportunity for students to study things other than *Gemorrah*—to get into general studies. From Israel's standpoint, this should be very important to get the student into the mainstream.

With the kind of support Israel provides for educational institutions, the government should not discriminate. The minute the government discriminates in favor of some particular institution or set of institutions, it immediately causes a problem. People start raising a hue and cry because they know it's going to be at someone's expense.

The government should provide its support in all directions and give people a chance to study in the environment in which they would like to study. Again, religion is an important part of Israeli life. Certainly, it's a dominant part of the life of many Israelis. Therefore, it's not surprising that a good many Israelis want to do their studies in an establishment that is religious in nature—even if it's electronics they want to study. If that's what they like, then the government should be supportive of that.

Some people say that the government should provide more support for techno- logical education—engineering—than for liberal arts education. We could make a case for that, but we could make a case against it, too. Many people would be very upset if the government were to favor the Technion, for example, in the allocation of government funds. At the present time, the government is not favoring the Technion. On a per-capita basis, the Technion gets the same funds as does the Hebrew University or Tel Aviv University. If it could be shown that favoring religious technological institutions would result in their attracting more people who are presently outside of the normal educational framework and not fully participating in the life of Israeli society, then perhaps such a government decision would warrant support. However, it's not at all clear that the government really could, or even should, do that. It means that the government, in effect, would be allocating funds in favor of certain institutions at the expense of others.

JEWISH SUBGROUPS

It is the perception of American Jews that a basic societal problem exists in Israel between Ashkenazi and Sephardic Jews. It is thought that the Ashkenazim control or run the institutions of the government, and the Sephardim, who have not reached the levels in society attained by Ashke- nazim, take a secondary role. Is this a proper perception reflecting the realities as they exist in Israel today? Do you foresee the resolution of this struggle within the next decade or two?

No, it's not a proper perception; it's simply a projection of a certain stereotype—perhaps applicable to American society thirty, forty, or fifty years ago—being applied to Israel. I'm referring to the tendency to look for the hewers of wood and the carriers of water—the disadvantaged in the society—who, because of their ethnic background or country of origin, are not given equal opportunity, are discriminated against, and are perhaps even persecuted. All that is totally inapplicable to Israel.

The very essence of Zionism is *Kibbutz Galyot*, the ingathering of the exiles— bringing Jews back from the four corners of the earth—back to their ancient homeland. That in itself is an ideal. Every Israeli takes pride in seeing Jews from all parts of the world coming to Israel and playing their role in the Israeli society—in the army, in the political establishment, in the academic institutions.

It is true, of course, that Jews coming from the four corners of the earth come not only from different countries but from different cultural backgrounds with different levels of education. Clearly, the Jews who came to Israel from Europe were disadvantaged as compared to the Jews who came to Israel from the United States. The Jews who came from Iraq, Libya, North Africa, and Yemen were disadvantaged, to some extent, as compared to the Jews who came from Western Europe and some of the Eastern European countries. They didn't have the same opportunities and, on the average, didn't have the same level of education.

Most of the Jews who came from the Oriental communities arrived in Israel bereft of everything, starting from scratch—living in tents, getting started in development towns, starting in agriculture without ever having had any background in that area. In many ways, Israel's greatest achievement is that within the span of one generation, we've managed to close the gap of many, many generations. If we look at Israel's society today in all its aspects and dimensions, we'll find that the sons of immigrants who came from Yemen or Iraq have attained the same level of achievement as the sons of immigrants who came from Poland, the Soviet Union, or the United States.

If we look at the Israel Defense Forces today, we will find that people whose parents were of Oriental background—Sephardim and immigrants from Arabic-speaking countries—fill some of the very top positions. The chief of staff at the present time is not an Ashkenzai. I had the privilege of appointing Moshe Levy as Chief of Staff, but he's not the only senior officer who is not Ashkenazi.

If we look at the business world in Israel, we'll find not only people whose parents came from Germany, Poland, Russia, or the United States but also people whose parents came from Greece, Iran, Iraq, North Africa, or Turkey. If we go to Israel Aircraft Industries and look at the people who are designing the Lavi, we'll find people from all the communities. If we go to Israel's academic institutions, we'll find professors from various backgrounds. So, the characterization that there is this segmentation in Israeli society between Ashkenazi and Sephardic Jews is totally inappropriate.

Look at the Knesset today. Look at Israel's cabinet and her cabinet ministers. We just had a president of Israel who's not an Ashkenazi Jew, Yitzhak Navon. Today, we have a speaker of the Israeli Knesset, Shlomo Hillel, who's not an Ashkenazi Jew. The interesting thing, and maybe the most significant, is that all Israelis take great pride in that. In other words, it's not only Jews originating from Iraq who take pride in the fact that Shlomo Hillel, who came from Iraq, is today the speaker of the Israeli Knesset. All Israelis take pride in that.

How long do you think it will be before the Jewish population of Israel, which emanates from seventy to seventy-five different countries, will be fully integrated so that their descendants will say they are Sabra, not Sephardic, Iraqi, or Ashkenazi?

We are already at that point. At least 25 percent of the Jews in Israel today already have difficulty identifying themselves when asked exactly where they come from or what kind of a Jew they are. Many of them can clearly tell you that their parents came from Iraq, Poland, or Yemen; if questioned further, they will tell you that their spouses come from families that did not come from that same country. So there are "mixed marriages" of Ashkenazi and Sephardic Jews. There is much of that and, of course, their children would not be able to identify themselves anymore with a particular country of origin. If we wait another five or ten years, the whole question of the countries of origin—although of interest and a source of pride to everyone in terms of the background and traditions they still try to maintain within the family—would really be of no significance in determining the demographic makeup of the Jewish population in Israel.

Will the Ethiopian Jews have a problem integrating into the society or intermarrying with other Jewish groups because of the color of their skin?

If we want to talk about that with certainty, it's probably too early to tell because immigration of Ethiopian Jews in large numbers is very recent. A definitive answer to that question can be given only ten or twenty years from now. But based on what has happened so far—and, after all, we've undergone the process of ingathering of exiles for many, many years now, even before the creation of the State of Israel—the answer is no. They will be fully integrated without any problems whatsoever into Israeli society, despite the fact they come from a background very different from that of most of Israel's present population. Israel has shown herself to be very successful in integrating people from all kinds of backgrounds—regardless of the color of their skin or the language they speak when they come here—and turning them into full partners in Israeli society.

Will the Ethiopian Jews have a problem intermarrying with Jews from other countries or Sabras because of Halachic doubt of their real Jewishness?

The answer to that is no, as well. It's a subject that has been discussed and debated—whether Ethiopian Jews must undergo some additional steps in order to confirm their Jewishness. Most of that is behind us. Whatever is not behind us, I am sure will be shortly. In the Israeli press there are already reports of "mixed marriages" of Ethiopian Jews or Jewesses with Jews who are not from Ethiopia. I'm sure it won't be a problem.

There is a widespread perception in the Diaspora that there is a widening of the gap between religious Jews and nonreligious Jews over the imposition of Halachic laws on the society and that this situation might lead to serious violence and civil disobedience. Do you believe this perception is well-founded?

There has been no deterioration in Israel over the years in the relationship between religious and nonreligious, or secular, Jews. As I indicated before, most of Israel's Jewish population is secular. What characterizes that secular population is a very high degree of understanding for the religious community in Israel and a readiness to bend over backwards in order to accommodate the very specific needs, requirements, and desires of the religious community—but up to a point.

That segment of the religious community that is very extreme—that makes demands not only on themselves but on other sectors of the population as well—is a small segment of the religious population. That element has always been with us. It has really not been getting any more extreme in recent years. If anything, the situation is probably improving. Why do I say that? First, if we look at the membership in the Knesset and the results of Knesset elections, we will find that, over the years, the number of Knesset members who have been elected to represent religious parties in Israel has decreased—and decreased very significantly. That doesn't mean that the percentage of Israel's population that is religious has diminished. It has probably stayed pretty much the same. But it does mean that the percentage among them who insist upon being represented by members of a religious party rather than voting for one of the major parties, Labor or Likud, is decreasing. And that to me means that the degree of polarization is actually decreasing, not increasing. It means that there are more and more people in Israel who are religious but don't feel they must express themselves by voting for a religious party in the Knesset, or by having a religious person represent them in the Knesset.

Also, the extreme wing of the religious organizations in Israel, Agudat Yisrael, in past years—before the establishment of the State of Israel—would have nothing to do with the Zionist movement. They insisted on isolating themselves and erecting barriers between them and the Zionist movement. Today, we find they are an integral part of the Israeli body politic. Agudat Yisrael is a member of the present government coalition. It is true that they would not agree to have any of their members be members of the cabinet—be ministers—but their representatives in the Parliament are members of the coalition. So, I see that bridges and connections are being built rather than the other way around.

ISRAELI ARABS AND
ARABS IN ADMINISTERED TERRITORIES

Israeli Arabs

What is your attitude toward Moslem and Christian Arabs serving in Israel's armed forces?

I'm all for it, and more than that, as Minister of Defense, I started a program of encouraging the service of Israel's Arab population in the Israel Defense Forces. Jewish citizens of Israel have an obligation to serve in the armed forces—men and women alike. Male Druse citizens of Israel are obligated to serve in the armed forces, just as Jews, but Druse women are not obligated to serve. This is a deferral to Druse religious sentiment and the opposition that exists in the Druse community to their women serving in the armed forces. Circassian males or "Cherkassim," as they're called in Israel, serve in the IDF, just as do Jews and Druse, but, currently, that's all—no other ethnic minority community in Israel is obligated to serve in the armed forces.

We have an increasing number of volunteers from the Bedouin community doing regular service. Bedouins have served in the IDF over the years but, in the past, only in very specific areas—mostly as trackers, where their native ability to track in the surroundings of the Middle East topography has been utilized. We're starting to encourage Bedouin young men to volunteer for regular army service for the three-year service period, going through regular basic training as do the Israeli recruits. We must continue in that direction.

I believe that everyone who is a citizen of Israel must not only ask for equal rights in Israel but also be ready to bear equally the burdens of citizenship. There's no way of obtaining equality of rights and opportunities without simultaneously obtaining a share of the burdens of citizenship. That is a problem that Israel's Arab population must face. It's something they did not have to face until now, yet, in effect, they have equality before the law. We hear demands on the part of the Arab population—they insist on having equality of rights. In the future, they will also have to attain equality when it comes to the burden of Israeli citizenship, which includes service in the armed forces.

It is apparent you believe that Israel's Arab men should serve in her armed forces, just as her Jewish men do. What about the Arab women? Should they serve in Israel's armed forces, or is there some other form of service that you think they could fulfill?

We're not yet addressing the issue of Israeli army service for Arab women. Many of Israel's Arab citizens do not want to serve in the Israeli armed forces. We can judge that from the fact that, in the last election, 60 percent of Israel's Arab electorate, in effect, voted for the PLO. The PLO is a terrorist organization that is dedicated to the destruction of the State of Israel. The 60 percent who voted for the PLO voted either for the Communist party or for what is called the Progressive Party for Peace. These are two parties that competed with each other as to who was the true and real adherent of the PLO—who it was that had the recommendation and the endorsement of Yasir Arafat.

An Arab-Israeli citizen who votes for the PLO is really not very eager to serve in the IDF. I'm not even sure how good a service it would be. That's really the first barrier that must be overcome. Israel, as a country, will have to deal with it, as will her Jewish and Arab citizens. The question of the service of Arab women in the Israeli armed forces will be addressed later.

What do you think about integrating Arabs with advanced education into Israel's government service?

We should do it. This comes, of course, as part of the issue of providing equality of opportunity. Israel owes equality of opportunity to all those who share equally in the burdens of Israeli citizenship. She owes equality of opportunity to her Druse citizens, and we have made good on that in the IDF where we have a number of Druse in high positions. All ranks and ratings are open to Druse, and today we have a number of full colonels who are Druse. I'm sure that soon we will have a Druse general in the IDF.

We haven't really done as well in civilian areas. I can't honestly say that there is an equality of opportunity for Druse in all government services. Certainly, if we look at the proportions of Druse in senior government positions, we will see that the proportion is far smaller than their proportion in the Israeli population. We must improve that situation.

When it comes to Israel's Arab citizens, equality of opportunity, including the opportunity to serve in senior positions in the various government ministries, will come only when there is a sharing of the burden of military service among the Arab community.

What is your attitude toward having an Arab minister in the Israeli cabinet?

It all goes together. It's really part of the political process. It's something that's quite possible today. We have Arabs who are members of Israel's Parliament. If one of the parties that has Arabs among its parliamentary faction joins the coalition government, it's quite possible that an Arab would become a minister in the government. Again, it goes back to the question of the sharing of the burdens of citizenship. The cabinet very frequently discusses security questions of ultimate importance to the country and deals with highly classified information. It's not even reasonable to expect that a man who didn't serve in the IDF—or would not serve in the IDF—would suddenly become privy to these kinds of sessions.

What do you think about Israeli Jews and Arabs intermarrying?

That is a very personal question that I would leave to the couples involved. I think it is a private matter.

What is your attitude toward Israeli Arabs maintaining close relations with other Arabs outside of Israel?

That may be quite natural, and there would be no objections to it, as long as it doesn't get into the area of communicating with the enemy. Israel's Arabs have a problem which they must face in that most of the Arab countries surrounding Israel are hostile to her—are her declared enemies—and insist that they are in a state of war with Israel.

We've had some very specific problems in past years, even in recent months, of Israeli Arabs and an Israeli Arab member of the Knesset who wanted to have direct contact with the PLO. Darawshe, an Israeli Arab who is a member of the Israeli Labor party, left Israel in order to meet with Yasir Arafat. Due to some miscommunication, the meeting didn't take place, so he came back. But, as a result, the problem came to prominence and was discussed in Israeli society and the Israeli press.

The appropriateness of such activity was questioned. It's totally inappropriate—even illegal. It's illegal for an Israeli citizen, regardless of whether or not he is a member of Parliament, to have contact with the enemy; the PLO is an enemy of Israel. The PLO is dedicated to Israel's destruction. It is a terrorist organization and, in my view, contact with the PLO by any Israeli citizen, Jew or Arab, should be punishable by law.

You've indicated that you think Israeli Arabs who fulfill full responsibility as citizens should have equal opportunity provided to them. Do you also believe that they should have full protection of their rights under the law?

Of course. At the present time, all Israeli citizens, including Israeli Arab citizens, have protection of their rights under the law, regardless of whether or not they carry the full burden of citizenship. And I believe it should continue that way. From the legal point of view, in terms of the rights of citizenship, we can't create a class of second-class citizens, with only partial rights to citizenship. We don't want that. But the claim to equal opportunity is tied to sharing the burdens of citizenship.

Arabs in the Administered Territories

Do you believe Israel should continue to encourage Arabs living in the administered territories to work during the day in Israel proper?

No, I don't believe that. I don't consider the very large-scale employment of the Arab population of Judea and Samaria within Israel's cities and industries a healthy phenomenon, either for the Jewish population of Israel or for the Arab population in Judea and Samaria. The use of so many Arab workers from Judea and Samaria in Israeli industry represents a large-scale deviation from everything that Zionists believe in.

Israel was built on the principle of self-labor, on the principle that people who came here did the labor that was required. They didn't come to Israel to be the bosses, to be the overlords over some other sector of the population that would do the dirty work for them. I don't think it's good for the Arab population to have the feeling that they're being utilized to do the jobs that the Jews don't want to do. As time goes by, we should be looking for ways and means of doing away with that phenomenon.

Should Israel cooperate with and help American groups that sponsor development projects for the Arabs in the administered territories?

I had to deal with that question directly while I was Minister of Defense, and I've had a number of conversations with Secretary Shultz on the subject. As I've communicated to him on a number of occasions, we are in favor of industrial development in Judea and Samaria—not only industrial development but agricultural development as well. There has been a great deal of agricultural development, and quite considerable industrial development, too, by the way, since 1967. We're all for that, and I think the statistics show that Judea and Samaria, industrially and economically in general, have advanced more rapidly than any other part of the world since 1967.

We encourage additional investments, but we do not believe in mixing business with politics. We do not encourage investments by American groups that are politically motivated—groups that have an axe to grind and that would like to see their investments contribute to some political changes they desire. So, as long as we're talking about individual private investors, yes, I'm all for it.

Do you support Jewish settlements in the heart of those sections of the administered territories densely populated by Arabs, for example, Hebron? Nablus?

I support Jewish settlements in Judea and Samaria, in fact in all of Israel. I really have no qualifications about that. I'm not among those who believe that Jews should not be seen by Arabs and that the very sight of a Jew is liable to antagonize an Arab or make him angry. Jews and Arabs have to live together in this part of the world, and it doesn't matter whether it's in Jaffa or in Haifa or in Hebron.

Hebron is a special case, because Hebron has had a Jewish community, in effect, forever—certainly for over a thousand years and, prior to that, in Biblical times. The Jewish community in Hebron was massacred. There was a pogrom in Hebron in 1929 and that was the end of the Jewish community there. Now, I can't see how anyone, including the Arab population of Hebron, and certainly no Zionist, would want that to stand as a final verdict of history—that the Jewish community in Hebron was wiped out in that way. So, I have looked upon Jewish resettlement in Hebron and the rebuilding of the Jewish community there as a very special case that really is symbolic of Zionism itself—the return of the Jews to the places where they lived before. There's no sense in differentiating among events that happened throughout Israel 2,000 years ago, in the Jewish quarter of the old city thirty-seven years ago, and in Hebron fifty-six years ago—in 1929. I've told this to the Arab notables in Hebron, and I think they understand. In my view, the rebuilding of the Jewish quarter in Hebron is symbolically one of the most important things that Israel has to undertake in future years.

Are you in favor of providing Israeli citizenship to Arabs who live in East Jerusalem?

The Arab population of East Jerusalem has the option of taking out Israeli citizenship. Actually, it's a very unusual offer. They have an open-ended option. They received that option when Israeli law was applied to East Jerusalem back in 1967. That's twenty years ago now, and any Arab who lives in East Jerusalem can exercise that option any time. Most of them have not. There are not more than a hundred or so Arabs of the population there who have taken out Israeli citizenship. But giving them that option was certainly the right thing to do.

Do you foresee the Arabs in the administered territories undermining Israel in a time of war, thus, perhaps, requiring mass expulsion?

First of all, let's use correct terminology. What is the correct term? If what you want to do is apply a term that indicates the type of control in the area, whether it's an integral part of the State of Israel or not, then I suppose the administered territories is appropriate. Somebody who has an anti-Israel bent might use the term occupied territories.

If you want to use a geographic term, then it's well-known that the land west of the Jordan River, since Biblical times, has been divided into the Galilee, the Sharon Plain, Samaria, Judea, and the Negev. That whole area is Western Palestine. It was referred to as that by the British during the mandatory administration. They used the terms Galilee, Sharon, Negev, Samaria, and Judea. Those who insist on using West Bank, clearly, for some reasons I suppose we can suspect, do not want to use the appropriate geographic term. The term they use really makes their motivation suspect. Other appropriate geographic terms for the mandated territory of Palestine are East Bank and West Bank. The East Bank is what is today the kingdom of Jordan, and the West Bank is everything else on this side, including Tel Aviv and Haifa. So when the PLO uses West Bank, we know what they mean. They mean the entire area west of the Jordan River.

If what we're talking about is the area that came under Israeli control during the Six-Day War, then we're talking about Judea and Samaria, which comprise the area that the Jordanians took over and occupied in the War of Independence in 1948, and Gaza, which is the area that the Egyptian army managed to occupy at that time.

The Golan Heights is a separate entity in that it was under Syrian control prior to the Six-Day War in 1967. East Jerusalem, also, is a separate entity in the sense that it is that part of Jerusalem which, having been conquered by the Arab armies in the War of Independence, was occupied by the Jordanian Legion until it was liberated by the Israeli army in the Six-Day War.

Now let's discuss whether the Arab population in Judea, Samaria, and Gaza is likely to undermine Israeli presence in wartime. If we talk about individual acts of terrorism, then we're dealing with that problem in those areas right now and have been, in fact, since 1967. Since 1948—before the establishment of the State of Israel—we've had to deal with terrorism that emanated from certain segments of the Arab population throughout Israel.

At the very present time, we're dealing with what is clearly Arab terrorism directed at the Jewish population in Israel within the green lines—the pre '67 borders. You may have noticed that every few weeks some Jew has been murdered on the roads, not in Judea or Samaria, but within Israel—in that part of Israel which is in the pre 1967 borders. Not all of the Arab population on either side of the armistice line of '49 holds to the norms of Western society. A significant segment of that population does not believe in those norms at all, and some significant portion of that population is engaging in terrorism today. They are ready to kill innocent people, even women and children. Many of them are supporters of the PLO. This problem of Arab terrorism, or in recent years PLO terrorism, is a problem that clearly we have dealt with in the past, are dealing with presently, and, if we're going to be realistic about the future, will continue to have to deal with.

Would this kind of terrorist activity become more extensive or assume mass proportions in time of war? Past history has indicated that such is not the case. It is just in times of war that there has been an absence of these kinds of phenomena and that the population has been far more quiescent and disciplined. I suppose it's because of the fear that during a war, certain emergency measures might be taken in response to terrorist activity. So, the past has indicated that just in times of war, terrorism has not been a source of concern. It has been in times of peace that we've had to deal with it.

But it's not impossible to experience terrorism in time of war. The population is liable to excitement, and certainly groups outside of Israel are liable to try to incite terrorism in wartime. If Israel were to be attacked again, say by a coalition of Arab states, it's possible that their leaders would try to incite the Arab population in Israel on either side of the armistice line—in Israel proper as well in the pre 1967 borders. If that were to happen, we would have to find the appropriate measures to deal with that situation.

There is a trend toward Islamic Fundamentalism among the Arabs, whether they are Shiites or Sunni. This has not yet spread to Israel, but if it were to spread to the Israeli Arab population on either side of the green line, then Israel would have to deal with a really hostile Arab population. Can you envision a set of circumstances, then, in which forced expulsion of large numbers of Arabs would be required?

First of all, we do have Islamic Fundamentalism in Israel at the present time. If we look at the Arab population, certainly in Judea, Samaria, and Gaza, and, to some extent, in Israel, among those Arabs who are citizens of Israel, we will find radical leftist movements and Islamic Fundamentalists. In the Arab universities in Samaria and Judea, there is a considerable following for Islamic Fundamentalism. These are all Sunnis. We don't have Shiites living in Israel. But I can't foresee Israel's expelling any large numbers of the Arab population.

We have deported people in the past who have been involved in inciting or engaging in terrorism. Recently, the Minister of Defense talked about the need to return to that policy. It's a policy that I have been advocating the last few years. It's a deterrent that is essential in order for us to deal with terrorism—to let people who are involved in terrorism and inciting terrorism know that they are likely to be deported from the area. But under no circumstances would I approve of the indiscriminate deportation of people.

How do you account for the impression, among a large portion of the Israeli population, that eventually the Arabs—those who live in Israel as well as those who live in Judea, Samaria, and Gaza—will, because of their own behavior, require mass expulsion?

I'm not sure how sizable that segment of the population really is. What we do see in Israel—and it's a phenomenon that is a source of great concern—is a very high level of frustration about the possibility of Jews and Arabs living together and about our ability to deal effectively with Arab terrorism. Israelis don't want to keep living with this kind of insecurity. They look for all kinds of solutions. Sometimes these solutions are very extreme and outlandish; they are inappropriate and will not be used.

When you ask me, then, why it is that there are some people in Israel who talk that way—which represents a minority opinion among Israelis—my explanation is that frustration with terrorism is most probably the reason. I certainly don't agree with or condone that opinion. The only thing we can say in the realm of understanding it is that Israel has been living with terrorism for a long time, and, clearly, it wears on people. Israelis are tired of it and search for ways to put an end to it.

Do you believe that Israel should encourage Arab emigration from Judea, Samaria, and Gaza?

It has been said over the years that there are many rich Arab countries short of manpower. For example, Saudi Arabia at various times in recent years has had as many as 3 million workers imported from all over the world. Some people think it might be better for everyone if that part of the Arab population that did not feel at home here, that did not have a feeling of loyalty to the State of Israel, and that had sympathy for Arab extremist groups—perhaps even for the PLO or other Arab terrorist groups—were to move into those Arab countries where there is a demand for their skills and labor. In such Arab countries, perhaps they would feel more at home. I have no quarrel with that position. Over 100,000 Arabs, from Judea and Samaria primarily, have moved into the oil-producing countries during the past twenty years or so. But such moves in the past were made—and if ever in the future should be made—at the volition of the people who made the move.

Certainly, it's nothing for the Israeli government to decide to implement, and not even something for the Israeli government to try to encourage.

Do you foresee the Israeli government perhaps being forced to establish conditions that will encourage a long-term process of emigration from Israel and/or Judea, Samaria, and Gaza?

No, not at all. The conditions that I talked about are conditions of attraction and not rejection. A country like Kuwait, for example, probably has the highest standard of living in the world. Many Arab professionals living in Israel, Judea, or Samaria can probably make ten times the income over there that they can make here. That's a magnet that exists in many of the oil-producing countries— probably in all the oil-producing countries of the Middle East—so that's not a situation that we have brought about. I dare say that if Kuwait was ready to hire Jewish engineers, we'd probably find that some Jewish Israelis would be going there to make those kinds of salaries. As it is, those opportunities are open only to the Arab population in Israel.

Arab universities in some Arab countries have been closed for political reasons. Do you anticipate that Arab universities in Judea, Samaria, and Gaza will have to be closed because they are hotbeds of unrest and revolution?

The Arab universities that exist in Judea, Samaria, and Gaza were all established since 1967—during the years of Israeli administration. For the nineteen years between '48 and '67, the Jordanians did not permit any universities in Judea and Samaria to be opened. Israel created the conditions and provided the opportunities for these universities to be established and to develop. We have no quarrel with these universities. Quite to the contrary, where there is a need for education at the university level, it must be satisfied; there is probably no way of satisfying that need other than by these universities. Sometimes the question is asked, why don't the students in Judea and Samaria want to study at Israeli universities, as do many of Israel's Arab citizens? One reason goes back to a subject we talked about before. With a diploma from the Hebrew University, they're not going to get very far in Kuwait. However, a diploma from a university in Samaria or Judea does open doors for them in those countries.

Since there has been terrorism and incitement to terrorism among the population in Judea and Samaria, it's no surprise that we find such activity occurring in the universities, where there is a collection of young people. There are centers of Islamic Fundamentalism in these universities, and there are centers of support for the PLO and all its factions, whether it's Arafat, or Abamusa, or Jabril. They all have groups that cheer them and lend them support, so we've had a need in the past to close down some universities for a certain period of time in order to contend with this kind of incitement. It may happen again in the future. But I don't foresee the possibility of closing the universities permanently.

In the Camp David Accords, there is a section on autonomy for Arabs in Judea, Samaria, and Gaza. How do you interpret that autonomy? What is your definition of that autonomy?

Autonomy is quite well defined in the Camp David Accords, and it really isn't a matter for personal interpretation. The differences of opinions that existed during the Israeli-Egyptian negotiations, which were supposed to establish the details at that time, had to do with questions of how large the self-governing body was to be and by just what electoral procedure it was to be elected. But the fundamentals of the autonomy as it appears in the Camp David Accords are clear.

The intention is that a self-governing body be elected by the population of Judea, Samaria, and Gaza. That self-governing body should have the authority to deal with various matters that concern the Arab population in the area—not the Jewish population—and that it should have nothing to do, of course, with matters of defense policy or foreign policy.

The present Arab population of Judea, Samaria, and Gaza is not indigenous to the area. They immigrated from several Arab countries and became refugees as a result of wars created by the Arab nations themselves. If Israel maintains jurisdiction over Judea, Samaria, and Gaza, do you believe these Arabs should be provided with Israeli citizenship, or should they be absorbed by Arab nations?

First of all, the origin of the Arab population in Judea and Samaria is not uniform. There are Arabs living in these areas today whose ancestors have been living in this part of the world for centuries, maybe more. There are also Arabs living in Judea and Samaria who have come into the area during the past fifty to sixty years, as a result of Jewish settlement and Jewish economic development. Additionally, there are Arabs in these areas, regardless of their origin, who moved from the villages they lived in as a result of the fighting there and today are living in refugee camps.

Secondly, the major responsibility for the settlement of all Palestinian refugees lies with the Arab countries. There's no other way of judging that issue. They bear the direct responsibility for the fact that these people are refugees because they called on them to leave their homes when the Arab armies invaded Israel. They bear the direct responsiblity for creating the refugee problem and for not solving the problem during the past thirty-nine years. They have insisted on not solving the problem and keeping these people in refugee camps in Arab countries such as Lebanon and Syria. Therefore, I feel they bear the direct responsibility for the settlement of the refugees.

The best solution to the problem is the settlement of the Palestinian refugees within the Arab world. Since they have the means and the land at their disposal, the Arab world, and especially the rich part of the Arab world, should take it upon itself to solve the problem once and for all, and put an end to that human tragedy and human misery.

Now, in Judea and Samaria, a good portion of the Arabs, but not the entire population, are refugees—perhaps 150,000. However, in Gaza, I think perhaps 70 to 75 percent of the Arab population are refugees—more than 250,000. So we're talking about nearly a half million Arabs with refugee status in Judea, Samaria, and Gaza.

What's going to happen to those half million? Should they be resettled in the Arab world?

I don't know what's going to happen there. They need to be settled. It's terrible for people to go on living from generation to generation in the status of refugees and under conditions of refugee camps. In Gaza, some of them have been settled in permanent housing and permanent dwellings by Israel; however, the correct solution is their resettlement in Arab countries with the Arab countries taking the responsibility for providing them with permanent homes. We don't have much reason to be very optimistic, however, because so far they haven't done it. Maybe in time they'll come around to that view.

Should the balance of the Arabs become Israeli citizens?

The balance of them should be offered the option of becoming Israeli citizens, just as the Arabs living in East Jerusalem were offered the option. Then it would be up to them. All of the Arab population in Judea and Samaria are Jordanian citizens. When they are presented with the option of becoming Israeli citizens, they will have to decide whether to abandon their Jordanian citizenship, and take upon themselves Israeli citizenship, or whether to remain in the area as Jordanian citizens. In the case of East Jerusalem, all the Arabs, with the exception of perhaps a hundred people, decided to maintain their Jordanian citizenship and not become Israeli citizens. What the case will be in Judea and Samaria when the time comes, I don't know.

What percentage of the land in Judea, Samaria, and Gaza is presently owned by Arabs, and how much of it is available to be bought? Is any of it being sold today?

Large portions of the land in Judea and Samaria are state lands and not under private ownership. However, the vast majority of the agricultural land is owned by the local population. Can that land be bought? In principle, yes, and some of the land is being bought from those land-owners who are interested in selling it. However, Jordan has a law on its books that any Arab who sells land to a Jew is subject to the death penalty. That serves as discouragement to some of the local landowners, even though they don't live under Jordanian rule. Many of them, of course, have connections with Jordan, want to travel to Jordan, and/or have family in Jordan. They are concerned that if they have that kind of a death penalty hanging over them, they may someday actually be executed. So that is somewhat of a barrier to the sale of land in the area.

Do you anticipate that it will be necessary to buy territory forcibly from the Arabs, identifying it as public-domain territory, in order to build roads and other projects in Judea, Samaria, and Gaza?

No more so than what is done in any country in the world where land is appropriated by the State for public purposes like road building. We've had some of that in the territories. We've had a lot of that in Israel itself. Many Israelis have had land they owned appropriated by the State for public domain, with proper compensation. Something like that could occur in Judea, Samaria, and Gaza, but there has not been extensive use of these measures in the past.

Do you believe Israel should return any territory in Judea or Samaria in order to obtain peace with Jordan or any territory in the Golan in order to obtain peace with Syria? If not, do you foresee any conditions under which Israel could be forced to make territorial concessions to Jordan or Syria for peace or for a settlement?

I don't believe Israel should turn over any more territory. Israel is small enough as it is—one of the smallest countries in the world. She is a country facing very serious security problems and is under the constant threat of attack by at least some of her neighbors. Relinquishing control over areas like Judea, Samaria, Gaza, or the Golan Heights would endanger the very existence of the State of Israel and our ability to defend ourselves.

LIBERATED TERRITORIES

Upon conclusion of the Yom Kippur War, the political climate was one which dictated third-party negotiations with the Arab nations, with the United States acting as the broker. Shimon Peres stated at a press conference in Washington at that time that Israel would pursue establishing peace with her Arab neighbors based on a policy that provides "a piece of territory for a piece of peace." Since that statement, the entire Sinai has been returned to Egypt as part of the Camp David Accords in which Israel and Egypt signed a peace treaty. Has the return of the Sinai to Egypt in exchange for a peace treaty been beneficial to Israel or, in retrospect, was it an error?

We have not yet come to the point where we can finish the accounts and determine what the bottom line is. In twenty or thirty years, we'll be able to say more definitely. But even then different people will answer in different ways. Israel paid a tremendous price for the peace treaty with Egypt and in many ways is worse off today than she was before the peace treaty was signed.

First of all, Israel paid a heavy economic price. That's a price that's easy to estimate because Israel turned over, to the Egyptians, the oil wells she had discovered and was working in the Gulf of Suez—oil wells that were about to make her energy-independent. That can be translated directly into dollars and cents. Israel has been importing—until the recent drop in oil prices—all of her oil from abroad to the tune of $1 1/2 to 2 billion a year. These imports represent a huge expenditure of foreign currency. Israel's GNP is about $22 to 24 billion, so we are talking about close to 10 percent of the GNP. For the oil we were producing in the Gulf of Suez, the cost of the production was minimal. Compared to the cost of importing, it essentially was zero. Giving up those oil wells placed a heavy burden on the Israeli economy, and part of our economic problems today are the direct result of that burden.

Also, as part of the agreement with Egypt, we had to remove all of our military installations—depots, air bases, naval bases—from the Sinai and duplicate these installations in the Negev. The cost of that was about $4 or 5 billion. The total economic consequences of the peace treaty with Egypt are, to date, on the order of the Israeli GNP—over $20 billion—by my reckoning. If any country, including the United States, is suddenly burdened with an economic price tag the size of her GNP, she is very likely to buckle. That's one price we paid.

Today, Israel is a quarter the size she was before the peace treaty. She's become a tiny country compared to what she used to be. She has lost strategic depth. We had to remove settlers from the northeastern part of the Sinai— perhaps the most advanced agrricultural settlements in the world at the time.

Those settlers were Israeli pioneers who went out there with the encouragement—and in some cases on the orders—of the Israeli government. We had to pull farmers off their fields and people out of their houses. We paid a tremendous price.

To answer the question of whether or not it was worthwhile, we must assess what we received in return. Perhaps what we received in return is worth more than the price we paid. If we are to assume that had it not been for the peace treaty, there would have been another war—or another two wars, G-d forbid—between Egypt and Israel, in which thousands of Israelis might have been killed and for which the economic costs might have been even greater than the economic price we paid for the peace treaty, then, perhaps, we could say it's been worthwhile, perhaps we've come out ahead.

My own view is that that was not the alternative—we were not faced with a situation in which we either signed a peace treaty with Egypt on Egypt's terms or went back to war. We haven't signed a peace treaty with Jordan, and we haven't had a war since 1973. During the same period, too, we have not had a war with Syria, even though we've not signed a peace treaty with her. For the same period, we have not had a war with Egypt. Israel has established an image of being strong militarily and of having a very considerable deterrent power. Prior to the peace treaty with Egypt, we had signed a number of interim agreements, so I don't think we were on a collision course. However, the expectation was that the peace treaty would lead to the kind of relationships between Israel and Egypt that would make a war in the future impossible. It would be a one-way street towards peace. If thirty or forty years from now we say, it's true—that the kind of relationships that have been established between the two countries are such as to make war impossible between them—then most Israelis, and I among them, would say it was a price worth paying. But we're not at all sure we will arrive at that point.

Not a single Israeli will tell you the peace treaty and the relationships between Israel and Egypt have lived up to their expectations. They are far from our expectations. Mainly, that intense interchange of Israelis and Egyptians in trade relations, in tourism, and in cultural relations has not occurred. We had expected to build on that so as to establish a network of relationships between the two countries that would make war impossible. Those relationships have not progressed. They have not developed because the Egyptian government has not allowed them to develop.

Everyone in Israel—and probably most people in Egypt—will tell you today we are in a precarious situation. Considering the fact that Egypt is not a democratic country and has an autocratic regime and considering all the problems that Egypt has, including a characteristic basic instability, we could open the paper tomorrow and find that everything is changed in Egypt, and that there's no more peace between Israel and Egypt. Then we'd find Israel, having paid this tremendous price, without the Sinai and all that it entails and without peace with Egypt. This was the big risk we undertook. If we expected by signing the peace treaty there would be a steady, gradual decrease of that risk because of the relationships that would blossom between Israel and Egypt, we were wrong. We find today, seven years after the treaty was signed, that has not happened at all. The instability that characterized the Israeli-Egyptian relationship then is essentially still the same today.

Do you foresee the continuation of this process of "a piece of territory for a piece of peace" being extended to the balance of the territories liberated as the result of the 1967 War—East Jerusalem, Judea and Samaria, Gaza, the Golan Heights?

I don't, and it shouldn't. It depends, of course, on the people of Israel, on the people who are elected to govern Israel, and on the authority they are given either to follow that course of action or not to follow it. As I said, today Israel is a quarter the size she was before the signing of the Israeli-Egyptian peace treaty. We're a tiny country, which means we're a very vulnerable country in terms of our security, especially considering the fact that we live in a very hostile part of the world.

If we look at Western European countries today, none of them are described as vulnerable—none of them have to contend with security threats. It really doesn't matter whether their borders are defensible or not. They don't have to defend them. Holland doesn't have to defend herself against Belgium, or Luxembourg doesn't have to defend herself against France; but, Israel must be able to defend herself against her neighbors. The moment that she's incapable of defending herself, or the moment that she is perceived as not being capable of defending herself, we have a war on our hands—a war we may win, but at a price that we don't want to pay, although we're ready to pay if we must.

The areas of Judea and Samaria are essential to Israel's defense. They are right in the heart of Israel. They border on the municipal boundaries of Israel's population centers. Under the circumstances, losing control of these essential areas is not paving the road to peace. It's paving the road to war. I think most Israelis understand that. Most public opinion polls indicate that the vast majority of Israelis are against making these kinds of concessions and don't believe that such concessions actually would lead to peace. Since Israel is a democratic country and the Israeli government essentially must represent the feelings of the people of Israel, I don't think we will see governments in future years pursuing the course of giving up territories in the quest for peace.

Since the liberation of Judea and Samaria, there have been two basic types of settlements. There are created towns, such as Ariel and Kazrin—

small settlements along the Jordan River, where economic viability is based on agriculture—and small settlements in the heart of Judea and Samaria, where economic viability is based on small industry or the employment of residents who commute to work each day over the green line. How do you foresee the future development of Jewish settlements in Judea and Samaria—along the lines envisioned by Yigal Allon after the 1967 War, along the lines of Ariel Sharon, or along some other lines different from both?

We must remember that Judea and Samaria are very small areas in terms understood by the people who live in the United States or even in Western Europe. They are, however, an integral part of Israel, so I don't expect that settlements in those areas would be essentially any different from what they are in the rest of Israel. The topography in Judea and Samaria is different from the topography in the Negev. That would reflect on the way people settle and live there and on what they do there. They are not, however, that different from the Galilee; topography in Judea and Samaria is very similar to the Galilee. The Jordan Valley has a topography all its own. It has particular climatic conditions and a particular security situation, but, it's really not too different from the Arava—the area that leads from the Dead Sea to Elat.

In future years, we'll find that settlement in Judea and Samaria is not so very different from settlement in other areas—we will find all kinds of settlements. We'll find agricultural settlements in areas in which the conditions are conducive to agriculture. We'll find industry in areas in which it makes sense to establish industry. We'll find lots of suburban settlements—which we already have—of people who live east of what used to be the green line, or the armistice line of 1949, and work west of the area. We have the mirror image of that as well—people who live in Netanya but who go to Samaria every morning in order to work in the factories that have been established there. In future years, we really won't be able to tell the difference.

Do you favor the establishment of towns or settlements in the liberated territories? What do you see as a function of these towns or settlements? How would they support themselves? Do you envision the settlers continuing to work on the other side of the green line and return at night to sleep?

Today, we have a number of towns in Judea and Samaria. The largest is Ma'ale Adumim, which, geographiclly, is in Judea or perhaps on the border between Judea and Samaria—east of Jerusalem. It's a town that currently has a population of over 11,000. We have Qiryat-Arba in Judea, just outside Hebron, which has a population of over 5,000. And there is Ariel in Samaria, which has a population of 6,000 or so. Today, there are small industries in these towns. Like them, there are other towns which, in future years, will have populations of perhaps 40 to 60 thousand. That means there will inevitably be industries in these towns which will grow to be cities.

Today, we have people who live in Samaria and work in the Sharon Plains, but we also have the opposite—people who live in the Sharon Plains and work in the factories and industrial facilities in Samaria. In Israel, small as it is, we will continue to have some people living in Ariel and working in Tel Aviv, and others living in Tel Aviv and working in Ariel. It's no different than people who live in Long Island and commute to Manhattan or vice versa.

The Jewish settlers in the towns and settlements of Judea and Samaria are and will be Israeli citizens, while the Arabs who settled in Judea and Samaria are citizens of Jordan. The law that applies to Jews is different from the law that applies to Arabs. How do you envision the application of the law to Jews and Arabs in the future in Judea and Samaria, especially in those areas such as Hebron and Nablus where Jews will be living in densely populated areas among the Arabs? How do you treat the Jews in one way and the Arabs in another way when they are living among each other?

There is no doubt in my mind that eventually Judea and Samaria will have a more normal status. They will be under either Israeli sovereignty, which is my wish, or Arab sovereignty—whether Jordanian, Palestinian, or PLO—as advocated by others. I don't foresee these territories continuing to live in the present nondescript state as administered territories or, as some people refer to them, occupied territories, which, of course, means the entire population does not enjoy full civil rights. It's an anomalous situation—one that should not and cannot go on indefinitely.

Since control over Judea and Samaria is essential to Israel's security, sooner or later there must be Israeli sovereignty applied to these areas and Israeli law governing them. Under those circumstances, the Arab population living in the area, who are all Jordanian citizens, will be faced with a choice—whether they want Israeli citizenship or not. Some will become Israeli citizens, and some will decide that they would rather continue to be Jordanian citizens. Those who decide not to become Israeli citizens will share the status that many have in Israel today—residents of Israel but not citizens. It will be their choice.

That's a choice that has faced over 100,000 Arabs living in East Jerusalem since Israeli sovereignty was extended to East Jerusalem shortly after the Six-Day War, twenty years ago. The Arab population in East Jerusalem has had the choice, and still has the choice, of taking out Israeli citizenship. Most of them have decided they do not want Israeli citizenship and prefer to continue living as Jordanian citizens. Those who have taken out Israeli citizenship are equal citizens of the State of Israel and enjoy the same rights and privileges as other Israelis. Eventually, they will share the same burdens of citizenship as the Jewish citizens of Israel.

The Arab population of Gaza, Judea, and Samaria has been decreasing since Israel liberated these territories in 1967; however, in East Jerusalem the Arab population has been increasing. What do you foresee as the status of the Arab population in East Jerusalem and its economic relationship? How will they live and work in East Jerusalem?

The answer to that can be seen now because East Jerusalem has been an integral part of the State of Israel now for twenty years. The Arab population in East Jerusalem has increased because we have a process of urbanization going on. It's what's happening all over the world. There is a tendency to leave villages and come into the big cities because of the opportunities that exist there. The Arab population of East Jerusalem work and earn a living. Their standard of living has advanced tremendously in the past twenty years, and it will continue to go up. Their standard of education has grown tremendously as has their standard of health. All in all, their quality of life has improved considerably, and I would expect that trend will continue.

Given the fact that the total income of the Arab world from oil is dropping, and has dropped dramatically during the last few years, many of the imported Arab workers are being asked to leave, and are leaving, places like the Arab emirates, Baharain, and Saudi Arabia—the oil-producing countries. Do you believe the Palestinians or other Arabs will try to come into Judea, Samaria, or Israel? If so, what can be done to prevent it?

The Palestinian Arabs who left Gaza, Judea, or Samaria in order to take jobs and seek fortunes in the oil-producing countries—and many did that—are free to return. We had something resembling the California Gold Rush here in past years because of the opportunities that developed in oil-producing countries. Considering the economic problems that are developing today in the oil-producing countries because of the drop in the price of oil, I suppose some of those Palestinian Arabs will return. Others, undoubtedly, will stay where they are. Not all of the Palestinian Arabs who left these areas went to Kuwait or Saudi Arabia. Some of those who did, however, are well-established and are certainly capable of riding out whatever change in economic fortunes may take place there. Many went to the United States and to South America. Again, some of them have or will come back; others will stay permanently where they have gone. But all are free to return.

During the period of the spirit of democracy—during one of the past Israeli governments, Peres permitted free election of mayors in Judea and Samaria, and it turned out to have many negative ramifications. Do you believe this policy should continue to be pursued to create democracy within Judea and Samaria for free election of mayors?

We must realize that terrorism is still rampant in Judea and Samaria. In an area where terrorism is rampant, it's very difficult, if not impossible, to have free elections. What happened during the time that Mr. Peres was Minister of Defense—in the period after the Yom Kippur War—was that he permitted the holding of municipal elections in the towns and cities of Judea and Samaria. Those elections, although held under Israeli auspices, were not really free, democratic elections. The PLO, in effect, manipulated those elections, scared moderate candidates out of running, and scared people out of voting for moderate candidates who did run. The end result was that almost all of the mayors that were elected were members of the PLO or agents of the PLO. It simply lead to radicalization in the area and brought about a situation in which, eventually, the Israeli government had to remove those mayors because it was impossible to work with them—it was imposssible to administer the area in cooperation with them.

We had a recent tragic episode in Nablus. For many years after the man "elected" during those PLO-manipulated elections was deposed, Nablus had an Israeli-appointed mayor—an Israeli military administrator. Then a well-know Arab businessman from Nablus was contacted and agreed to take upon himself the task of being an appointed mayor of Nablus. This was Zaafar al-Masri, a very fine person. As Minister of Defense, I met him. It was clear to me that he was very intelligent and a man with values. He wasn't a Zionist, but he believed that ways must be found for Jews and Arabs to live together. He managed to be mayor for just a few months before he was assassinated. So, until such time as we are able to establish the kind of environment in the area where people don't have to fear being shot, where the democratic election process can be carried out freely, where people can run for election without being intimidated, and where people can vote without being intimidated, the area is really not ready for the election of municipalities and mayors. But I believe we must get to that point, and we will.

We have free elections for municipalities and mayors in the Arab cities and villages within the pre-1967 borders of Israel. We managed to arrange a climate in which these elections are held without people being intimidated. I don't doubt that we will get to that point in Judea and Samaria, as well.

ZIONISM

Is it a correct perception that the most significant deeds of the Zionist movement in pre-State Palestine in establishing national institutions were achieved by the Socialist Zionists, for example, Histadrut (Labor Federation of Workers), Kibbutzim, Moshavim? If not, please explain.

It is difficult to get Israelis to agree as to what were the most significant national institions. There was a whole gamut of institutions founded in pre-State Palestine. Most of them, if not all, made important contributions to the settlement of the country and to the establishment of the State of Israel. Those who were involved in building certain institutions are quite naturally likely to view them as the most important ones. It's no surprise, for example, if people from the Labor party say that the Kibbutz was the most important institution—or among the most important ones—and that the Labor party had the major share in establishing Kibbutzim in the country. But if we look at the country's institutions, including her agricultural settlements, villages, towns, cities, universities, industrial enterprises, and manufacturers' associations, we find that we can't give special credit to any particular group. It's the sum total of the work and dedication of everyone involved.

Israel was settled by some very dedicated people of all branches of the Zionist movement, including the Socialist branch. They all had their impact, and they all created very unusual things—in some cases miracles. If we talk about the contribution of the Labor movement, certainly the Kibbutz is an outstanding achievement. The Kibbutzim have made contributions to the settlement of the country and the establishment of the State of Israel out of all proportion to the segment of Israeli society that they represent. But it's not the only outstanding achievement in the development of the State of Israel. With all the due respect that I have for Kibbutzim, or for the Histadrut as a labor union, I would say it's not the dominant achievement in Israeli society—it's one of a number of very significant achievements. Many have been partners in those achievements.

What has been the achievement of the non-labor sector—the Herut or general Zionists?

If we talk in terms of institutionalized achievements, I would start with the cities. The most famous and characteristic of Israeli cities, Tel Aviv, was in large measure the product of the settlement, not by organized labor, but rather by the more bourgeois, or middle class, elements of Israeli society. As a result, the Tel Aviv municipal government, throughout the years—with some few exceptions after the State of Israel was established—has been in the hands of the parties associated with the middle class not the Labor party.

The urban development of Israel was not a Labor or a Socialist development. That is true not only about Israel's major cities but also about her small towns and villages, places like Zichron Yaakov and Binyamina, which were, at least originally, agricultural villages. They were not agricultural villages established within the Socialist framework. They were established, more or less, in the free enterprise framework. Individual farmers came and settled the land and then joined the Farmers' Association in order to protect their collective interests. So, as we examine Israeli society and Jewish settlement in Palestine, we find that all those involved have made their contributions.

Is it a correct perception that the great Zionist thinkers and writers in the formative years of the Zionist movement were all Socialist Zionists, for example, Borochov, Sokolov, Syrkin, Katzelson, Chazan, Gordon, Greenberg, Ben Zvi, Ben Gurion? If not, can you explain?

First of all, in my view, the greatest Zionist leader was Jabotinsky—the greatest by far. With all due respect for all the Zionist leaders since Theodore Herzl, I think Jabotinsky overshadowed them all. As time goes by, and we're able to distance ourselves from the party struggles that characterized the Zionist movement throughout the years and view in perspective the contributions of different people in the Zionist movement, the stature of Jabotinsky looms larger and larger.

But if we want to go back to the original Zionists, then let's go back before Herzl. There was settlement by what was called the first *aliyah* to what was then Palestine under Ottoman rule. They were the Biluim—mainly from Russia and some from Rumania, but they were not Socialists. That was individually orientated private enterprise—farmers who came on their own to settle on the land of Zichron, Rishon Lezion, Nesziona, and Rehovot. After Theodore Herzl founded the Zionist movement, it didn't take long before various political parties, including Socialist parties, appeared. They were not the dominant parties at the beginning. There were religious Zionist, middle-class Zionist, and Socialist Zionist parties.

As I've said, in my view, the outstanding leader after Herzl was Jabotinsky. He also had major impact on the development of the Zionist movement, even though throughout most of his life, he was in opposition and did not command a majority in the Zionist movement. As so frequently happens in history, we find that those who were in the majority and those who were in control, in time, adopted his ideas and his precepts.

Has the Zionist movement moved toward Jabotinsky's views?

It certainly has. What characterized Jabotinksy's views on things was his realism—his ability to size up a situation correctly and then draw the appropriate conclusions. This became apparent on three major issues which became conflicts within the Zionist movement between Jabotinsky's views and the views of others. We can look at every one of these issues and gauge to what extent Jabotinsky was right in a historical perspective, as well as to what extent his views were eventually adopted by other Zionist leaders and other Zionist parties.

The first issue on which Jabotinsky saw things differently from most of the other Zionist leaders was the fate of the Jewish community in Europe. Back in the thirties, even before Hitler came to power, Jabotinsky envisioned the Holocaust. Although he may not have foreseen all the details, he saw the approaching tragedy facing the European Jewish community. That is why, as early as 1933-34, he called for the evacuation of the Jewish community in Europe and its transfer to Palestine.

This was in contrast to the views of the established Zionist leadership, who felt that his was an alarmist view —that the Jewish community in Europe was not facing that kind of tragedy and that, therefore, there was no reason to take emergency measures. They felt that immigration to Palestine should be selective immigration. They were concerned that if suddenly there were an evacuation and masses of European Jewry were brought to Palestine, there would then be many people in Palestine who were not properly prepared for life there. This was the attitude of most of the rest of the Zionist movement. This was the view of Chaim Weizmann. Although that view had been held by many people for a long time, it especially came into focus in the thirties when the Zionist leadership had to face Jabotinksy's call for evacuation.

Was the Socialist Zionist movement in favor of selective aliyah?

Absolutely! It was in tune with their desire to build a Socialist state here. They wanted to bring people here who wanted to be Socialists, those who they felt had the proper background and mental make-up to become members of the Socialist society they wanted to establish. So it's not difficult to understand why, from their point of view, they were not enthusiastic about mass evacuation of European Jewry to Palestine. I'm sure that they, too, would have called for it, or would have supported it, if they had been convinced, as Jabotinsky was, that the Jewish community in Europe was facing destruction and carnage.

So, in regard to that issue, in retrospect, there is no question that Jabotinsky was right. He was almost prophetic in his vision of the fate that awaited European

Jewry if it didn't leave Europe. It is generally recognized that much of the established Zionist leadership —certainly the Labor wing—did not evaluate correctly the situation of European Jewry and did not draw the appropriate conclusions because of their incorrect evaluation. There are probably still people in the Labor movement who are hesitant to admit that.

The second issue on which Jabotinsky was opposed by most of the established Zionist leadership—especially the Socialists—was the attitude toward Britain as a mandatory power. Here again, Jabotinsky, very early, realized that Great Britain was not going to implement the mandate that had been put in her trust—to establish a Jewish state in Palestine.

Most of the Zionist leadership, primarily the Labor Zionists who became dominant in the *Yishuv*—the Jewish community in Palestine—felt that they could get Britain to carry out the mandate, if not fully, then at least partially. Therefore, everything had to be based on cooperation and collaboration with the mandatory power. Jabotinsky realized that pressure would have to be applied to Great Britain—political pressure and eventually military pressure, as well—if a Jewish state was going to be established. In that, also, there is no question that he was right.

In the later years preceding the establishment of the State of Israel, more and more of the Zionist leadership, including Ben Gurion and other Labor leaders, began to adopt Jabotinsky's view. It was late, and they certainly did not always give proper recognition to Jabotinsky for the correctness of his view. However, during those last years of the British mandate, even the Hagana began to engage in underground activities against the British. Again, it was late, and much of what they did was more moderate and limited than what was done by the Irgun and the Lechi, the underground movements that drew their inspiration from Jabotinsky. But they did also join the struggle, and I think that was a demonstration of their recognition that Jabotinsky's view was correct.

The third issue on which there were differences of opinion between Jabotinsky and most of the rest of the Zionist leadership was the issue of the Arab-Jewish conflict. Jabotinsky, again very early, recognized the conflict for what it was—a conflict between two nations for the same piece of territory. He had no illusions about being able to do away with that conflict.

The Socialist Zionists talked for years about building a binational state and about cooperation between the proletarians of both nations—between the Jewish working class and the Arab agricultural workers. In other words, the "oppressed" sections of the two peoples, Jewish and Arab, would join hands against the exploiters, regardless of whether they were Jewish or Arab, and form the basis for the state that would be built. Well, in retrospect, you'd almost call that foolishness, right? Certainly, it was a most unrealistic and idealized view of life in the Middle East—of life in Palestine. And it was very far from the truth.

Jabotinksy went on to say that what was essential if the Jewish State was going to be established and survive, and if an accommodation was going to be reached with the Arabs, was the building of a strong Jewish military capability. That would convince the Arab world that they had no military option and that they would have to reach an understanding with the Jewish population living in the area. Eventually that view, too, was adopted by the others but once again, late.

The best student that Jabotinsky had was Ben Gurion. He realized late, but in time—in the late forties, just prior to and during the War of Independence—that unless Israel had a strong military force, there was not going to be an accommodation with the Arabs, and there wasn't going to be a State of Israel. He laid great stress on building the Israel Defense Forces—then and during the years thereafter.

Is it true that the Socialist Zionist movement had an orientation toward Russia as an ally and partner, rather than toward the West?

The Socialist parties and their leaders—including Ben Gurion, not just those on the far left—were believers in carrying on a class struggle in Israel. They talked about the alliance that they foresaw between the Israeli proletariat and the Arab agricultural workers. They believed in engaging in a class struggle against what they called Jewish capitalists and entrepreneurs. Jabotinsky, of course, saw that as destructive to the whole settlement effort. He believed that Jewish entrepreneurs had an important role to play in the settlement effort. He was concerned that the whole settlement effort could be aborted if the Socialists had their way— if Jewish laborers were engaging in a struggle against Jewish entrepreneurs and Jewish owners of factories, plants, and businesses, instead of building the country and dealing with the adversaries of Zionism.

The ideas that people in the Socialist Zionist party brought with them from Russia in revolutionary days have fallen into disuse. The Labor people themselves have been disabused of those ideas. Many people would find it difficult to believe that in the thirties, in what was then Palestine, in addition to all the problems the Jews had with the British mandatory administration and with Arab terrorism, the Socialists waged a struggle against what they called Jewish business interests.

It's not too surprising to find that those political groups that believed in carrying on the class struggle in Palestine—before the Jewish State was ever established—also felt a particular association with and an affinity for the Soviet Union. There were some among the Zionist settlers in Palestine who, at various stages in the game, went back to the Soviet Union—left Palestine and returned to the Soviet Union! In recent years, with the opening of the gates of Russia, a few of them have returned to Israel with dramatic tales of the years just after their return to Russia and the years they spent in labor camps in Siberia. They have reported that most never survived that experience.

Among the Socialist Zionist parties, there were many years of almost blind support for the Soviet Union, even in the days of Stalin. Gradually, people in the

Labor party began to abandon that pro-Soviet view. The final abandonment, of course, was in '67. The immense event that really disturbed many people in the far left of the Israeli Labor party—in Mapam—was the arrest of two Mapam emissaries in Czechoslovakia and their participation in the Prague trials. Although these trials took place in 1953, the full truth was not revealed until they returned to Israel and told the whole story of what had happened to them—how they had been framed and how they had suffered in prison over the years. That was really the watershed for the far left of the Israeli Labor party and their disenchantment with the Soviet Union. But there are some remnants of that Soviet orientation in certain parts of the Labor party to this very day.

Is it a correct perception that when Israel achieved her independence, all the national institutions established as government agencies emanated from the shadow institution that had been formed by the Jewish Agency, which had been an instrument of the Socialist Zionist movement?

The Jewish Agency appears in the wordings of the mandate of the League of Nations. During the mandate days, it was called a state in the making. That was its intention under the mandate. As Britain carried out the provisions of the mandate and created a Jewish state, it was gradually to have turned over the governmental responsibility in Palestine to the Jewish Agency, which then would become the government of Israel.

The Jewish Agency was not a Socialist institution. It was the institution that represented the Zionist movement, and through most of the years, it had a representation from the various branches of the Zionist movement. For a number of years starting with the thirties, the Labor party became the prominent, and later even the dominant, party within the Jewish Agency. The conflict between Jabotinsky and his movement, on one hand, and the Labor party, on the other, as well as the severity and tenure of that conflict, finally caused Jabotinsky to leave the Zionist organization. He created the New Zionist Organization—the NZO. As a result, he was not represented in the Jewish Agency.

Is it a correct perception that the great generals and political leaders who took the State of Israel through five successful wars and built the foundations of present-day Israel all came from the ranks of the Socialist Zionist movement, for example, Abba Eban, Moshe Dayan, Yigal Allon, Shimon Peres, and Yitzhak Rabin? If not, please explain.

It's difficult to evaluate the roles played by people representing different facets of the Zionist movement without seeing those roles in the context of the conflicts that characterized the Zionist organization and the Zionist movement. If we talk about the roles people have played in the Israeli military and the IDF, we have to go back to the pre-State period—to the undergrounds and to the conflict between the underground and the Zionist establishment.

The people who played the most prominent role in the fight against the British were the followers of Jabotinsky—the Irgun and the Lechi. The people who were the pioneers of Jewish seamanship—of the Israeli navy—were the followers of Jabotinsky who set up a school for naval officers in Civitavecchia, Italy in the thirties. The first fledgling attempts to build the nucleus of a Jewish air force by providing pilots' training were carried out by Betar, both in Israel (Palestine then) and in other parts of the world.

Of course, the military effort that was most instrumental in getting the British to leave—and, therefore, most instrumental in setting the stage for the establishment of the State of Israel—was the underground, the Irgun and the Lechi. At the very last stage of that effort, the Hagana also joined in. Even though the period of direct cooperation among the three groups was limited, there were activities by the Hagana against the British.

When the State was established, Ben Gurion was the first Prime Minister and also the first Minister of Defense. Initially, there was not a readiness to allow the people from the Irgun and the Lechi—people who had amassed considerable military experience and had shown themselves to be well-qualified in the military field—to participate. Even with their good military credentials and military experience, they were simply kept out of the Israel Defense Forces when they were first established.

The Altalena happens to present a good example of the personalities involved at the time. The Altalena was a ship that brought arms to Israel at the most crucial of times. The effort had been organized by the Irgun and supporters of the Irgun in the United States. At the time, right in the midst of the War of Independence in June/July of 1948, what Israel was missing most were arms and, of course, the people who were ready and capable to use those arms. The fate of Israel was hanging by a thread. It was not at all clear if Israel was going to be able to survive militarily. Close to a thousand trained young men and women were on that ship—ready to come and join the fight for independence. With them, they were bringing a significant amount of arms that had been collected in Europe. Despite that situation, as the ship approached, Ben Gurion gave orders to fire on it. The ship was finally sunk. Most of the arms were lost, and some of the people on the ship were killed.

There is one particular related incident that is simply characteristic of the situation at the time. The captain of the Altalena was an American Jew from Chicago who had been a lieutenant commander in the U.S. Navy during World War II. Actually, he had never been associated with and didn't know anything about Zionist politics. After his discharge from the Navy, he saw an ad in *The Chicago Tribune* stating that they were looking for people to help the Jews in

Palestine. He volunteered, and he ended up being the captain of the ship. Well, not only was the ship shot at and sunk, but when he swam to shore and immediately volunteered to serve in the fledgling Israeli navy, they wouldn't accept him. He was, at the time, the most qualified naval person in Israel, but because he had come on the ship and was suspected of being close to the people in the Irgun, they refused him entrance into the Israeli navy.

That's just an example of the kind of discrimination that was practiced in those early days against anyone who did not come from the Socialist part of the spectrum. As a natural result, if we look at the prominent Israeli personalities in the IDF in the first ten years or so of the State, they were people who were associated with the Socialist Zionist parties. That's changed by now. We don't have that kind of discrimination in the IDF any more.

Have there been any prominent generals who didn't come from the Labor movement?

Shlomo Erel was an admiral who became commander of the Israeli navy, I believe, in 1966. He had been in the Israeli navy ever since 1948, and, although some people may have different views on the subject, he was probably the most experienced man among the officers. He had graduated from the Betar Naval Officer's School in Civitavecchia, Italy and had been at sea from the time he graduated from that school in the thirties. He had been in the Merchant Marine during World War II. It took almost twenty years before he became commander of the Israeli navy, not because he was the youngest man there—he wasn't—and not because he was the most inexperienced man there—he wasn't. It took a long time before he got the job he was most qualified for because he had been a member of the Betar.

So people were kept back, and for many years we did not have any prominent Israeli generals who were associated with Betar or the Likud. Thereafter, we entered a period when generals, for the most part, were not associated with movements, which, of course, is the way it should be. If we ask the Israeli generals today what movements they belong to, most can't give an answer because they don't belong to any movement.

Were Weizmann and Sharon part or products of the Labor movement?

Weizmann was never a member of the Labor movement and in his earlier days had some association with the Irgun. Sharon was a member of the Labor movement before he took up membership in the Likud. The fact that someone is or was a member of the Labor movement, however, doesn't necessarily mean he was a product of it. It may mean that at a certain time, he felt it was appropriate or convenient to have membership in that movement. I believe it is correct to speak of people as products of the Labor movement only when they came from Kibbutzim and grew up in the *Palmach*, like Yigal Allon.

Speaking of Yigal Allon, we were very good friends; he told me there were two events in his lifetime that created disappointment and sadness. One was that he was the commander who, under orders, had to fire on the Altalena. He felt that was a great tragedy. The second was that after the '67 War, Israel didn't depopulate the West Bank. Can you comment on that?

The Altalena incident is truly one of the great tragedies of the history of Israel. With all the respect that we have today for Ben Gurion as a man, as a founder of the State of Israel, and, if any man can be given that title, as the man who led and won the War of Independence, that was an inexcusable act, even in historical perspective. It was a totally inexcusable partisan act to fire on a ship that brought guns and soldiers at the most crucial time of the War of Independence, bringing about the deaths of many Jewish volunteers who came from various parts of the world. Two of the boys who were killed in that incident were Jewish volunteers from Cuba. Some of the volunteers came from the United States. It's easy for me to understand why any of the military people involved in the action, like Yigal Allon, would have pangs of conscience right to the end of their days. It's an almost unexplainable incident and certainly an indication of the level of partisanship and intensity of hatred that existed—but which clearly offers no acceptable excuse.

In regard to Allon's second comment, I suppose he meant that if a larger part of the Arab population in Judea and Samaria had left the areas during the fighting and had gone to Jordan, perhaps some problems that we're facing today might be less challenging than they are.

During the mid-1940s, a book called Perfidy, *written by Ben Hecht, a famous playwright, made grave accusations against the leaders of the Jewish shadow government in Palestine. Can you comment on the subject?*

I don't remember the details of the book, but it's based on the tremendous chasm between the Socialist Zionist movement and the Revisionist Zionist movement throughout the pre-State period—from the 1920s right up until 1948. Although the Altalena incident well represents the level of brutality and fanaticism that people sank to, it's not the only example. In 1946-47, when only the Irgun and the Lechi were active in underground activities against the British, we had a period that was called the Sezon, the "season." It was a time when Revisionist Zionists were sought out by members of the Kibbutzim—by the Socialist Labor party—on orders of Ben Gurion. They were hunted down, arrested, beaten, and tortured. They were held in Kibbutzim, chained to beds, chairs, and posts. They were murdered. They were turned over to the British in large numbers by orders of the Socialist Zionist leadership or the various paramilitary arms of the Socialist Zionist movement.

Some have said that the Socialist Zionist fervor during that period was one in which their socialism—their Socialist ideology—was no less important to them than their Zionist theology or ideology. Was the Kastner affair an outgrowth of that kind of thinking?

I wouldn't say that. I wouldn't even tie it to the Kastner affair. That was a very individual situation. It was a reflection of the tragedy of the Holocaust and the dilemmas that Jews had to face during that time in various parts of Europe. In particular, it represents the dilemmas faced by Jews who were in leadership positions. Should they collaborate with the Nazis in an attempt to save a small number of people, or should they lead the Jewish masses in resistance to the Nazis? Kastner simply made the wrong choice there. He was a leading Jewish personality in Budapest during the very last months of the war. It's been well-established that he took the wrong path. Halevi, the judge who pronounced sentence in the Kastner liable case, said that Kastner had sold his soul to the devil.

Will you comment on the work and death of Alozoroff?

That's another milestone in that long and unnecessary strife that existed between the two parties—the Socialist Zionists and the Revisionist Zionists. Alozoroff was a prominent Zionist leader—one of the younger generation of Socialist Zionist leaders at the time—and of very considerable talent and capability. He really had a future among the leaders of the Socialist Zionist party. In 1933, he was murdered on the beach in Tel Aviv while walking with his wife one evening. What happened immediately thereafter is that the Socialist Zionist party tried to fix the blame for the murder on the Revisionist movement. They were very busy manufacturing evidence and suborning witnesses in an attempt to produce proof that the two men who had been arrested—who belonged to the Revisionist movement—were the perpetrators of the crime.

Eventually, the two were acquitted by the British courts. Just recently, the investigating committee that had been set up by the Israeli government to review the case cleared them positively and declared them totally innocent of the crime. At that time, however—in 1933 and for a number of years thereafter—the Socialist Zionist parties and their leaders were very active in doing everything possible to create an impression that it was a politically motivated murder, that the murderers were Jews, and that the murderers had been sent by people in leading positions in the Revisionist Zionist party.

The commission that just issued the report says that it cannot state definitively, even at this time, who murdered Alozoroff. There is a theory that Arabs murdered him. In fact, there is an Arab who, at one point, admitted to the murder. But there are differences of opinion as to whether his was an honest admission or whether he had some other motivations for coming forth and admitting to the murder. We don't know. We do know that it was not carried out by the two people who were accused of the crime.

After the State of Israel successfully fought the War of Independence, Prime Minister Ben Gurion called for the Zionists in the Diaspora and the Jewish Diaspora youth to come to Israel to settle the land. There was a groundswell of good will and excitement within the Western-educated, affluent Jewish communities, yet they failed to come to drain the swamps and turn the deserts green. Do you believe that the Socialist Zionist approach to aliyah at that time was correct?

I believe that another approach could have been tried—could have been and should have been. Not that it was wrong to ask them to come, but it was wrong not to approach other groups.

The social and economic environment that was established in this country by the Socialist Zionist leadership was one that really was not conducive to mass immigration of Americans to Israel. We had immigration of American citizens to Israel in small numbers. We had Americans who came to join Kibbutzim. We had Americans who were themselves members of Socialist Zionist organizations, and many of them made important contributions to Israel. Golda Meir came to Israel from the United States. She was a Socialist Zionist. She joined a Kibbutz when she came to Israel in the twenties. But it was foolish to assume that we could have a large number of Americans come and join Kibbutzim and take their place in the ranks of the Socialist proletariat in Israel.

In order to create the necessary conditions for American immigration, we had to create a climate that was much more attuned to people from Western countries, both economically and socially, and that was not done. I can't say that if it had been done, we would have had mass immigration, but I think that it was a first necessary step. Even today, we're still looking for a large-scale influx of Jews from the United States to Israel, and I still believe it is an essential prerequisite that the country be liberalized. It is vital that greater opportunities be given to private enterprise, that the economy progresses, and that employment opportunities be opened so that people who come to us from the West really feel that socially and economically it's not too different from the Western world they're accustomed to.

In the early years of the State of Israel, wealthy Western Jewish businessmen, especially in America, showed not only a willingness, but also a great desire, to establish businesses in Israel. However, the ideologically Socialist-oriented government attempted to funnel this good will through investment in the Histadrut or charity. Why did this approach fail to harness the Jewish businessmen and their capital to take part, at that time, in building the State?

The answer to that is obvious. When you tell a Jewish entrepeneur who comes from the United States—or for that matter from England or France—that the condition for his making an investment in Israel is that he take in the labor union, the Histadrut, as a partner, he's not likely to be too enthusiastic.

How do you explain the fact that during the first decades of the State, the Socialist Zionist government was able to harness so much financial support and good will from the American Jewish leadership who were and are Capitalists?

They managed to create the impression—which to some extent was true—that, in effect, they were Israel. If American Jews wanted to support the State of Israel, they had to support her government—even realizing that Israel did not have frequent changes of administration over the years. Not only was the Labor party in power from 1948 until 1977—a period of twenty-nine years—but it had also been in power in the Jewish community, in the *Yishuv*, in Palestine prior to the establishment of the State of Israel. They had been in power for fifty years.

So, it really should not be surprising that the State's Socialist Zionist government managed to create the impression that the Labor party really wanted the same end goal for Israel as American Jews—even though their ideological position, especially in the area of economics, was probably strange and not particularly attractive to most in the American Jewish community. American Jews just began to accept the situation, saying that this was Israel, where perhaps conditions were different from those in the United States, and letting the Israelis decide what was good for themselves.

But there was a change of administration on May 17, 1977. That's an historical date in the history of Israel—the date when the Likud came to power. The differences of opinion that existed in Israel on economic issues between Labor and Likud became apparent to the American Jewish community only after 1977. Only after the change of administration when Likud came to power did American Jews have a chance to see that a very significant part of Israel's population, and possibly the majority, had views quite different from those of the Labor party.

Just prior to statehood, you were the leader of the Betar movement in America—the Zionist youth movement of the Herut party. Jabotinsky was your ideological leader. Do you believe an Israel structured by your ideological perception thirty-eight years ago would be a different kind of nation today?

I have no doubt about that. First, our perception in 1948 was that the War of Independence, once having started, should have been pursued to the Jordan River. It was obvious that, otherwise, Israel would not be properly defensible and would, in fact, invite aggression if the borders were to be those of the armistice of 1949. Again, what came to the fore was the idealized and unrealistic view of the Labor party regarding the Arab-Israeli conflict. Ben Gurion felt that if we were moderate and limited the areas that were controlled by the IDF, we would have a very good chance of making peace with the Arabs immediately upon conclusion of the fighting. There was anticipation that peace agreements would come in the wake of the armistice agreements. The IDF were called back from areas that they already controlled in order not to create an impression of an Israel that was too "large."

The history of Israel would have been different—better—if the war had been pursued at that time. It really would not have involved any more serious fighting. The Arab armies were beaten on all fronts. We would not have all the problematic situations in Judea and Samaria that we have today if the IDF in 1948 and 1949 had continued on to the Jordan River.

Beyond that, our view of Israeli society and the Israeli economy was what you might call a Western view. We wanted a much more liberal approach—and that would have brought much greater progress to the development of Israeli society and would have avoided the very serious economic crisis that we are in today. I believe our economic crisis is a direct result of the government's overinvolvement in Israeli society and Israeli economy.

Can you define your particular brand of Zionism and would you compare it with the general definition of Zionism?

As we've discussed, I am a product of the Jabotinsky school of Zionism. As a young man, I was a member of Betar and became one of its leaders in the United States. I've continued my association with the Jabotinsky movement, today, the Likud. What characterizes that movement? We have to review what characterized Jabotinsky during the time that he was one of the leaders of the Zionist movement—to my mind, the greatest of Zionist leaders.

In summary, what characterized him for me was his realistic approach. He didn't look at situations in idealized terms. He had no illusions. Based on a realistic appreciation of the situation, he called for taking appropriate measures. You may recall, too, he was a realist regarding the ultimate fate of European Jewry. He was a realist, too, in appreciating the fact that Britain was going to betray the trust that she had been given by the League of Nations to establish a Jewish state in the area, and he was a realist when it came to evaluating the relationship between Jews and Arabs and the intensity of the conflict between them. I would say to this day what differentiates the Likud from the Labor party is absence of illusions; that is, we take a realistic approach to our problems and draw the appropriate conclusions from that realistic appreciation.

Can you define in today's terms and today's reality the differences between the ideological Zionist goals of the Herut movement and those of the Labor Zionist movement?

The ultimate goals are the same. They have to do with the welfare of the Jewish people and the establishment of a Jewish state that will be a haven for Jews throughout the world—a haven so attractive that the majority of the Jewish people on this earth will want to come to Israel and will eventually live here. It is the goal of all Zionists. The differences in opinions all have to do with the means that are suggested for achieving this goal.

In the area of foreign and defense policy, the major difference between Labor and Likud—some people in Israel say left and right—has to do with the attitude toward territory. It has to do with whether we believe that peace in the area, which is everyone's goal, can or cannot be achieved by conceding territories and by making Israel more vulnerable. The Likud does not believe in territorial compromise, a term that sounds benign but could involve a mortal danger to the State of Israel and the people who live here. I have always believed that this whole concept of territorial compromise—of buying peace by giving up pieces of our territory—is based on illusions and a lack of understanding of the part of the world we live in and the environmental conditions under which we live.

As ambassador, I used to tell audiences in the United States that the Middle East is not the Middle West. This is a different ball game. It's a hostile, volatile area with a long tradition of intolerance and a long history of brutality. Look at what's going on between Iran and Iraq. Look at Qaddafi. Look at Assad in Syria.

If you don't take care of yourself, you don't exist in this part of the world. The Lebanese have learned that sad lesson, tragically.

Some have ideas that if we show only good will and if we aim to compromise and give up areas that are important to us to show how dearly we want peace with our neighbors, it actually will achieve peace. Such notions are illusions—really delusions—and, even when put forth with the best of intentions, could be of ultimate danger to the State of Israel and the people who live here.

The other major difference between Labor and Likud has to do with the economy of the country. The Labor party is essentially still a Socialist party, although many of its members will say that they are not classical Socialists anymore. But the Israeli economy is what I call a Bolshevik economy. It's an economy in which the government and the labor union play outsized roles. The problem, although not one of ideology, is the inefficiency this introduces in the Israeli economy and, therefore, the obstacles it creates on the path to achieving those goals that are common to all of the Zionist movements. If Israel cannot become a country with a high standard of living and have an economy that knows how to utilize the wealth of talent that exists here, then she's not going to be the kind of country we want her to be. She will not attract other people and, in fact, may not even be able to hold the young people who grew up here. That's the second difference.

The Israeli economy must be a free economy, must be a haven for private enterprise. I don't claim there is no role at all for a government in regulating the economy or taking part in it, but there's no doubt in my mind that that role must be a fraction of that which is presently being played by the Israeli government. I am all for labor unions. I think they play a very important role—an essential role in modern society, but I don't believe the labor unions should be in the business of being in business. Eventually they will have to get out of being in business.

How does your view of the kind of Israel that you would like to see differ from that of some of your old comrades in the Hatchiya—*the party of Zionist revival, or is it just a difference of means?*

There are no substantial differences between *Hatchiya* and Likud or *Hatchiya* and *Herut.* You have to remember that most *Hatchiya* members, if they were active in politics before *Hatchiya* was established, were active in Likud and *Herut. Hatchiya* was established in the wake of the Camp David Accords—in the wake of the Israeli-Egyptian peace treaty—because of the opposition some of the people had to that treaty. But, as you know, there were people in *Herut* who remained in *Herut,* even though they did not agree with the treaty. Such a disagreement cannot be a *raison d'etre* (a sufficient reason) for maintaining a political party. It may be the cause of very severe differences of opinion when it happens. It may even be the cause of a split in the party at the time it happens.

But it cannot continue to be the reason for maintaining a separate political entity seven years later. That's behind us.

The treaty has been signed. All of Israel is committed to it. The people in *Hatchiya* are committed to it, just as the people in Likud and in the Labor party are. Israel is a modern Western country that follows the tradition of adherence to international obligations undertaken regardless of which party was in power at the time they were undertaken. The United States signed a treaty giving away the Panama Canal. Those who voted against that treaty are committed to the treaty just as those who voted for it. So, in my view, there's really no reason that would justify the continuing existence of *Hatchiya* as a separate political entity. There's no doubt in my mind that in time they will remerge with the Likud.

Why is it that, after eight years in a leadership position and the fall of the Labor party's control over government institutions, the Likud-Herut has failed to obtain support for its viewpoint from the Diaspora Jewish leadership and the mass of the Jewish community?

I don't know if that's really true in the full sense of the word as you stated it. I have come across many in the Jewish communities of the Diaspora—several in leadership positions—who seem to be favorably inclined toward Likud. Most of these people are not citizens of the State of Israel, so they don't vote in Israeli elections. Some of them are hesitant to identify themselves with a particular party and would like to adopt a position of simply working for Israel without any particular political connotation. But among those leaders of the Jewish communities in the Diaspora who are ready to identify themselves, there are a large number who make no secret of the fact that they tend to agree with the Likud's position on the problems that face Israel.

I don't know whether you could say at this time that the majority of Diaspora Jewish leadership are in favor of Labor. If that's the case, then it's still the carry-over of those many, many years when the Labor party, in effect, was Israel and represented itself as being Israel to all the people it cultivated during those years. Also, some Jews in the Diaspora are very conscious of public opinion and are very concerned that if Israel's leadership takes too hawkish a position, she will be open to criticism. They are somewhat sensitive about this kind of criticism and, therefore, quite naturally gravitate toward more dovish positions—toward positions that involve mild concessions that won't call criticism upon Israel.

There are many people in the Jewish communities of the Diaspora who are very courageous and are not concerned about such criticism. They are ready to swim against the stream, if necessary. They are ready to explain Israel's security needs and are ready to support strong forthright positions when taken by the Israeli government. I have told Mr. Peres and people in the Labor party here that there's no trick at all to getting applause in the United States by talking about

Israel's concessions and announcing that we are ready to give up a piece of territory. It's very easy. The difficult thing is to be very outspoken about Israel's security needs and get applause for these positions.

Has Israel failed to provide its youth with a proper Zionist education and, if so, why?

There's no universal answer to that question. The problem of fathers passing on values to their sons is a problem in all generations and in all societies. On the whole, we in Israel have done a good job of that because this is a country that was founded on the ideology of continuous efforts through generations in attaining long-term goals. We have found, generation after generation—and it's now 100 years since the early settlement of Palestine by pioneers who came from Poland, Rumania, and Russia—that Israelis are pursuing these goals and making very strenuous efforts to reach them. They are ready to make very significant sacrifices for these goals.

We do have in Israel today, among all generations, a higher level of national motivation than can be found in any other country in the world. In the final analysis, that's the proof of the pudding. We may never be satisfied. We may think that there's always a need for more. In every generation there's sometimes a feeling that the young people are not as devoted Zionists as their fathers, and maybe not as good at being soldiers as their fathers. But then, whenever an emergency arises, we find that almost the opposite is the case. Our young people surprise us with the intensity of their commitment to the country and to her security with their readiness to do whatever is necessary.

Part Two

On Israel and World Jewry

On Israel and World Jewry

Moshe Arens' Overview

The Jewish people in the Diaspora share a common destiny with Israelis and the State of Israel. If there were not a State of Israel, then it would mean eventually the end of the Jewish people. Alternatively, if Israel prospers and triumphs, then the Jewish people will live, not only in Israel, but in the Diaspora as well.

The very establishment of the State of Israel—the War of Independence in 1948—needs to be seen in the context of the Holocaust. If that war had been lost, not only would that have been the end of all Jewish aspirations for establishing a Jewish state, but it would have been the end of the Jewish people. Why, then, was there not greater participation on the part of Jews throughout the world in that struggle for Israel's survival? People were still under the shock of World War II and the Holocaust. Also, communications in those days were not what they are today. Most Jews were really not aware of what an historic era it was for the Jewish people—that here a battle was being fought for their very survival, and if that battle were lost, the death note might ring for the Jewish people.

This is much better understood today. It explains the very large-scale identification of Jews throughout the world with Israel. The most dramatic demonstration of this identification of Jews in the Diaspora with Israel is the case of Soviet Jewry. After decades of Bolshevik rule under Lenin and Stalin and deliberate persecution of Jewish identity, Jewish history, Zionism, and the Hebrew language, we suddenly find that Russian Jewry is still Jewish. To many of them, being Jewish means demanding the right to come to Israel.

Starting from the premise that Jews throughout the world share a common destiny with the State of Israel, what obviously must follow is an obligation for Israel's well-being—ultimately, a commitment and a dedication to come to Israel and to participate personally in its upbuilding. There's much that a Jew can do for Israel in the United States, Canada, Argentina, or Western Europe, but none of this can measure up with personal participation—being in Israel, living in Israel, doing business in Israel, and raising children in Israel.

We live in a mobile world. People move around, and none of us should expect that 100 percent of the Jewish people are going to live in Israel. But we certainly do want to strive toward the objective that a significant majority of the Jewish people will live in Israel, will be anchored in Israel, or will personally participate in activities in Israel. Most of all, we want people to come to Israel because they want to come, not because they have to come in an effort to try to save themselves or their children, and not because they're convinced they'll do better materially in Israel than where they are.

Israel can become an affluent country that will provide great economic opportunities. But arriving at that point is dependent upon immigration from the West. This is an obligation of Jewish communities in the Free World. It is in their capability to accelerate the process of making Israel a very advanced country economically and, therefore, attractive to more and more people who, of their own volition, will leave the Diaspora and come to live here.

There is a partnership between Israel and Jews in the Diaspora because we share a common destiny, but it's not an equal partnership. From the formal point of view, those who live here are citizens of the State of Israel and participate in the election process. They also have to face the consequences for the decisions that are made here by the democratically elected authorities.

I don't mean that people who don't live here don't have the right to express their opinions on how to deal with problems in Israel. On the contrary, it would be unnatural if committed Jews in the Diaspora didn't have opinions on Israeli problems. And it would be unnatural to say to them that we would like to hear their opinions only after they decide to settle in Israel.

There is a question, however, as to whether or not Jewish communities in the Diaspora should express opinions that run counter to offical Israeli government policy, possibly weakening the government's position. There are no universal answers to that question, but committed Jewish supporters from the Diaspora should be somewhat reticent to voice opposing opinions, particularly, if they are a matter of crucial importance to the State of Israel or if they are a matter of life or death.

If you are not living in Israel, however, you are not less of a Jew. A Jew is a person who believes in Jewish survival, who believes in the unity of the Jewish people—that we are responsible for each other as Jews, and who believes in the centrality of the State of Israel.

Merrill Simon's Overview

The nature of Israel's present and future relationship to the Diaspora has spawned an emotional free-for-all among the Jewish people. Now that the State of Israel exists, the question of the legitimacy of Diaspora Jewry has challenged, troubled, and annoyed those Jews who have adamantly chosen to remain in the Diaspora. In many ways, the relationship, which should be interdependent, has become divisive and neurotic.

As a people, we have a tendency to focus on the wrong questions—questions that divide rather than unite. Instead of making frontal attacks on where a person chooses to live, perhaps we should concentrate on underscoring the contribution a person can make, given that the choice of residence has been made.

It seems that the polarization of Jewish religious movements—inflamed by such issues as the "Who is a Jew?" legislation in Israel—has brought reality to some of the gravest post-Holocaust concerns of the Jewish people. The continued polemics among the Orthodox, Conservative, and Reform branches can lead only to a deeper schism. Even more exasperating, the "Who is a Jew?" issue, ultimately, can only be destructive. It may be a stimulating focal point for those who study Halachic law and an interesting issue for those involved in theoretical discourse, but creating the traumatic impact of challenging the birthright of hundreds of thousands who have committed themselves to the Jewish people is not the way one guarantees Jewish survival.

The question for attention must be not "Who is a Jew?" but, rather, "What is a Jew?" From a reactive perspective, a Jew is a person who is perceived by others as being Jewish and is held accountable for the behavior of the Jewish people in Israel and in the Diaspora. The world, which demands that Jews must take care of each other in a unified fashion, has already decided that we, as Jews, must act as one people. It is our task to motivate and encourage the support that emanates from this grim reality. We can only do this with gratitude and sensitivity as we leave the divisive questions to the theologians.

From a proactive perspective, a Jew is a person who perceives himself (or herself) as being Jewish and accountable to demonstrate that Jewishness in a self-defined way. It may mean being strictly observant, being affiliated with a synagogue, being a member of a Jewish organization, and/or donating money or time to some Jewish cause. However demonstrated, it is an indication of commitment to being a Jew. If we want to avoid further alienation, this is not the time to scrutinize Jewish credentials. It is not the time to seek Halachic purity on the issue of "Who is a Jew?" Rather than focus on the divisiveness of the answer to that question, we must capture the cohesiveness of the answers to "What is a Jew?"

Another disturbing issue concerns the alarming rate of assimilation of Jews in the West through intermarriage. It is clear that the "Jewish heart" of two generations ago has not been successfully transmitted to our progeny. This may be due to our failure as Jewish parents and Jewish teachers. It may be attributable to the passage of time which has allowed significant Jewish events to slip into historical silence. Whatever the cause, we must decelerate this threat to Jewish survival by increasing the quantity and improving the quality of the existing commitment of Western Jews.

Jewish commitment has to be articulated through Jewish day school education—a place where Jewish subjects are taken seriously, a place where Jews primarily socialize with each other, and a place where cultural bonding, which may not be taking place at home, can, at least, occur in school. In these schools, commitment to the State of Israel should be of central importance because it is Israel that should be the unifying factor for all Jews. Israel's religious significance, her centrality to Jewish survival, and, therefore, her importance in all of our everyday lives must be the focus.

We should concentrate and care about the oppressed Jews in the Soviet Union and in Arab lands by actively reminding ourselves that our people are being persecuted for the mere reason that they are Jews, observant or secular. We who were born in the Free World are only here by chance. Our good fortune should only reflect the necessity for helping those who, through no fault of their own, suffer unspeakable indignities every day of their lives.

The Jewish people will be sustained only by three things: the continued unified support for a strong, safe Israel; the curbing of assimilation by heroic efforts in the promotion of Jewish day school education where Jewish subjects are central and not peripheral to the curriculum; and the demonstration of our responsibility for each other by focusing on concerns that draw the Jewish people closer together. Jewry is again at the crossroads where, ultimately, it is we who will determine the way in which we will survive—and, indeed, we will survive.

ECONOMY

In the past, what has been the impact of world Jewry's financial support of the State of Israel on Israel's economy, i.e., United Jewish Appeal (UJA), State of Israel Bonds, and private institutional fund-raising?

Many Jewish people from the United States have made very significant contributions to the economic scene in Israel. They have made these important contributions to Israel's economic strength either as employees or managers of some of Israel's best-known and most successful companies or as investors, partners, members of the board, and even chairmen of the board in business enterprises that also have been successful in and of themselves.

There are also the more institutionalized methods of participation—UJA and Israel Bonds. A percentage of the contributions to UJA comes to Israel. The money raised by Israel Bonds is transferred to the treasury of the State of Israel.

At the present time, what is the impact of world Jewry's financial support of the State of Israel on Israel's economy (UJA, Israel Bonds, donations to private institutions)?

We can examine the UJA contributions to Israel on a quantitative basis. During recent years, the UJA has contributed $250 to 300 million a year. The gross national product of Israel is about $24 billion. So we're talking about approximately 1 percent of the GNP of Israel. I don't want to minimize that, but, clearly, it's not something crucial to the Israeli economy. It's a reflection of the commitment of American Jews to the State of Israel.

Israel's GNP has grown almost exponentially over the years, but the American Jewish community's contribution has not kept pace. I have always been of the opinion that American Jewry's contribution to Israel could be and should be far larger than it is, especially when taking into account the American Jewish community's stated commitment to and interest in Israel and considering that the American Jewish community and Israel share a common fate.

Israel and her taxpayers carry a tremendous burden because of the extensive security problems we face; the six wars we've fought in the past years; and the ingathering of the exiles to this haven for Jewish people from all over the world— whether from Arabic-speaking countries as in the past, from Ethiopia or the Soviet Union in the present, or from South Africa as may be in the near future.

Given these facts, the American Jewish community must carry its share. "What is its share?" My answer is that that share should be far larger than an amount which represents 1 percent of the GNP of Israel, and which, I'm sure, represents far, far less than 1 percent of the GNP of the American Jewish community. That's not a contribution that is commensurate with the relationship that exists between the American Jewish community and Israel. I'm sure the statistics are available to show that, since the establishment of the State, the Israeli economy has grown much faster than American Jewish institutional contributions to Israel's economic growth.

The greatest impact of world Jewry on the State of Israel and Israel's economy comes by virtue of personal participation. That is my recommendation and appeal to anybody in the Jewish community in America or in any other country of the Diaspora who wants to make a contribution to Israel's economic well-being. It is not only an economic contribution to Israel's strength and independence, but it has great value from a political as well as a security point of view. Personal participation can range from making an investment and being a partner in a business in Israel to moving to Israel and participating in economic enterprise here as an employee, employer, president of the company, or chairman of the board of the company.

Next to personal participation by actually working in or managing an enterprise here on a day-to-day basis comes being a partner or investing in an enterprise here and, perhaps, sitting on the board of directors helping to guide that enterprise. Next comes direct contributions to a particular institution. Here again, we still have that direct connection and direct involvment of a person who has taken the trouble to target an investment or contribution to a particular institution considered worthwhile. In most cases, that involves a certain bond that grows between that contributor and the particular institution. We have this on a very large scale; many of Israel's institutions are supported in this fashion.

In the future, what do you believe will be the importance of world Jewry's financial contribution to Israel's sustenance and growth through the traditional fund-raising vehicles such as UJA, Bonds, and private institutional fund-raising?

I can only tell in a normative manner what it should be. The American Jewish community must carry a much larger share of the economic burdens that the people of Israel have shouldered. Most of these economic burdens are burdens of world Jewry, or they are missions that represent goals of Jews throughout the world, not just the Jews who happen to live in Israel. I hope in time the gap will close by virtue of a greater level of partnership of world Jewry, in particular American Jewry, resulting in an easier economic situation for us in Israel.

What do you see as the future role of the massive fund-raising organiza-

*tions established by the UJA and the State of Israel Bonds in the United
States? Do you see their continuing their traditional role of raising money
for Bonds and UJA?*

In recent years, there have been discussions as to whether there is still any
rationale for having two separate organizations—Israel Bonds and UJA—or
whether it is appropriate that fund-raising for Jewish institutions and Jewish
causes in the United States be merged with fund-raising for Israel. Such is the
case with UJA—part of the funds stay in the United States to serve the needs of
the American Jewish community and part of the funds are sent to Israel. There
are ongoing discussions, debates, and sometimes even arguments about what
proportion should come to Israel. This needs to be examined more closely.

There should be one organization in the United States that is concerned with
raising funds for Israel and only for Israel. Within the framework of that kind of
organization, we stand a real chance of raising the level of participation of the
American Jewish community in the growth and development of the State of
Israel.

*Over the next decades, the income raised by these two organizations,
Bonds and UJA, will continue to become a smaller percentage of the State
of Israel's financial resources; yet, a monumental effort,
organizationally—in time, in money, and in involvement—is spent by
most of the committed Jewish community in pursuing these funds. For
many, it is their only vehicle for Jewish identification, and, for most, it is
their only contact with the State of Israel. Do you believe the time to be
ripe to redirect the efforts of these organizations, or can you envision the
creation of a third fund-raising vehicle, sponsored by the Israeli government, dedicated to raising investment capital to finance Israel's emerging
high-technology industries?*

First of all, we should separate investments which are on the level of personal
participation in business enterprises in Israel from contributions that the American
Jewish community makes to the State of Israel. The latter is really nothing other
than a sharing of the burden that has fallen on the shoulders of the people who
live in Israel. I wouldn't even call it a contribution. It is an obligation that the
American Jewish community must share.

The measure of the giving of American Jewry to Israel through the UJA and
Israel Bonds as a percentage of the Israeli GNP—1 percent—is an indication of
just how significant that "contribution" is to Israel's economic well-being. The
more appropriate measure is the percentage it represents of the total income of the
American Jewish community. That will tell to what extent people are really
hurting—giving till it hurts—and really carrying their share of the burden. It's

appropriate, correct, and necessary for the American Jewish community to carry its share of the burden, which is far larger than what is being carried at the present time.

The notion of American Jews providing capital for investments in the State of Israel—a level of personal participation—is very important. In many ways, it is much more important than what people give through UJA or whatever organization they believe is appropriate. This is not only because of the money invested but because of the economic climate it helps to create. If the economic climate in Israel is good, there will not be a shortage of money. Money goes where money is to be made. Certainly, there's some correlation between reaching such an objective and the organizational structure that's charged with the task of obtaining the capital for investment. I'm inclined to think that a single organization devoted solely to the raising of investment capital for Israel should be handling the matter in the United States.

Today, we have non-Jewish people investing in Israel, and, if the economic climate improves—as I'm sure it will, we'll have more and more people without any personal connection who will invest here because they'll think it's good business. The primary importance that I attach to Jews investing in Israel is that it brings about a personal participation on their part. Eventually, this may lead to their living in Israel, or, for that matter, their children coming to live in Israel—part of the time or all of the time—and that's what's important.

Do you believe there are any other methods of harnessing Diaspora Jewish capital and know-how to assist in the massive task of catapulting Israel into the post-industrial revolution—the high-technology revolution?

There's a great deal that needs to be done to bring the facts before the American Jewish community. There are many good Jews in the United States, active in business, with financial resources of their own and/or access to financial resources, who could invest in a business enterprise in Israel. Many of them have a great deal of know-how—in many cases, far more important than financial resources. They are not very well versed as to Israel's economy, Israel's economic climate, the kinds of industry that we have in Israel, or the natural resources—primarily, the human resources—that we have in Israel. There is room for a "marketing campaign" to bring facts and figures before that particular audience.

Do you believe that the method of harnessing Jewish capital for investment in high technology should come from an institution similar to AMPAL, which is bank sponsored (Bank Hapoalim), rather than from a government-sponsored agency? Should the instrument be long-term bonds with fixed interest, stocks, or a combination of both?

It should be handled from a business vantage point. This means working with a concept of a portfolio offering people various options. Many investors will want to have their own Israeli portfolio. Some may decide to be in bonds, some in stocks, and some in venture capital. Others may decide to make a direct personal investment in a particular business known to them.

The American Jewish community, as a whole, will want a portfolio. There will be some for whom Israel Bonds is the only reasonable or attractive option, some who will insist on making a personal investment in a particular company, others who will want to invest in venture capital funds that deal only in investments in Israel, and so on. We want to be able to present the entire spectrum of business opportunities to the American Jewish community.

Do you envision world Jewry continuing to participate in financing private institutions in Israel such as Yeshivot, or do you believe that eventually that source of revenue will dry up?

I don't think it will dry up. Throughout Jewish history, giving has characterized Jews. This will be true of Jewish communities throughout the world in future years, as well. The recipients will be various cultural, religious, educational, and health institutions in the countries in which they live. Very naturally, however, since Israel is, and will continue to be, the focus of Jewish life, many of these contributions from Diaspora Jewry will come to institutions in Israel.

POLITICS

Should the World Zionist Organization (WZO) be involved in political decisions made by the government of Israel? Is there a true partnership between the WZO and the Israeli government?

The WZO should not be involved in political decisions made by the government of Israel. Israel is a sovereign democratic state that is run by a government elected by the people. It represents the people of Israel, and it has the legal and moral authority to make decisions for the State of Israel and for the people of Israel. It carries the responsibility for the State of Israel and its future; therefore, only the Israeli government can make the decisions in Israel.

This is not to say that other people who have a concern for Israel or a commitment to Israel cannot or should not make their voices heard. The WZO is comprised of people who are committed to the State of Israel. Many of its members intend, eventually, to settle in Israel and become Israeli citizens. It's perfectly appropriate for them to make their voices heard on issues on which they have strong feelings. They can give their advice, and they can lobby—but that and not more than that. They cannot be participants in making the decisions.

There isn't a full partnership between the WZO and the Israeli government. The WZO is not a pseudo government. Israel is not governed by two governments. It can't be. The State of Israel, like any other state, can be governed by only one government—the government that is elected by the people of Israel.

Should a new kind of organization or agency be created in the Diaspora, particularly in the United States, to provide the leaders with more of a say in helping formulate some policies of the Israeli government?

The people outside of Israel cannot and should not formulate the policies of the Israeli government. But they can and do give advice. That advice is given not only by the WZO and its leaders but also frequently by individual Jews—Jews of stature who have an association with Israel or who feel very strongly about some particular point and know their public stature will make their voices heard. There's no need for additional organizations to provide this kind of advice—the Israeli government isn't lacking in advice. The channels of communication among the Israeli government, the Israeli society, and Diaspora Jewry are open. There are many contacts and exchanges among them. I've never heard leaders of Jewish organizations in the Diaspora complain that their voices cannot be heard or that they don't have access to the people who make decisions in Israel. That's all that's required and really nothing more.

Conversely, shouldn't American-Jewish leaders have a voice in those policy decisions of the government of Israel which may affect the American-Jewish community?

That's like asking, shouldn't Americans have a voice in the decisions of the French government that may affect the people of America? This is a small world, and it's interconnected. The French government makes some decisions which may have an affect on people in the United States, but that doesn't give people or organizations in the United States the right to be partners in that decision. When the French government has to make a decision on matters that affect the United States, I'm sure there are many contacts and plenty of lobbying. It could be directly by the U.S. government, vis-á-vis the French government, or by Americans in leading public positions who are trying to influence or convince—but no

ON ISRAEL AND WORLD JEWRY • 139

more than that. In that sense, with all the differences there are between the relationship that exists between the French government and the people in the United States and the relationship that exists between Israel and the Jewish community in the United States, there is really no difference.

Israel has a sovereign government that is elected by the people of Israel. It's responsible to the people of Israel and only to the people of Israel. When the Israeli government makes decisions, there's no doubt that many of those decisions, in some way or another, influence the Jewish community in the United States. All of these decisions may influence Jews in the United States who intend to emigrate to Israel. But again, they cannot be partners in making those decisions until such time as they come to live in Israel and become Israeli citizens.

Should Israeli political parties be allowed to raise money in the United States to finance their activities in Israel, as well as the elections?

I see no objection to that, but I doubt it's a very common phenomena for political parties in one country to raise money in other countries. There are hundreds of thousands, if not millions, of people in the United States who have a very real interest in Israel, who have a love for Israel, or who have a commitment to Israel to the point where they take an interest in the detailed workings of the Israeli democracy and feel an attachment to or support one of the Israeli political parties. There is no reason why these people cannot express that support by making financial contributions if they have the capability to do so.

Should American Jewry have a greater say in how the funds they raise are spent in Israel?

The American-Jewish community has a say in how funds raised in the United States for Israel are to be spent. It is done quite adequately through the instrumentality of the Jewish Agency.

Would a political dialogue between a roof Jewish organization and the Israeli government conflict with Israel's relations with countries at a governmental level?

No. I am a great believer in communicating and, therefore, in dialogues. There is an ongoing dialogue between Israel and America and between Israel and the American-Jewish community. That dialogue is carried on in a multitude of channels through roof organizations, other organizations, individuals, and through various academic and research institutions. It's all to the good, and it should continue.

EDUCATION AND CULTURE

Is the Jewish day school movement and Jewish day school education in the Diaspora important for Israel and world Jewry?

Yes, it is vital. Much of the commitment to Judaism and to the State of Israel expressed by past and present adult generations of world Jewry is rooted in their having lived during the period of the Holocaust and its immediate aftermath, during the time of the creation and early struggle for survival of the State of Israel, and during periods of extreme and blatant anti-Semitism. To the youth of today in the Diaspora, the Holocaust is past history, the State of Israel exists, and particularly to those in the Western world, anti-Semitism, where it stills exists, is more covert than overt, and, therefore, less observable.

Today, more than ever, it is of critical importance that new generations are steeped in Jewish education—that they know Jewish history, culture, and the Hebrew language and understand well the history and significance of the continued existence of the State of Israel. It appears that the synagogue schools, in general, have not produced a generation of such well-educated Jewish youth, committed to being Jewish. For the sake of the survival of Diaspora Jewry, a more intense Jewish education for new generations is required to combat Jewish alienation and assimilation and to stop the erosion of intermarriage. Jewish day school education in the Diaspora is essential, too, for the continued existence, well-being, and further development of the State of Israel, because the most committed Jewish youth are from the ranks of Jewish day school graduates; and the majority of young people who consider making, and eventually do make, *aliyah* are products of the day school movement.

I hope that all three major branches of Judaism will expand their day school movements. The Orthodox, of course, have done a fine job of creating a large network of day schools through both the Yeshivot and the Orthodox Hebrew Day School operations. During the past few decades, the Conservative program, the Solomon Shecter Day School system, has blossomed. And most recently, as I understand, the Reform movement, which for years resisted day schools in support of public schools, passed a resolution to create and operate a day school system. The expansion of the day school movement among the Orthodox, Conservative, and Reform branches is vital to the survival and well-being of not only Jewish communities in the Diaspora, but also the State of Israel.

Today, the story of Israel—the music, the art, the people—is becoming more and more familiar to Jews in the Diaspora. Multitudes of Shlichim are roaming through every community in which there are Jews residing, spreading the message about Israel. Do you see a need for a cultural dialogue to enhance the understanding of Israel and Israelis by Diaspora Jewry?

I'm all for anything that can contribute to that understanding—dialogues, seminars, and conferences; interchanges of students, teachers, and performing groups; study tours; international competitions; communications through organizational activity; visitations and tourism.

Of course, the reverse is true also. The better the understanding by Israelis of the Jewish community and its status in the United States, Canada, Argentina, or even in the Soviet Union, the better, because the Jewish people are one, and all Jewish people share a common destiny. It is important to have as high a level of understanding as possible in order to have as great a cohesion as possible. Understanding each other and the different facets of the Jewish people located in different parts of the world is the first requirement for unity.

Can the Israeli government provide the financial support necessary to continue the development of Israel's cultural institutions and maintain her active participation in the international interchanges required to enhance understanding and unity among Jews throughout the world?

The Israeli government wants to support all activities that foster cultural development and international understanding. At the present time, however, our grave security problems and economic concerns are financially draining. We must rely, even more than previously, on the Jewish communities and private individuals in the Diaspora to encourage and finance such activities. A larger portion of the responsibility to preserve and share Israel's cultural heritage, to support the further development of Israel's cultural institutions, and to foster the cohesion born of international understanding among Jews in Israel and the Diaspora must be undertaken by Jewish communities throughout the Free World.

RELIGION

There is a perception among Jews in the Diaspora that since the Likud came to power in 1977, the Orthodox community in Israel, led by the rabbinate, has been garnishing greater influence within the political arena—forcing upon the majority in Israel, who are nonobservant Jews, more and more Halacha and impacting more upon the conduct of their daily lives. This being the case, how do you expect to sustain the level of support for Israel among the Diaspora Jewry, most of whom are not affiliated with any Jewish religious institutions?

I don't think that's the case. The relationship between the religious establishment in Israel and the rest of the population was determined back in 1948 under Mr. Ben Gurion's stewardship. That relationship is the basis of various discussions that continuously come up on issues about whether buses in a certain part of Israel will or will not run on the Sabbath or whether soccer games will or will not be played on the Sabbath. It is what people refer to as the "status quo," which has become something of a "sacred cow" in Israel. Everyone says let's not change the status quo. Essentially, it has not changed much since 1948; if anything, it has changed in favor of the secular population.

How do you expect to influence these non-Orthodox Jewish communities in the Diaspora to make aliyah, given their growing concern that they would be second-class citizens or be forced to live in a way that they find objectionable?

I think that's a red herring. I don't think it's a real problem. We've had immigration from the United States to Israel—far less than what we would like to see—but we have had it. In retrospect, we've had periods in which immigration seemed fairly large-scale—the period after the Six-Day War, for example. At that time, thousands were coming to Israel on an annual basis. I've never encountered anybody who wanted to come here but was prevented from doing so because of concern about the religious environment in Israel or because of the relationship between the religious and secular populations in Israel.

Aliyah is important to Israel and an integral part of the goals that are shared by everyone here—religious and nonreligious. I have no doubt that if we suddenly found ourselves faced with a tremendous urge for *aliyah*, say from the United States, and it became clear that the only obstacle to the fulfillment of that urge by tens of thousands, hundreds of thousands of Jews was the religious establishment in Israel—the relationship between the religious and the secular segments of society—I'm sure we'd settle that problem by removing the obstacle.

The growing concern in the United States of some non-Orthodox Jews, due to this perception, has manifested itself in their financial and other support of the political activists in Israel who would diminish the role of religion in politics. Can you comment on this?

There are American Jews who take intense interest in what's going on in Israel to the point where they begin to identify not only with Israel as a whole but with certain segments of the Israeli political spectrum, the Israeli society, or Israel's cultural institutions. Those people tend to direct their financial and other support in certain directions—those they're inclined to favor. This is perfectly legitimate and perfectly appropriate. I'm sure there are American Jews who are very religious and support religious institutions in Israel, while others, who feel that the center of gravity in Israel has swung too far in favor of the religious community, extend their support to those organizations in Israel opposed to the present status quo.

Do you believe that the growing concern with Diaspora Jewry about an Israel that is becoming polarized by the Jewish antireligionists, that is, secular humanists, on one hand, and the Orthodox Jewish community on the other, is justified?

I don't think that polarization is increasing. I think it's decreasing. If you pick a number of parameters that we could agree on as being characteristic of the extent of that polarization, you'll find it's not on the increase. If anything, the Israeli society is becoming more secular rather than less secular.

In the last decade, the vast majority of those who have come on aliyah to Israel from America have been those in the spectrum of Orthodox Jewry. Since their Jewish and Zionist commitment is rooted in Judaism and an attachment to the land of Israel, they are a natural group within the United States to develop and from which to promote aliyah. Do you believe enough has been done to tap this natural resource for aliyah? What more should be done to encourage aliyah by the observant Western Jews?

Not enough has been done to encourage *aliyah* generally. *Aliyah* has not been anything like what we want it and need it to be. As long as we believe, as I do, that *aliyah* is not like the weather—it's not something you can't do anything about, then it's obvious we haven't done enough about it. Since we can do something about it, if it has not lived up to expectations, it follows that we haven't done enough in order to bring about the level of *aliyah* that Israel needs.

It is easy to understand why the tendency for *aliyah* to Israel is somewhat stronger among people in the United States with a strong religious orientation. Many Americans in Israel have not come from a religious background and have not been primarily motivated by religious convictions or religious upbringing. When we talk about *aliyah* from the United States, we want to appeal to all segments of the American Jewish community—to the religious as well as the secular, and to the Orthodox as well as the Conservative and Reform.

ZIONISM

Since the U.N. resolution equating Zionism with racism, which was passed in the mid-1970s, there has been much questioning within the American Jewish community on just what is Zionism. Would you please define Zionism?

In the days of Theodor Herzl, Zionism was the movement whose object it was to create a Jewish state in what was then Palestine. Today, that State exists—the State of Israel. Zionism's objective now is to make Israel a strong state—one that will serve as a haven to Jews throughout the world who are in need of such a haven. Zionism's aim is to have the State of Israel serve as a magnet to Jews throughout the world who decide they want to live a full Jewish life in a Jewish state and who will turn that State into "a light unto the nations" that will become a center of learning, knowledge, wisdom, culture, and technology. That's Zionism.

In the early days of statehood, then Prime Minister David Ben Gurion declared that the only persons entitled to refer to themselves as Zionists were those who either live in Israel or are planning to make aliyah. Do you support this position on who is a Zionist?

No, not really. It is a problem of semantics. Surely, to be a Zionist means to make a commitment. Zionism is not just a dispassionate interest in a particular cause. It involves a real commitment, and the ultimate commitment, of course, is personal participation.

Certainly, there are different kinds and various levels of personal participation. A person can be a Zionist and make immigration at some future date. I believe all people who have come to live in Israel are Zionists who, during those periods of their lives before immigration, were Zionists who had not yet made *aliyah*. You might ask the question, "Can a Zionist be a person who has definitely decided that he will never come to Israel?" If a person feels a deep commitment to the State of Israel and to the goals of Zionism, in my opinion, he's a Zionist; I would never give up hope that he'll eventually find his way to coming to live here.

Do you believe that Ben Gurion's approach not only eroded but undermined the Zionist movement in the Diaspora at that time?

No, I don't believe that. Actually, the Zionist movement in the Diaspora—if you define it as being the movement of those Jews who feel a very strong commitment to the State of Israel—has flourished since the State of Israel was established. We can look back at the American Jewish community in the days before the State of Israel was established. At that time, there was a debate going on in the American Jewish community among those who did and those who did not feel that establishing a Jewish state was a positive thing to do in terms of Jewish interests. At that time, too, there was a strong assimilationist trend in the American Jewish community. I'm not sure that the majority of American Jews then were Zionists in the sense of supporting the establishment of a Jewish state.

Today, the vast majority in the American Jewish community are very strong supporters of and are committed to the State of Israel. In that sense, they are Zionists. The Zionist organizations that existed in pre-State days, to which all those Jews in the United States who felt a commitment to the establishment of the State of Israel belonged, have become smaller, less powerful, and less alive than they used to be. A reason for that, of course, is that since the State of Israel was established, people feel they can be committed to, can contribute to, and can travel to the State of Israel without being members of a particular Zionist organization or party. And there is some logic in that.

After the Six-Day War of 1967, the Jewish Agency for Israel, American Section, was expanded to include a number of non-Zionist organizations. In retrospect, do you believe that this was a good decision? Was it good for the State of Israel?

Yes, it was a good decision—if you mean the inclusion of American Jewish leaders who were not members of Zionist organizations in the United States. It simply reflects reality, namely, that there are many Jews in the United States with a great commitment to Israel who are very firm supporters of Israel. Many of them, by the way, are investors in Israeli businesses; many of them have residences in Israel. They are not members of the Labor Zionist Federation, the Herut party, or the Mizrachi religious party and are not members of one of the other Zionist political parties—which is what you must be if you want to be an institutionalized Zionist in the United States. These people have the right to be and should be represented in that agency that deals with relationships between Israel and the Diaspora as well as with contributions to Israel by the Jewish communities in the Diaspora. They should have the right to be represented there no less than the people who happen to be the official representatives of the Zionist parties in Australia, Canada, or the United States.

The whole concept of the Jewish Agency is in need of reform, and, in many ways, today it is an anachronistic structure. Most people in Israel are inclined to believe that there's a lot of money being wasted there, and that it's a bureaucracy that is needlessly duplicating the work of the Israeli governmental bureaucracy. To some extent, it has become a bureaucracy that is trying to perpetuate itself. There's a real need for taking a new look at the whole concept and structure of the Jewish Agency.

Have the proliferation of non-Zionist organizations in America and the rest of the Diaspora, which have undertaken political and project fundraising on behalf of the State of Israel, made obsolete the need for a Zionist movement and Zionist organizations in the Diaspora?

I wouldn't go that far. After all, we are interested in providing all those frameworks that serve to attract Jews in the Diaspora to activities in support of the State of Israel. To that end, the more, the better. Give everyone the chance to work in the framework they find appropriate, attractive, and convenient.

If there are American Jews who are attracted to, and would like to be active on behalf of, Israel within the framework of a religious Zionist organization which has an affiliation with a religious Zionist political party in the State of Israel, so be it. I don't know how many there are like that, and I doubt the number will increase in the future; but even if it is a small segment of the American Jewish community that would like to participate within that particular framework, I say, let them.

What do you see as the present and future roles and functions of Zionist organizations in the Diaspora in helping to contribute to the future quality growth of the State of Israel?

The quality of the State of Israel is a direct function of the people who live in Israel, and it's a function only of that parameter. Therefore, contributions to Israel's quality are contributions that involve personal participation in the life of the State of Israel. The more *aliyah* we're going to have, the better the quality of the State of Israel will be.

Can a Diaspora Zionist movement assist the State of Israel in meeting her ideological goals?

Yes. Israel is in need of support. The problems and challenges facing Israel are of such magnitude that our chances of meeting these challenges and overcoming the problems are immeasurably better if we enjoy the support of the world's Jewish communities. If, for a moment, we were to visualize ourselves as not enjoying the support of Jewish communities throughout the world and being dependent only on the population that happens to live in Israel at the present time, we would be facing great risks. So, that support is essential to the future of Israel and the future of the Jewish people, because they are one and the same.

Part Three

On Israel and Her Foreign Relations

On Israel and
Her Foreign Relations

Moshe Arens' Overview

The dominant objective of Israel's foreign policy is Israel's security. Most countries in the world don't feel there is any real threat to their security, so they have other primary objectives. We are still under the influence of the Holocaust where 6 million Jews were killed; we still see Jewish communities in various parts of the world being persecuted; and we've had to fight six wars since the State of Israel was established in 1948. Had it not been for our ability to withstand these onslaughts, Israel could have ceased to exist within a matter of days. This threat of destruction is still directed against us today by surrounding hostile Arab countries supported by the Soviet Union.

From a purely military standpoint, Israel is outmanned—and outgunned—by the Arab standing armies by a ratio of fifteen to one. Israel has a fighting chance only after we have our reserves mobilized, bringing the force ratio to four or five to one. But it takes time to mobilize the reserves, so we need space within which to absorb any initial onslaught to give us time. If not, our population centers could be hit in the initial hours of a war, and Israel's ability to defend herself would deteriorate. Territory, therefore, is an essential element of Israel's defense posture and of eventual peace in the area.

Another objective of our foreign policy is to strengthen our relationship with the entire Western world and with the United States specifically. Israel is a Western nation, and she has the same ideals as other Western nations—particularly the United States. Part of the hostility directed against us is a result of our being part of the Western world, so, in large measure, our security is tied to the security of the Western world. If the West were to fall to a Communist onslaught, it would be very difficult to be optimistic about Israel's security. Whether we like it or not, Israel is part of the East-West confrontation.

151

The United States attaches a great deal of importance to Israel and to her relationship with Israel. Although the relationship between the two countries is based on a great commonality of ideas, ideals, and strategic interests, only recently has it reached the high level where it is today. We want to continue to build and strengthen this relationship. The United States and Israel must work in concert and must be seen working in concert by everyone.

The first objective of Israel's defense policy is to attain the kind of posture that will deter aggression. There is little question that U.S.-Israeli relationships are a very important part of that posture. But that deterrent effect is not the only component of the relationship that's important. It is important that a country such as Syria, and the Assads of the world, see strategic cooperation between the United States and Israel. They will then see clearly the consequences, both from Israel and her ally, of planning an attack on Israel.

To Israel, next in importance after the United States are the countries of Western Europe and, perhaps, before them, Japan. Common ideas and common values lead to common strategic objectives and interests, which means that Israel should have common interests with these countries—and I'm sure she does—just as these countries have common strategic interests with the United States. Because we live in this ideologically polarized world, they all must see themselves in the context of the East-West conflict. If the United States goes down vis-á-vis the Soviet Union, G-d forbid, they'll all fall together, and they know it.

To gain uniform support for her position in the Middle East in international forums, Israel wants to emphasize the commonality of interests and strengthen the ties that bind together all democratic nations. Currently, these major democratic countries after the United States—Japan, the United Kingdom, France, and West Germany—are not on the list of those Western nations that vote with, or abstain from voting against, Israel in the United Nations. We want to improve our ties with Western European countries and Japan. Commercial relations between Israel and Japan could have great benefit to Israel's economy.

We must not forget that the underlying tenet of our foreign policy is to continue the peace process with our Arab neighbors. I believe, however, that the most important development in the Arab world that will advance the peace process is the westernization and democratization of the Arab countries. I'm sure they cannot remain frozen in their present state of totalitarian rule for much longer. They are confronted with Western thoughts and Western values more regularly than ever—through the current print media explosion and through television which, with the use of satellites, brings the world closer together. As the Arab countries perceive the value of westernization and democratization, they will move in that direction. Only then will the area contain the right ingredients for real peace between Israel and her neighbors.

Merril Simon's Overview

Since the establishment of the State of Israel, American-Israeli relations have expanded to the point where the Reagan administration, in its second term, sees Israel developing into a strategic ally—in deed, if not by formal proclamation. Israel has sought this improved status between herself and the United States throughout the nearly four decades of her existence. There have been many tense and rocky periods. There now exists, however, an interrelationship between these two democracies—the world's largest and one of the world's smallest—that is unparalleled any place else in the world. It is one of almost complete interdependence.

As Americans, Jews, and supporters of Israel, however, we must never forget the fundamental difference between what motivates American policy in the Middle East and what motivates Israel's policy in the area. For the United States, Middle East policy is based primarily, if not solely, on a perception of American interests as determined by those formulating, financing, and implementing that policy—the Congress, the State Department, the administration, and groups of vitally interested citizens through lobbies and political action committees. For Israel, however, Middle East policies are based not on a perception of vital national interest but more on one of national security and survival.

While the United States may view Israel as an important, essential, or even vital element in her Middle East policy, she still attempts to maintain cordial relations with as many of Israel's neighbors as possible—despite the fact that these neighbors have taken a public posture as Israel's mortal enemies bent on her destruction. The United States, especially since the Yom Kippur War and the ensuing oil crisis, has attempted the vigorous pursual of a policy in the Middle East of "evenhandedness"—a policy formulated and developed under the Nixon administration in 1969 and represented by the Rogers Plan.

In order to offset the tremendous support for Israel—not only among the Jewish population but also within non-Jewish communities—the Nixon, Ford, and Carter administrations attempted, through various representatives, to manipulate public opinion against Israel. They did this in order to strengthen American ties with Israel's Arab neighbors, even though they were pursuing policies inimical to Israel's vital interests. During this period, the lowest point of American-Israeli relations was during Israel's incursion into Lebanon, culminating with the Sabra and Shetilla massacre. At that time, tremendous public abuse was poured upon Israel by the communications media, not only within the United States but throughout the entire Western world. It was after that situation that the tide turned toward Israel.

Events since the Reagan decision to send U.S. Marines into Lebanon to stabilize the situation in the fall of 1982 have only focused on the folly of some of the premises of a so-called evenhanded policy. The blowing up of the American embassy and the Marine barracks in Beirut and the spread of reckless terrorist activities against Western and American targets—not just against Jews and Israel—are representative examples. Such incidents, carried out by Arabs from a number of Arab countries and by Moslems from non-Arab countries, exhibited the political impotence of Saudi Arabia. Although the United States had supported Saudi interests that were in conflict with those of Israel, there was no indication that the Saudis used their political goodwill to influence the Syrians, state-supported terrorists, or events in Lebanon, as had been anticipated. Nor did the U.S. sale of AWACS to Saudi Arabia significantly strengthen her military position in the area. Saudi Arabia and the Arab Gulf States remain at the mercy of Iran, whose chances of wearing down Iraq in their war of attrition become more likely as that war enters its eighth year. All such events and activities have only drawn Israel and the United States closer strategically.

While Israel's relations with the United States have continued to strengthen considerably since 1983, her relations with the nations of Western Europe have not. Those nations have continued to pursue myopic policies based on narrow, marginal, commercial interests. No longer is the Arab oil price and availability driving these policies; now they are determined by arms sales and other commercial interests. As Arab buying power has increased, the nations of Western Europe have been feeling the sting of Arab and Moslem terrorism, made possible by years of their relaxing security while permitting PLO offices to be opened in their major cities.

As Americans and Jews, we want to fight every place where the sickness of anti-Semitism rears its ugly head. Understanding that the new wave of anti-Jewish expression finds its way through declarations and acts against Zionism, we must fight with every legal means at our disposal against this evil. We must attempt to repeal the U.N. resolution equating Zionism with racism, while keeping in mind that Israel's position within the United Nations is extremely precarious due to her regional isolation, the anti-Semitic and anti-Israel nature of the Eastern Bloc nations, the lack of backbone by Third World nations, and the narrowly perceived commercial self-interest of Western European nations.

It is essential that no American supporter of Israel—Jew or Gentile—ever forgets that America is a democratic society where freedom of speech and political activity is fundamental, and that there exist, within our society, many influential friends of Israel's enemies who are constantly attempting to influence adversely American policy toward Israel. The Middle East is a volcanic area where events move so rapidly and so unexpectedly that the unpredictable event has become commonplace. We cannot relax our vigil in showing our political support for stronger American-Israeli relations. As Americans and supporters of Israel, we must maintain a vigilance to see that Israel is treated fairly by the media and to make certain our policymakers understand how we feel about controversial Middle East policies.

I've asked Moshe Arens to answer a series of questions covering these topics—understanding that his early childhood was spent in Eastern Europe in an area where vicious anti-Semitism was rampant and in an area overrun by Nazi Germany only a short time after he and his family emigrated to the United States. While serving as the Israeli ambassador to the United States, he dealt with U.S.-Middle East policies on a day-to-day basis. In his capacity as Minister of Defense, he dealt with the export arms policies of all the nations selling arms to Israel's enemies, the problems of purchasing weapon systems from the United States, and the difficulties in obtaining financial assistance in support of Israel's arms industry. As Minister Without Portfolio, he has been dealing with the problems of Soviet Jewry and Israeli-Soviet relations.

ISRAEL AND THE WESTERN WORLD

United States

What is the basis for long-term strategic interests between Israel and the United States?

The basis for long-term strategic interests between Israel and the United States is the common ideological foundation of the two countries—the commonality of values that characterize life and the body politic in the United States and Israel. We live in a world ideologically polarized between the Communist states and the Western society of nations; thus, common values and common ideals translate into common strategic interests. The United States is the leader of the Free World. Israel, while one of the smallest in size, is not one of the most insignificant members of that community.

Israel and the United States share common strategic interests of very considerable importance. The United States understands and appreciates that Israel makes a contribution to the Western alliance and to the strength and pursuance of the goals of the Free World that is completely out of proportion to her small size. This is why the strategic alliance between Israel and the United States is a meaningful one to both countries.

Why have strong strategic political/military ties developed between Israel and the United States since 1983?

Since the establishment of the State of Israel, ties—including strategic ties—between Israel and the United States have developed monotonically. They have been improving all the time. If we want to see the rationale behind this constantly improving relationship with an increasing dimension in the area of strategic cooperation, we must reflect on the history of the State of Israel and U.S.-Israeli relationships.

At the beginning, there were doubts in Washington that Israel could survive at all, and, as a result, Israel was looked upon certainly not as a partner but, rather, more as a burden. We know that those who argued with President Truman against recognition of the State of Israel even argued that Israel would eventually be a country in the Communist bloc—that she would not be a Western country at all—and that she would have strategic interests that would be opposed to those of the United States.

Shortly after the establishment of the State of Israel, it became clear to everyone in the United States that Israel was a Western nation, with Western values, committed to the Western cause and to the community of free nations. In time it became apparent that Israel was a partner of value. The War of Independence made it clear that the tiny country of Israel did have the strength to beat back the surrounding Arab armies. Israel's astounding victory in the 1956 Sinai Campaign—reaching the Suez Canal in 100 hours—enhanced the appreciation for Israel's military capability. During the Six-Day War, Israel demonstrated dramatically the strength and ability of her military forces. During the War of Attrition, the Israeli air force shot down Russian-piloted MIGS over the Sinai. This was just one more expression of the capability that existed here. So, over the years, there grew an increasing appreciation in the United States for Israel—a small country but a country with very signficant potential for strengthening the Free-World partnership.

Does the United States have long-term fundamental interests in supporting the State of Israel? If so, what are they?

Yes. The common strategic interests are obvious. There are two primary goals of the United States in the Middle East, and they happen to be the two primary goals of Israel. Blocking Soviet penetration of the Middle East is of great concern to the United States. If the Soviets were to penetrate this area, it could have catastrophic consequences for both the Free World and Israel. Add to that the goal of the United States that there be peace in the Middle East—that there be an accommodation and reduction of tension in the area. In effect, the United States and Israel have identical interests.

It is important to point out that we are talking about the commonality of interests between the United States and Israel. Everyone knows that, although there are no conflicts of interest between the two countries, there have been differences of opinion. This could be a definition of the relations between the two countries—no conflicts of interests but differences of opinions on how to pursue common interests. It happens quite often that nations disagree on the means of pursuing their common interests.

Does the United States have long-term fundamental interests in supporting the Arab states? If so, what are they?

Considering the United States' goal of a reduction of tension and an accommodation in the area, certainly, she would not like a move by Arab countries to the Soviet orbit. These are Israel's interests, as well. Therefore, U.S. interests in the area, particularly with regard to the Arab states, are no different than Israeli interests. What is frequently at issue is the best way of pursuing these interests.

The differences of opinion usually stem from differences of perception between Israel and the United States. Is it essential that in order to keep Saudi Arabia from moving into the Soviet orbit, the United States sell her F15 aircraft and AWACS aircraft? Neither Israel nor the United States would want Saudi Arabia to move into the Soviet orbit. However, Israel's opinion has been, and continues to be, that selling the latest weaponry to Saudi Arabia entails much greater risks to Western interests, including Israel, than the potential benefits. Saudi Arabia is a medieval state, and I don't believe the risks facing her are such that she would move into the Soviet orbit. The real risks are internal. Basically, Saudi Arabia has an unstable and anachronistic government with a limited life expectancy. It is very difficult to prove that selling the Saudis F15s or AWACS is going to extend their government's life expectancy. Actually, it might even shorten it.

Do you believe that the present strategic military cooperation between Israel and the United States will be expanded to include prepositioning of military hardware in Israel, not just hospital equipment?

Yes. The level and dimensions of strategic cooperation are growing all the time; therefore, I am sure that in the future they will include additional elements that are not included at the present time.

Do you believe the present level of military aid provided to Israel by the United States can remain constant, that is, independent of changes in administrations within the United States?

The United States' level of military aid to Israel should be determined by both the surrounding Arab countries' level of military expenditures as well as the Soviet Union's level of military aid to those countries. The level of military expenditures in the surrounding Arab countries is far larger than the level of military expenditures in Israel. As a result, the balance of forces, at least in terms of equipment and number of men under arms, has been deteriorating over the years.

The situation has been getting continuously more difficult for Israel. Actually, the level of U.S. military aid to Israel has not been keeping pace with the level of the security threat to Israel, which means the security threat to the Free World's interests in the area. In the immediate future, a significant increase in U.S. military aid to Israel is going to be needed to enable Israel to keep pace with the present Middle East arms race. Perhaps the level of Arab military expenditures may eventually decline, if the lower prices of oil are sustained.

In what direction do you see strategic cooperation between Israel and the United States developing, and do you believe it will change with subsequent administrations?

I am sure strategic cooperation between Israel and the United States will continue to broaden, deepen, and include additional elements as time goes by. I have no doubt that it will continue in future years regardless of whether a Republican or Democratic administration is in the White House and regardless of who happens to be in power in Israel. This is so because strategic cooperation reflects the fundamental interests of the two countries.

The Reagan Plan for the Administered Territories in Israel calls for the return of Judea and Samaria to Jordan in exchange for peace. In your assessment, how committed to that plan is the United States in the long run?

This is a question that needs to be addressed to the people in the administration in Washington. It is clear to the present administration that the plan was rejected by both Israel and by the surrounding Arab countries. It's simply not pertinent at the present time.

If the United States and the Soviet Union start to cooperate politically on problems of the world, will it have a negative impact on the United States' relations with Israel?

No. Israel, as well as the United States, would like to see a relaxation of tension between the East and the West throughout the world. Since that would mean a relaxation of tensions here in the Middle East, as well, it would only be to our benefit.

What is your perception of the ability of the America Israel Public Affairs Committee (AIPAC) to influence American policy on Israel and the Arab states?

AIPAC has been a very effective organization in Washington in marshaling support for Israel. I don't in any way, manner, or means intend to diminish the high opinion I have of AIPAC in this leadership capacity when I say that the support for Israel they've been so successful in marshaling is founded on the very broad level of support that exists for Israel among the population and in the Congress of the United States.

Jerry Falwell and his Liberty Foundation, formerly known as the Moral Majority, have indicated that they consider themselves an extension of AIPAC. Do you believe that this involvement or support of AIPAC by Jerry Falwell will enhance AIPAC's success in reaching its goals?

Generally, any support for Israel in the United States among a group that is prominent and has influence is in Israel's favor. There's a certain amount of interdependence among the capabilities of the various organizations—and there are many in the United States—who work for and try to marshal support for Israel. In that sense, the support of one organization for Israel, in some ways, perhaps indirectly, helps other organizations garner support for Israel.

How important is it to the State of Israel to have the political support of men like Jerry Falwell and the Evangelical Fundamentalist Christian community which individuals like him represent?

It is very important for Israel to have the support of the United States. Because she is a democracy, the actions and policies of the United States reflect the wishes and opinions of her people; therefore, it is important to have the support of each and every group in the United States that is ready and wants to lend support to Israel. The larger and more influential the group, of course, the more important that support is. The Evangelical groups in the United States, including Falwell's Moral Majority organization, apparently enjoy large memberships and the support of millions of Americans. If they provide widespread support for Israel, then that is very important for us.

The majority of Jews in the United States are represented by Jewish organizations which tend to be domestically liberal. They have had, and continue to maintain, a close dialogue with the National Council of Churches, which has become very anti-Israel, pro-PLO, pro-Third World, and pro-Marxist. On the other hand, the conservative church, represented by Evangelical Fundamentalist Christians, whose domestic position is much more conservative than the mainstream of the Jewish population, has developed and is developing stronger and stronger political support for the State of Israel. They also provide most of the tourists to Israel from the United States. How do you reconcile this situation, and what can be done in order to enhance political support for the State of Israel?

First of all, I don't know that the National Council of Churches is a pro-Marxist organization; I am not in a position to confirm or deny that. Israel welcomes and is grateful for the support it gets from the United States—from all quarters. The larger and more influential the group, the more important that support is for us. This really doesn't have any connection to and doesn't even interface with the relationships of the leadership of certain Jewish organizations with other organizations in the United States.

Some Jewish organizations in the United States, as well as some leaders in the American Jewish community, carry on a dialogue with organizations that are not fully committed or supportive of Israel. Some of that may be inevitable. It doesn't make us too enthusiastic here in Israel. The American Jewish organizations and their leadership, however, must deal with problems facing the American Jewish community; they must deal with various segments and different organizations within that community. It is not to be expected that they will have dialogue only with those organizations that have a total commitment to Israel.

During this decade, within the "leadership" of the Black community, as represented by men like Rev. Jesse Lawrie, Rev. Jesse Jackson, Andrew Young, and Louis Faracan, there has been growing support for the Arabs and the PLO and continuing development of a strong anti-Israel posture. How do you reconcile this with the American Jewish community's desire to maintain the Black-Jewish political coalition? Do you foresee this trend among the leaders of the Black community trickling down to the masses, and, if so, what can Israel do to combat the situation?

I am not fully informed on all the currents and cross-currents within the Black community in the United States or on their impact on the relationships between the Jewish and Black communities. I know, however, that there are many Blacks in the United States who are fervent supporters of the State of Israel. I've met Black members of the Congress who fall into that category and who frequently visit here. I find it difficult to believe that the majority of the "leadership" of the Black community in the United States is not supportive of Israel and is supportive of Israel's enemies.

I don't doubt, however, that there are some segments of the Black community who have anti-Israel views. In pursuance of maximizing the support of all people in America for Israel, we need to invest efforts to bring about a larger level of support for Israel within the Black community. I am sure we can count on the American Jewish community to participate in that effort and to make it effective. I hope that in future years less of Black leadership in the United States will be in the ranks of those supporting Israel's enemies.

Recently, the American press has given, and is likely to continue to give, much attention to the Pollard affair. Most coverage is both explicitly and implicitly anti-Israel. What is your understanding of the Pollard affair? What effect has it had, and will it have, on American-Israeli military, political, and economic relations?

The Pollard affair, an attempt to obtain information that was classified as "secret" in the United States for Israel, is something that never should have happened. It's something that no Israeli should have been engaged in. It's an aberration. It's certainly not a reflection of the policy of the government of Israel. It's contrary to the policy of Israel. The fact is that it happened, and now we are dealing with damage containment.

First, and most importantly, we are making sure that this sort of thing can never and will never happen again. Secondly, we are mending our fences and bridging whatever gaps may have developed as a result of the reaction in the United States to that event. I don't believe it's going to leave permanent scars behind. The relationships between Israel and the United States are too strong and too firmly founded for this to happen. But, certainly, it's a very painful experience.

There has been excessive U.S. media coverage of the cluster-bomb incident. Can you provide any information on the circumstances surrounding this incident and its importance.

I don't know any details. To the best of my knowledge, nothing improper was done by citizens of Israel or officials of the Israeli government. My guess is that it will become clear in the near future.

For decades the American communications media has focused a disproportionate amount of attention on the small State of Israel, barely larger than the state of New Jersey. Can you explain why?

First of all, Israel has had many achievements—totally out of proportion to her size—which have attracted the attention of people throughout the world. As small as she is, Israel is a unique event in the history of man. The Jewish people have returned to their ancient homeland after 2,000 years of dispersion; they have renewed their ancient Hebrew language; they have made the desert bloom; they have established centers of science, technology, and culture; they have built a sizable and good armed force. All of this is news. It is not at all surprising that it rates with other news throughout the world and, therefore, interests the media.

Secondly, we are also in a region of conflict. We've been involved in six wars during the four decades of the state's existence, and that's news. It's not good for Israel—not good news for anyone—but it is news. So, we find ourselves in the headlines of newspapers and on television.

To those explanations, add the fact that Israel enjoys a very great level of support throughout the world, particularly in the United States. Most supporters of Israel are interested in the country and what happens here. Since we are of interest to many people, that, too, creates headlines.

Can you explain why the American communications media—the press, radio, and television—appear to be so hostile to the State of Israel?

I've met many representatives of the United States media who were not hostile, although there's no doubt there are many who are. I've met some of them, too. I've seen much coverage of Israel which has been grossly biased and clearly anti-Israel. It's not easy to find an explanation for that. It's probably too facile to say it's a reflection of anti-Semitism. We can't say whoever gives Israel negative coverage has an anti-Semitic bias, although it's probably true in some cases.

In many countries of the world, the media is biased in favor of the left in some manner. We know that the extreme left in the world has adopted the PLO and even has been supportive of terrorism. The only connecting link that I can find is that those in the media who are biased in favor of the left too easily adopt the far left's attitude towards terrorism and the PLO.

The Camp David Accords
You were opposed to the terms and conditions of the Camp David Accords at the time they were negotiated and signed by Israel. In retrospect, were your apprehensions realized?

In some considerable measure, yes. But first let me say in what measure they were not. There has not been a coup d'etat in Egypt, although it has come close to that. Sadat was assassinated, and, more recently, the Egyptian security police rioted and burned down a number of hotels in Cairo. I'm sure it gave Mr. Muburak some trepidations. Yet there's not been a change of policy in Egypt, as might have happened considering that Egypt is not a democratic country and that a total change can take place overnight. That's certainly something that was a concern to me at the time the Accords were negotiated. It is still of concern to me now. However, it is only correct to say that seven years have now gone by since the signing of the peace treaty, and there has been no basic change in the position of the Egyptian government towards the peace treaty with Israel.

On the other hand, the peace that exists between Israel and Egypt is not the peace for which Israel bargained. It is not the peace we paid such a tremendous price for. We expected the treaty to bring about a permanent, true, and stable relationship of peace between the two countries. That has not happened. There exists what Mr. Muburak calls a "cold peace." Now, seven years after the treaty was signed, we still have the fear, which is realistic and not paranoid, that we could wake up one morning and find ourselves without the Sinai and without peace.

What role did the United States' administration play in getting the Israeli negotiating team, led by Begin, Weizmann, and Dayan, to make concessions which went beyond what it felt might jeopardize Israel's long-term economic, political, and/or military security?

The facts are in—books have been written by participants in the Camp David talks about the negotiations held before and after. The historical record is clear that the Carter administration applied very severe, undue pressure on Israel to make concessions that really were contrary to Israel's best interests.

Why did the Israeli negotiating team fail to understand the disastrous economic ramifications that would result from the Camp David Accords?

Although it may not be appropriate for me to answer that question, since I was not a member of that team, my understanding is that they never assigned a high degree of importance to the economic dimensions of the peace treaty. To the best of my knowledge, no one even made a rough calculation of what the economic consequences of the peace treaty were likely to be. Some felt it was not honorable to look at the economic dimensions in the framework of the peace treaty and the relationships between Israel and Egypt. However, we all know that economic dimensions are dominant dimensions in the relationships between countries.

Many of us have read at one time or another John Meynard Keynes' great book, *The Economic Consequences of the Peace*, which he wrote shortly after the Versailles Peace Treaty. Based on economic considerations, he predicted many of the tragic events that were to follow that peace treaty due to its economic

ON ISRAEL AND HER FOREIGN RELATIONS • 165

consequences. Yet here there was almost total disregard for the economic consequences of the peace treaty.

Why did the Israeli negotiating team fail to obtain a larger economic commitment from the United States to underwrite more of Israel's costs of implementing the Accords, which they should have known would exceed one year's GNP of the State of Israel?

Part of the answer is what I just discussed—that lack of attention was paid to the economic dimension by the people involved. Knowing this, it's understandable why, during the bilateral talks between the United States and Israel, the United States was not asked to make a contribution to help carry that burden.

You might ask an additional question. How is it that representatives of the United States, who are more conscious of the economic dimensions of events and relations between countries, did not, on their own, realize the tremendous economic impact of the treaty they were trying to promote and, therefore, volunteer to carry a significant part of that burden?

Did Begin have an option of holding out for a better deal, or was he placed in a position of no choices by the Carter administration?

I don't believe that Israel was in a position of "no choice" or "no alternative." I believe that Israel had alternatives and that we did not have to give in to pressure. We talked before about the U.S.-Israeli relationship—a relationship that's founded on a very broad base of support among the people of America for Israel. The Israeli leadership could have appealed to that support in the United States. In that manner, they could have outflanked or blunted any pressure that was applied, but that was not done.

One of the major reasons the United States pursued the Camp David Accords was to ensure that Egypt would become an integral part of the Western world by being armed with American weapon systems and, thus, removed from the Soviet sphere of influence. From a United States perspective, has not the Camp David Accords proven to be successful? Is it not in Israel's best national interest to have Egypt armed with American weapon systems and, thus, part of the Western sphere of interest rather than armed with Soviet weapons systems and, thus, part of the Soviet sphere of interest?

It is certainly in Israel's interest to have Egypt, or for that matter any Arab country, in the Western orbit rather than in the Soviet orbit. The major contribution to Egypt's moving into the Western orbit was made by Israel. It was not so much through Camp David, but rather during the Yom Kippur War—by defeating an Egyptian army that was armed with Soviet weaponry, by proving conclusively that Soviet support was not sufficient to allow Egypt to defeat Israel, and by proving that if Egypt was going to achieve any or even part of her objectives, she could achieve them only through negotiations, including the participation of the United States but not the Soviet Union. These are the factors that moved Egypt into the Western orbit. Of course, it's good for both Israel and the United States.

It is not essential to sell Egypt the most advanced weaponry in order to keep her in the Western orbit. The question that needs to be asked is, "Since Egypt signed a peace treaty with Israel, why does she need weaponry?" Today, Egypt has a very large army. There is talk about a Libyan threat to Egypt, but Libya is no match at all for Egypt or the Egyptian army as it is today. Why, then, is Egypt continuing to arm herself on such a vast scale with American support and mostly American weaponry? There is grave concern here that if there were to be a sudden change in Egypt's position toward Israel—and that's not only possible but could happen in a matter of twenty-four hours, we could suddenly find ourselves faced on our southern border with a very large, hostile army equipped with the latest military weapons from America, as well as from France and England. We must prepare for the contingency that these arms someday might be turned against us, and the preparations for that eventuality, which we hope will never materialize, must be made today. As the Egyptian army grows, Israel must make allocations of her resources in order to keep pace with that growth.

Why didn't the Carter administration and the American media give Begin and the State of Israel credit for making tremendous sacrifices in signing the Camp David Accords?

That's a good question to address to Mr. Carter. As more and more of the facts on Camp David surface, including Mr. Carter's own statements since he left the presidency, it is becoming very clear that Mr. Carter had a very strong anti-Israel bias.

Western Europe

WEST GERMANY

Is it true that Israel has aligned herself militarily and politically with West Germany more than with any other European country. If so, how do you reconcile this, considering Germany's Nazi past?

This is not true. Israel is not militarily aligned with any Western European country. As a matter of fact, some Western European countries, such as Britain, have an embargo on arms sales to Israel while freely selling arms to all Israel's enemies. France has been very reticent to have any dealings with Israel and has been selling whatever weaponry the market will buy in the Arab countries. West Germany probably sells less weaponry to Arab armies than does France, Britain, or Italy. Her publicly announced policy is not to sell arms to Arab countries, but as is well-known, some weaponry that is produced in cooperation between West Germany and France has been sold to Arab armies. Anti-tank missiles, such as the Hot and the Milan, which are co-produced by the Germans and the French, are in the hands of the Syrian army. West Germany does not, however, sell any arms to Israel.

Israel is a member of the democratic community of nations of which the United States is a leader and, in many ways, Israel is aligned with the United States. There exists extensive strategic cooperation between the two countries, which began in 1983-84. However, I don't believe the governments of most Western European countries, including that of West Germany, view Israel in the way she is viewed by the United States. As a result, there is not the same kind of cooperation taking place between Israel and any of the Western European countries, including West Germany.

Why hasn't West Germany cooperated in trying to stop terrorism—particularly terrorism against Israel?

I wouldn't say there's no cooperation at all. Until very recently, all of the Western countries were very hesitant about cooperating to an extent that would be effective in the fight against terrorism. Most of the Western European countries tried to make separate deals with the terrorists —in effect, giving in to terrorist blackmail—by trying to buy protection from them. Under the leadership of President Reagan, the Declaration of Tokyo—which spoke very clearly about cooperation in the fight against terrorism—was adopted by the leaders of the

Western industrial nations. I hope that will be the direction that will be followed by West Germany in future years.

Can Israel develop and depend upon long-term strategic ties with West Germany, considering the past Hitler experience and the emergence of the Greens?

There aren't any such ties, and I don't see them in the offing. Certainly, there seems to be no indication from West Germany that there is interest in such ties. If there were such indications, there would be a great deal of reticence here in Israel to establish them. Why the Israeli reticence to establish strategic ties with West Germany? It is because of the history of the Holocaust and the role the German people played in the destruction of European Jewry. At the present time, the subject is totally hypothetical.

Is it correct to say that Germany is the best friend that Israel has in the Common Market and, if so, why?

No, it is not correct to say that. We would have to determine and establish a criterion by which we should measure the friendship of Western European countries or Common Market members. As I have already pointed out, to Israel's disappointment, none of the Common Market members, including West Germany, view her as an ally. They don't view Israel as a member of the democratic community of nations of which they are also a member, nor as a country that shares strategic interests with them by virtue of that commonality.

One way we might measure the attitude of Western European governments toward Israel would be by their votes in the United Nations on issues that relate to Israel. Unfortunately, issues relating to Israel come up at the United Nations constantly. West Germany does not stand out as a better friend of Israel's than some of the other Western European countries. As a matter of fact, most Western European countries have a rather sad voting record in the United Nations on issues relating to Israel. Only the United States has an excellent voting record, which, incidentally cuts both ways, in that a recent State Department study found that Israel voted together with the United States in over 90 percent of the votes. Aside from the United States, only Australia and Canada have supportive voting records in the United Nations on issues relating to Israel, but they haven't been that closely aligned. None of the Common Market countries has a good voting record on Israeli-related issues before the United Nations.

In which areas can economic ties with Germany develop?

Primarily, as an export market for Israel. The Israeli economy is moving rapidly into the area of high technology. The markets for high-technology products are, first of all, in the United States, secondly in Japan, and thirdly in Western Europe, which, of course, would include West Germany.

Do you believe cultural ties with Germany will develop to such a degree that German as a language will be taught in Israeli high schools?

I really can't foresee that happening in my lifetime and probably not in the lifetime of my children. We know how long the aftereffects of the Spanish Inquisition stayed with the Jewish people, and the Spanish Inquisition was child's play compared to the Holocaust. My guess is that the scars of the Holocaust will remain with the people of Israel, and with the Jewish people throughout the world, for quite a number of generations.

FRANCE

France leads other Western European countries in her anti-Israel posture in political forums. Why?

The French have a large arms industry that works primarily for export. Their arms exports are larger than their sales to the French armed forces. The majority of their export sales are to the Arab world, which they appear to view as their major market. The French are primarily motivated by commercial advantages, and they appear to give up whatever political and ideological motivations they may have in Israel's favor in order to gain these commercial advantages.

Can you foresee political ties with France becoming as good as they were prior to 1967?

It is possible. There is no barrier from Israel's point of view. The question is whether the French will adopt an attitude toward Israel based on the recognition that she is the only democracy in the Middle East and that both countries share, not only common values, but also common strategic interests. France's policy could be then directed toward very close relationships with Israel, possibly an alliance. It could happen.

It's something that did happen in the fifties. The relationship between Israel and France at that time was an alliance. During the past ten or fifteen years, however, I haven't seen many signs of the relationship moving in that direction again. Some people thought they saw some warming of the relationship between Israel and France, on France's behalf, when Peres became Prime Minister of the National Unity government. He had what seemed a very warm visit with French President Mitterrand. In retrospect, though, despite these public signs of diplomatic warmth, nothing concrete has developed to effect a more positive direction to Israeli-French relations.

Do you see the very strong cultural ties that exist between France and Israel having any influence on the political and military relations between them?

Cultural ties can, at most, help to pave the way, but they can't point the way toward important political and military relations. What points the way is usually the common strategic as well as common political interests between two countries. The fact that both France and Israel are democracies in this ideologically polarized world should be sufficient foundation, since democracies do have common strategic interests. That will point the way, if and when the French ever decide that they are ready to sacrifice some of their commercial interests in order to maintain a coherent foreign policy.

Do you foresee the development of any strategic common interests between Israel and France, considering France's relationship with the Arabs?

It's quite possible. France shares common strategic interests with Israel as do all democratic countries in the world today, with the possible exception of India. (India has some differences which are not too difficult to understand.) All democratic countries, whether it's the United States, Norway, Australia, Canada, or certainly the Western European countries, share common strategic interests by virtue of their sharing common values.

Since we live in an ideologically polarized world, the common strategic interests stem from the rightful concern that all the democratic countries have with Soviet expansion and penetration. For example, Soviet penetration into the Middle East would certainly be of very serious consequence to France. Soviet penetration into Western Europe would be of more serious consequence to France. The

French realize that Israel's serving as a barrier to Soviet penetration into the Middle East makes life easier for them in terms of their trying to block Soviet penetration into Western Europe. These are, in effect, two parallel approaches that need to be blocked simultaneously in order to prevent the Soviets from moving forward. Until now, the French have simply depended on Israel's taking care of her own interests in the Middle East and, by virtue of doing that, taking care of France's strategic interests as well. Therefore, presumably, no explicit French cooperation is required.

On occasion, people in Washington feel that this is the French position in Europe as well, since they are not active members of NATO and appear to be counting on the American umbrella there. They pursue divergent policies from those of other Western democracies in order to concentrate primarily on commercial interests. In order to seek these commercial interests in the Soviet Union or in the Eastern bloc, France relies on the United States to take care of the strategic interests of the Western democracies. The day may very well come, and I certainly hope it does, when the French will realize that their policy is not a consistent one, not a very honorable policy, and not even a very good policy from the French point of view.

Given the fact that France is such a major arms supplier to the Arab world, can you foresee military cooperation between France and Israel?

We did have it once in the past, or, certainly empirically we can say that it happened in the past, and, probably, in principle, it could happen again.

France has consistently opposed Israel in the Common Market and even supported the admission of Spain and Portugal under conditions detrimental to Israel's agricultural exports. Do you foresee any fundamental changes in France's attitude in the future?

It's possible. But change would come about only if a French government came to power that would pursue a principled, honorable foreign policy designed to lead to cooperation with those countries that share common interests with France—even if on occasion it would be at the expense of some French commercial interests.

There was hope that when the Socialist government of Mitterrand came to power in France, there would be a change in policy. What are your observations regarding the attitude of the Mitterand government toward Israel?

This is an indication that things are not always what they appear to be. It is true there was hope that when Mitterrand came to power, there might be a shift to a more sympathetic policy toward Israel. This has been true in the area of pronouncements. If we examine official pronouncements, we'll find that Mitterrand's probably sound a little better to Israeli ears than did those of Giscard d'Estaing.

In particular, there was considerable hope here in Israel for improved relations with France once Peres became Prime Minister. Mitterrand and Peres were both members of the Socialist International and presumably had developed a close personal relationship. Peres' visit to Paris had all the trappings of a very warm reception; however, nothing of substance has changed. French policy has remained just as it was during the days of Giscard d'Estaing. Certainly, when it comes to the Middle East, French policies are being dictated by commercial interests which have been independent of the administration or the parties in power.

Can you foresee the development of joint civilian projects between France and Israel?

No, not between France and Israel. However, considering the very great assets that Israel has in the area of high technology and its applications in many commercial as well as military fields, I foresee a trend toward cooperation between Israel and other countries that, likewise, have capabilities in the area of high technology, or that would like to develop capabilities and believe there is something to be gained by such cooperation. This may be on the basis of two commercial companies cooperating, not necessarily government cooperation. Such is the case between Israel and the United States. There are many American companies involved in high technology in Israel. It would be quite natural if that kind of cooperation also develops with some Western European countries; however, it is least likely to develop with French companies.

What do you see as the impact of the large Moslem population in France on French policy toward Israel?

I'm not sufficiently knowledgeable about French party politics to determine what effect the French Moslems have on French policy. We might ask the same question about the French-Jewish population's influence on French policy. There are half a million Jews in France, which approximates the Moslem population, and it's a very active population—successful in both cultural and academic endeavors, as well as in the business world. However, considering France's policy toward Israel, it becomes obvious that the Jewish population has not been effective in influencing that policy in any way.

Is the fact that France is such a strong Catholic country influencing French policy toward Israel?

I doubt it; the answer to your question simply lies in looking at recent history. This Catholic country has gone through a period of a very close relationship with Israel, through a period of a very distant relationship with Israel, and, on occasion, even through a period of a rather hostile attitude toward Israel. It's clear that this Catholic country of France can go either way.

GREAT BRITAIN

Do you believe the British have shed their Lawrence of Arabia mystique, their mandate syndrome, or their blame of Israel for the breakup of the British Empire?

I'm sure there are people in Great Britain who remember the British mandate. There are still people in the foreign office who were involved there during mandate days. Some probably served in Palestine during that time and still carry with them memories and prejudices from that period. However, I don't believe that this is the dominant influence in setting Great Britain's policy on the Middle East today. Very much as in the case of France, the dominant influence in setting Great Britain's policy on the Middle East today is commercial interest. Again, it's the sale of arms to the Arab countries and the realization that those countries represent the major market for British arms. How is it at all possible that a country like Great Britain would maintain an embargo on the sale of arms to Israel, while selling to the Arab world whatever the Arabs want to buy? The answer to that is purely commercial interest.

I had a meeting with Michael Haseltine, the British Secretary of Defense, while I was Minister of Defense, during which we discussed that very subject. I was in the fortunate position of being able to tell him that even if they removed the embargo, Israel would want nothing from Great Britain. I reminded him that Israel had an advanced weapons industry—maybe even a little more so than the British—and that we also had the possibility of procuring weaponry in the United States. Therefore, there was really nothing that we needed from Great Britain. I pointed out how incongruous it was that during the Falkland Island crisis, Mrs. Thatcher talked about the need for all democracies to stand together when one of them is faced by a totalitarian enemy, while Great Britain, (a democracy) was maintaining an arms embargo against Israel (also a democracy) and at the same time selling arms to all of Israel's totalitarian enemies. Mr Haseltine responded that the British knew Israel had a very advanced defense industry, was able to satisfy many of her own needs, and could procure weaponry in the United States. He said they knew Israel was not in need of weaponry from Great Britain, while on the other hand, they felt that it improved their position in the Arab marketplace if they could say they had an embargo against Israel.

The world was told that Europe's attitude toward Israel, after the 1973 Yom Kippur War, was based on the availability of oil and the Arab oil embargo. Given the fact that Great Britian is an exporter of oil, how do you explain the present anti-Israel posture of the British in international forums?

It really doesn't have very much to do with oil. It mainly has to do with the sale of arms to Arab countries and possibly with the sale of other equipment as well. Since the oil crisis of the early seventies, the Arabs have become the major oil-producing countries and have probably become, as well, the major market-place in the world for weaponry and many other items. The British have been out there trying to sell their goods as best they can. Certainly, Arab commercial considerations have been dominating their Middle East policy; that's probably true of most of the Western European countries.

Of all the countries in Europe, Great Britain has the closest ties with the United States in regard to strategic interests and strategic cooperation. Given the fact that the United States and Great Britain both believe in the containment of Russia in the Middle East, do you believe that Israel has, or will have, any interest in developing with Great Britian a strategic military relationship?

In principle, Israel is ready for, and even interested in, developing a strategic relationship with any of the countries that are members of the democratic community of nations, if there is a parallel interest on the other side. There has been no indication of that kind of interest on the part of Great Britain. You are right in saying that Great Britain has the closest strategic relationship with the United States—closer than any of the other Western European countries. Nevertheless, there were a number of cases in recent history when Great Britain took a position contrary to that of the United States on issues of great importance to the East-West relationship. The last such issue was probably the gas pipeline that they want to build through Europe.

In international forums, the British are sticking to their position. There has been no relaxation of their anti-Israel posture. Perhaps some people who would take a very detailed look might find that their position has improved a little under Mrs. Thatcher compared to what it was under the Labor party; however, I'm not able to make that fine a discrimination.

Do you believe there is anything Israel can do to effectuate improvement in cultural ties between Great Britain and Israel?

There is a certain assumption in that question that I'm not able to confirm, and that is that cultural ties between Israel and Great Britain are in need of improvement. I don't know about that. There are quite a few Israelis who study at British universities. I imagine the Israel Philharmonic plays in Great Britain, and I know Ted Heath was here to conduct the Israel Radio Orchestra. There is an English-Israeli Chamber of Commerce, a Conservative Friends of Israel in Parliament, and a Labor Friends of Israel. On the cultural level, the relationship is very good, because the two nations have very similar cultures, and Israel is almost an English-speaking country. Even if there were a problem in cultural ties, I don't believe it would effect the political relationship between the two nations.

ITALY

Do you believe that there has been or will be a change in Italy's negative attitude toward Israel's economic membership in the Common Market?

I really don't feel competent myself nor do I know anyone else competent enough to make that kind of forecast. When we talk about Israeli-Italian relationships, the basic issue is the same as it is when we talk about Israeli-French relationships or Israeli-British relationships. Italy is a democratic country and a member of the democratic community of nations, a community of nations led by the United States and of which Israel is a member as well. We hope there will come a point when the Italians will say to themselves, "Even at the expense of some of our immediate commercial interests, it is important for us to pursue our strategic interests and an honorable foreign policy; therefore, it is essential for us to have a close relationship with Israel, and, as part of that close relationship, look after Israel's commercial interests within the Common Market."

Are Italy's negative attitudes toward Israel's economic membership in the Common Market influenced more by her relationship with the Arabs—the oil or commercial ties, or are they more influenced by her own internal economic problems?

I know that her attitudes are influenced by oil. Italy is an oil importer and, therefore, does have, and will continue to have, concern as to where she gets her oil. Italy certainly is influenced, also, by the fact that the Arab world constitutes a very large marketplace for Italian products. Over and above these concerns, there may be some very detailed problems of incompatability between Italy and Israel with regard to the products that might be marketed in Europe. There really should not be any significant conflicts of interest. Any conflicts should be minor and localized and shouldn't be any greater than those that might arise between Italy and Spain.

Given the traditional politics in Italy and the major influence of the Communist party on the society, do you foresee, for Israel, any interest in establishing a strategic military relationship with Italy? What are the risks for Israel in establishing such a relationship?

There is a strong basis for establishing strategic relationships between Israel and any of the Free-World countries. I believe, specifically, that's true for Italy. Such relationships are essential to the containment of Soviet power—economic, military, and political—and to the maintenance of Western-oriented democracy.

In general, the risks involved in Israel's establishing strategic relationships with any country with a large Communist party are the same as those faced by the whole Free World, first and foremost, the United States. The major risks are information leaks, due to Communists holding important positions throughout the country, perhaps even in the military, and the possibility of Communist-supported leftist groups taking over the government. Those risks apply to Israel's establishing such a relationship with Italy or with France, although right now (in 1987) France has Communists in the government, while Italy does not.

Whether or not the risk is worthwhile is really a question Israel would have to consider, if and when we ever get to the point of establishing that kind of relationship with Italy. Right now, it's something that doesn't worry us, although I'm sure it worries the United States.

What areas of economic cooperation do you foresee developing between Italy and Israel outside the Common Market?

The potential for economic cooperation between Israel and Italy is similar to the potential for such cooperation between Israel and France, or Israel and Great Britain, or Israel and the Scandinavian countries. It lies in all those areas in which the Italian government or Italian business interests feel that it would be to their advantage to cooperate with Israeli firms and/or the Israeli government. Primarily, it would be in the areas of high-technology products.

Can you explain why Israel's cultural ties with Italy have been as good as they are, given Italy's relationship with the Arabs?

Good cultural ties between Israel and almost any other country in the world exist because Israel is a very cosmopolitan society. We find people in Israel speaking all languages of the world. This includes a relatively high percentage who speak Italian, even though we've not had many Jews come to Israel from Italy because of the rather small size of the Jewish community in Italy. Many people in Israel are interested in art, music, and literature, and so clearly in Italian art, music, and literature. The basis is there, and if the desire exists on both sides, then we have the makings of a very good cultural relationship.

Can you explain why the Vatican has such consistently adamant positions toward Israel? Do you think the Vatican will change its position and establish normal diplomatic relations with Israel, as they have with most other countries in the world?

I can't give you the reasons for the Vatican's anti-Israel posture. I believe that the first and most important step the Vatican would have to take, if it ever changed its position on Israel, would be a recognition of the very passive role the Vatican played during the Holocaust and, therefore, the indirect responsibility that it must carry for what happened in many parts of Europe where the majority of the population was Catholic and participated actively in the murder of the Jewish population. The most significant signal that there is going to be some change in the Vatican's attitude toward Israel and the Jewish people, would be facing up to that. It's something they haven't done yet. The Vatican has never faced up to that. I'm sure to them, also, it is a very painful problem.

GREECE

Why does Greece, while maintaining de facto relations with Israel, still refuse to establish de jure recognition of Israel, with full exchange of ambassadors, even though she is obligated to do so as an economic member of the Common Market?

This is an attempt on Greece's part to downgrade the relationship and not give it full status. There is an Israeli ambassador in Greece, and there is a Greek representative in Israel. We have a similar situation with Turkey, although I think the Turkish representation is at a lower level than that of Greece. On occasion, countries use the level of their representation in order to signal just how warm or cool the relationship is between the two countries. When Egypt recalled her ambassador and sent a minister here, it was meant to be an indication that it was a cool relationship and not a warm one.

At the present time, Mr. Papandreo, the Prime Minister of Greece, wants to signal to everybody who is listening to signals, including the people in Greece, that he is keeping his distance from Israel and that it's not a full, warm relationship. Why is this the case? The reason primarily has both commercial and ideological content. Greece, of course, has commercial interests in, and is a purchaser of oil from, the Arab countries. However, there is also an ideological basis to her foreign relations, in the sense that Papandreo's government is probably the most leftist government in Western Europe outside of the Iron Curtain. He's taken a very strong leftist stand. It was anticipated that Greece would leave NATO when Papandreo came to power. Although Greece didn't leave NATO, she quite consistently adopts anti-Western attitudes. Papandreo, on occasion, has even taken pro-Soviet positions on various issues that have divided East and West.

There is a long history of terrorism emanating from Greece. Why has she continued to maintain, over the years, relaxed security, allowing terrorists to run free in her ports of embarkation?

The Greeks have had a fairly close relationship with the PLO, and the PLO has been the lynch pin of international terrorism for all these years. To the best of my knowledge, there's a PLO office in Athens, and the Greeks have freed PLO terrorists who were arrested on Greek soil. As I've said, there's probably even some ideological content in that policy.

Do you see any possibility of economic ties between Greece and Israel developing?

It's possible, but it doesn't seem probable right now. What might make for economic ties is that the two countries are in close geographic proximity, and

Greece could benefit from Israeli know-how in areas of agriculture and industry. But we're still pretty far from that at the present time.

Do you believe that the fact that a large Greek Orthodox community exists in the Arab world has had any influence on Greek policy toward Israel?

There is not one large Greek Orthodox community in the Arab world. There's a fair-sized Greek Orthodox community in Lebanon, but that Greek Orthodox community found itself caught in the Christian-Moslem struggle in Lebanon. Zakla, a town which came to prominence in 1982, has a Greek Orthodox majority. I'm sure that there are Greek Orthodox in Syria; however, they're a relatively small minority. In Jordan, the Greek Orthodox are also a very small minority. The Christians of Eygpt are primarily Copts, but there is a small number of Greek Orthodox as well. The problem is that there are many small Greek Orthodox communities throughout the Arab world, which, cumulatively, appear to influence Greek attitudes toward Israel.

SPAIN

Given Spain's full membership in the Common Market, which, from its beginning, obligated her to establish diplomatic relations with all member countries, why did it take her so long to establish such relations with Israel? How do you envision relations between Israel and Spain developing—in what areas and in what directions?

I'm beginning to sound like a broken record, but, again, the delay was mostly due to commercial considerations. I think the Spaniards continually evaluated the pluses of establishing formal diplomatic relations, as opposed to maintaining the existent situation. Prior to establishing formal relations with Israel, they estimated that since there were de facto relationships and communications between Israel and Spain, they had no penalty to pay for not having full diplomatic relationships. Whatever they wanted to get out of Israel they received, whether it was in the area of expert advice, or assistance in various technical fields. By the same token, it is likely they felt that the very act of establishing diplomatic relations with Israel might have had an adverse effect on their relationships, including commercial, with the Arab world. Therefore, they kept postponing the establishment of full diplomatic relations with Israel.

Spain became a member of NATO after the fall of the Franco regime. She possesses one of the most backward military establishments in Europe—a military that must be modernized. Do you foresee Israel playing any role in modernizing the Spanish armed forces?

In principle, the answer is yes. Because Israel has a very advanced defense industry and because we have, unfortunately, gathered so much operational experience in the six wars we've had to fight, we have the capability of assisting any country that would like to modernize her military establishment. Certainly, this is dependent on the condition that there is a desire by both parties. This means that between Israel and the other country there would have to be common strategic interests.

We're presently going through a period of increasing cooperation between Israel and the United States. We are already seeing little Israel assisting the United States, the superpower, in some areas where Israel has developed expertise that the United States does not possess. The same, I'm sure, would be true for any NATO country that felt she would like to make available to herself Israel's assistance and utilize Israel's capability. If Spain decided she wanted to receive assistance from Israel in building her military capability, I'm sure that kind of relationship could be developed.

Your answers to prior questions regarding the influence of a country's large Catholic population on that nation's attitudes toward Israel have been consistent: that is, you believe commercial interests, not religious beliefs, have dominated. Do you feel the same about Spain? Do you think Spain's strong Catholic community will influence the quality of her future relationships with Israel?

The answer to both questions is yes. I believe that commercial interests, not religious beliefs, dominate Spain's attitudes toward Israel. I believe, also, that the strong Catholic community in Spain will have a positive influence on the quality of her relationships with Israel. Even though it's been nearly 500 years since the Spanish Inquisition, probably quite a few Spaniards have felt guilty about it and would like to erase that spot on Jewish-Spanish relationships. They'd like to make up for it. My guess is that they have been uneasy about the fact that for so long it was only Spain among the European countries that had not established diplomatic relations with Israel. They would like to see a good relationship develop between Spain and Israel.

The Jews enjoyed a golden era in Spain prior to the Spanish Inquisition

in 1492, but there have been no Jewish communities in Spain for hundreds of years. Will the large Spanish-speaking Sephardic community in Israel be an asset in establishing cultural ties between Spain and Israel?

To a certain extent that will probably be the case. In Israel, among those who speak Ladino or Spanish, there are Jews who have come from Turkey, from Greece, and some from Yugoslovia; the largest Spanish-speaking community in Israel is the Bulgarian-Jewish community. Three quarters of the Sephardic Jews in Israel are of Bulgarian origin. We have Sephardic Jews from Holland and from England in Israel, but it is doubtful if any are still Spanish-speaking. The very fact that we have a few hundred thousand people in Israel who are Spanish-speaking, however, is helpful in establishing cultural relationships with Spain.

TURKEY

Do you foresee the establishment of full diplomatic relations between Turkey and Israel?

Some people might be surprised to learn that there are diplomatic relations between Israel and Turkey, considering the fact that Turkey is a Moslem country. Almost the entire population of Turkey is of the Moslem religion. It is true that we've gone through periods when relationships between Israel and Turkey were better than they are right now. It is Turkey's commercial interests that dominate her policy toward us. The Turks in recent years have become very active, especially in construction projects, in the Arab world, including Saudi Arabia. Their very sizable income in foreign currency is the result of that kind of work. They have been under pressure from countries like Saudi Arabia to downgrade, or even break, their relationship with Israel. As a result, they've downgraded, but they haven't broken relations.

The Soviet Union is a common enemy of both Turkey and Israel. Additionally, there is tremendous animosity between the Arabs and the Turks (who ruled over the Arabs for over 500 years). Given these two common adversaries, do you believe that strategic military cooperation can develop between Turkey and Israel, in spite of the fact that 95 percent of the Turks are Moslems?

To that you must add that Turkey does not have a good relationship with Syria. Syria has territorial claims on Turkey in the Alexandretta region, so there certainly are some common strategic interests between Israel and Turkey. However, these strategic interests are primarily in the realm of blocking Soviet penetration into the area.

If you were to ask which countries in the Middle East play the most important part in blocking Soviet penetration into the area, the answer would have to be Turkey and Israel. In some ways, it is Turkey even more so than Israel, because Turkey borders directly on the Soviet Union, which, fortunately, Israel does not. In other ways, it is Israel more so than Turkey, because Israel is a country that is very strong militarily and has been, on a number of occasions, directly engaged in fighting armies that were equipped with Soviet weaponry. There were even a few incidents of direct engagement between Israeli military personnel—Israeli pilots—and Soviet pilots over the Sinai some years ago. Therefore, in the area of containment of the Soviet Union, there clearly is a common interest between Turkey and Israel, which will eventually come to the fore. Then I believe the Turks will realize that it would be beneficial to establish close relationships with Israel.

Speaking of Syria, she is the only country in the Middle East, except for South Yemen, that has very serious political, economic, and military ties with the Soviet Union. Syria has border claims on Iraq at the Euphrates Bend; she also has border claims on Turkey in the Alexandretta region, which date back, originally, to the breakup of the Ottoman Empire but which stem more recently from Turkey's takeover of the region in 1938-39. Syria has always had an aggressive attitude toward her neighbors and has never given up the claims anywhere on her borders. Do you believe, just as at times Iraq and Syria have flared up and just as Iraq and Iran flared up, that there is a possibility Syria might try to take advantage of some situation to fulfill, forcibly, her claims against Turkey?

The Syrian leadership is very pragmatic. Assad has shown himself to be a capable, pragmatic man, and my guess is that he would be very hesitant to try to start something unless he felt reasonably certain that he was going to be successful. Although he's made some mistakes in the past, and it could happen again, by taking on the Turks he would be engaging in a very significant undertaking. I don't expect he will do that in the foreseeable future. I am sure, however, that the Turks are keeping the possibility in mind. I would imagine that the Turkish government has a contingency military plan.

Do you foresee a role for Israel in the modernization of industry and agriculture in Turkey?

Israel would have quite a bit to contribute in those areas. There were assistance programs in the past that were successful. We have a program going on at the present time which could, in the future, be the basis for cooperation, but which, unfortunately, has not been, so far.

The Turks are going to be assembling F16 airplanes. Israel has a sizable quantity of those F16 airplanes on hand, and we've got more on order from the United States. I'm sure it could be to the benefit of both countries, Israel and Turkey, to cooperate on this program. We decided not to assemble F16s in Israel, and have been procuring them directly from the United States, because we felt we didn't require the planes on a sufficient scale to justify that kind of an effort. I doubt whether Turkey's assembly of the F16 only for her own purposes makes sense economically. If Israel and Turkey were to work on it together, then it might be justifiable economically.

AUSTRIA

Have there been military, economic, or cultural ties between Israel and Austria?

There have been no military ties. There were economic and cultural ties between the two countries, and the relationship was cordial.

Should Israel refuse to maintain diplomatic relations with Austria as long as Kurt Waldheim remains in the position of president?

The question of diplomatic relations with Austria is a question not only for Israel, but for all Western countries. That question should be addressed based on the final conclusion regarding Mr. Waldheim's background. If it should be proven that Mr. Waldheim was not only "on the scene" where war crimes were committed—that is very clear—but actually participated in war crimes—in other words, he is a war criminal—then, all Western countries face a problem regarding their relationships with Austria as long as he's the president. It's not 100 percent clear yet because there's no final answer to that question presently, but I'm sure there will be in due time. If it were to be the case that he is a war criminal, then there should be a consultation among Israel, the United States, and other Western countries. A common position taken by these countries would be most effective.

ISRAEL AND THE
EASTERN EUROPEAN COMMUNIST BLOC

The Soviet Union

THE SOVIET UNION AND ISRAEL

What is your assessment of the Soviet threat to Israel in the Middle East? Is it your perception that the ultimate aim of the Soviet Union is the destruction of the State of Israel?

The ultimate objective of the Soviet Union is to expand—to extend her influence and her presence in all directions throughout the world. Because Israel is located in the Middle East, not very far from the Soviet border, the threat of Soviet penetration and expansion is a very real and imminent danger. Although the earlier significant presence of the Soviets in Egypt is a thing of the past, today, the Soviets have that very significant presence in Syria, which is right on Israel's border. There, too, the threat is real.

If the Soviets, G-d forbid, were ever to extend their influence into this area, would their intention be to destroy the State of Israel physically, or destroy it as a state, or to incorporate it as a Soviet satellite? Who knows? We've seen what they've done in other countries. We don't want to follow the model of Eastern Europe or Afghanistan; therefore, we want to be very sure that the Soviet Union never gets that close to Israel.

Can you foresee a change in the attitude of the Soviet Union toward the State of Israel?

Nothing is sunk in concrete in this world and, in time, things can change. As long as the Soviet leadership is driven by Communist ideology, they will continue to have this ambition for constantly extending Soviet influence and Soviet presence; therefore, under present circumstances it is difficult to foresee a more favorable attitude toward Israel. My guess is that Russia will not be run forever by a Communist dictatorship.

Under what conditions do you believe the Soviet Union will want to re-establish diplomatic relations with Israel?

The Soviet Union wants to re-establish diplomatic relations with Israel at the present time. The Soviet leadership realizes it was an error to have severed diplomatic relations with Israel immediately after the Six-Day War. By breaking communications with Israel and formally putting themselves totally in the Arab camp, they were not able to carry on any dialogue with Israel. They understand that was a mistake and that it has worked against them. They realize they would have been better off during the past years if they had had some channel of communication with Israel—if they had been able at least to pose as a power that might mediate or assist the United States in mediating the Arab-Israeli conflict. Severing diplomatic relations with Israel has simply cut them out of that process, and they understand that.

They want to change that and are probably waiting for the appropriate moment to make that move. Decision making in the Soviet Union is really not that dynamic—it takes a long time. It could be that even in a few years nothing will have changed. But, as I understand their motivation, they would like to make a change and re-establish diplomatic relations with Israel.

Is it your perception that establishing diplomatic relations with the Soviet Union would be in Israel's best interest?

I don't think it's terribly important for Israel. We Israelis are believers in the universality of diplomatic relations. We don't believe we should have diplomatic relations only with countries with whom we agree or with whose leadership we can identify or support. Communications are important regardless of the conflicts of interest that might exist between countries. In that sense, although Israel and the Soviet Union are at opposite ends of the ideological spectrum, and Israel is solidly in the Western camp, I'm sure we would not reject any attempt on the part of the Soviet Union to re-establish diplomatic relations—on condition that Soviet Jewry were allowed to come to Israel.

Under what conditions do you see the Soviet Union's permitting a large emigration of Russian Jews directly to Israel from the Soviet Union rather than through a stopover in Europe?

That's difficult to say. Even with the experience we've gained in the past ten to fifteen years, it's difficult to understand fully the rationale behind Soviet policy on allowing or not allowing Soviet Jewry to leave or on facilitating their direct voyage to Israel. At the present time, the gates are closed, and they are closed almost hermetically. There are between 2 and 3 million Soviet Jews trying to get out and trying to come to Israel.

During the seventies, there was a decade of large-scale emigration of Jews from the Soviet Union. A quarter of a million Jews left the Soviet Union—160,000 of them came to Israel and are here today. When the Soviet Union opened the gates in the late sixties, it came as a surprise to most of us. People had not really expected it after so many years of Bolshevik rule and total antagonism by the Soviet leadership toward Israel, Zionism, Jewish culture, religion, and values. Yet, all of a sudden, the Kremlin leadership, presumably for reasons that they thought were beneficial to the Kremlin, opened the gates and allowed a significant number of Russian Jews to leave. Then, just as suddenly as the gates were opened, they were shut at the end of that decade; they have remained shut for about six years now.

It is impossible to envisage a quarter of a million Russian Jews being permitted to leave the Soviet Union in the seventies without great pressure having been applied by people around the world—especially by the Jewish communities throughout the world and by the State of Israel. The one thing we might say with some degree of certainty is that since the gates were opened then, it is not impossible that they will be opened again.

Whatever the reason Russian leadership found at that time for letting Russian Jews leave might become pertinent, appropriate, or relevant again this year or next. It's clear that the pressure that was applied to the Soviet Union to open the gates made a significant impact and played an important role. Today, efforts being made throughout the world, including Israel, to apply that kind of pressure on the Soviet Union and the Kremlin to let the Jewish people go are not sufficient. Much more could and needs to be done. Pressure must be applied, reapplied, and reinforced.

How do you perceive the attitude of the Soviet Union toward the State of Israel being affected by the recent strategic arrangements between Israel and the United States?

It's probably correct to say that the language the Soviet leadership understands best is the language of force—it's not the only language they understand, but it's the language they understand best. They think in terms of force and divisions; therefore, anything that is done to strengthen the Free World can only improve the chances of achieving our objectives. Anything that is done to make Israel or the Western alliance seem stronger, or to make the relationship between Israel and the United States seem stronger, can only work for the best in all directions, including the direction of improving Israeli-Soviet relationships.

How will the establishment of economic and political ties between China and Israel affect the attitude of the Soviet Union towards Israel?

We don't have such relationships now, but if China were to establish diplomatic relationships with Israel, it might give the Soviets an opportunity to do the same. It might make it easier for them to do something they want to do under any circumstances.

Do you see any possibilities of the Soviet Union and Israel establishing economic ties?

Usually, with diplomatic ties come economic ties, although sometimes there are economic ties between countries that have not as yet established diplomatic relationships. There is room for trade between the Soviet Union and Israel. I am sure the Soviets have certain products in which they have a comparative advantage over us, just as we have products here in which we have a comparative advantage over them. If there were diplomatic relations, there would be trade between the two countries.

If the Soviet Union does establish economic and political ties with the State of Israel, do you believe that all other Eastern bloc countries will follow suit?

Yes. From what we know of the satellite countries, they follow the cue from Moscow. There are both diplomatic and economic relationships between Israel and Rumania at the present time, but she's the only country in the Eastern bloc that has this kind of relationship with Israel. Whatever hesitancy exists within other Eastern bloc countries to establish relationships with Israel is based on their feelings of obligation to follow the Soviet model. I believe the only reason why countries like Bulgaria, Hungary, and Poland have not established or re-established diplomatic relations with Israel until the present time is that they know the Soviets have not. Obviously, they're waiting for Moscow to make a move. I believe they will follow the Soviets in establishing a relationship with Israel, if the Soviets were to do so.

Can you foresee the Soviet Union and Israel establishing at least cultural ties?

When countries have diplomatic relationships, many other things follow. They may not follow in a very large measure, but they do follow. The United States has diplomatic relations with the Soviet Union, and by virtue of these diplomatic relations, also has trade and a certain level of cultural relations. That model would probably be followed in the relationship between Israel and the Soviet Union.

THE SOVIET UNION AND ISRAEL'S NEIGHBORS

The Soviet Union, as an economic example, has been a dismal failure to the outside world. Can the Soviet Union, therefore, penetrate the Arab world as they did during the Nasser period when the Communist system had glamour and appeal to the Third World?

I certainly agree that Communist economies have shown themselves, without exception, to be failures and to be far less efficient than liberal or Western economies. But that is not the primary consideration of Arab dictators when they decide which way to lean. Dictatorships are not naturally inclined toward free economies or toward the Western way of life and the Western way of doing business. In many ways, a Bolshevik economy—a centralized bureaucracy that runs the economy—is much more attuned to the way of thinking of Arab dictators than is a Western economy.

Without an economic entree, is there any other way that the Soviet Union could penetrate the Arab world, other than through military sales?

The Soviets almost uniformly enter countries using military sales and military technicians. That has invariably been the case in all the Arab countries.

It has been reported that the Soviet Union has provided Arab nations with chemical weapons, including poison gas. Do you foresee her providing the Arab nations with nuclear weapons?

I cannot corroborate the statement that the Soviet Union has provided Arab countries with poison gas. The nuclear reactor in Iraq, which was bombed by the Israeli air force and which would have been the source for Iraqi nuclear bombs, was not built by the Soviet Union but by the French and Italians. So far, the Soviets have not provided nuclear weaponry to any of the Arab countries. They have been very careful not to do so. To the best of my knowledge, the Soviets have not provided nuclear weaponry to any other country. They have provided very advanced conventional weaponry to many countries, including Syria, but not nuclear weaponry. I can only interpret that as being a reflection of Soviet policy not to provide nuclear weaponry to any other country.

Is it possible that Soviet military personnel might become involved in any future war between Israel and any of her Arab neighbors?

That's not impossible. During the War of Attrition between Israel and Egypt, there was a very strong Soviet military presence in Egypt. Surface-to-air missile systems were manned by Soviet personnel. The Soviets piloted a significant number of fighter aircraft, flying out of bases in Egypt, and were actually engaged in combat with the Israeli air force. Five Soviet-piloted MIGS were shot down over the Sinai in 1969.

In the past, there were threats by the Soviets of direct physical intervention by Soviet troops at the end of both the Six-Day War and the Yom Kippur War. The Soviets have a significant military presence numbering in the thousands in Syria at the present time. They operated the SAM 5 missile systems in Syria for an extended period of time—almost three years. They are now manned by the Syrians.

I'm sure the use of military personnel against Israel is an option the Soviets would consider under certain circumstances. At the same time, however, they are quite realistic in their estimation of Israeli military capability. In weighing the option of military intervention in this area, the Soviets would not look with enthusiasm toward a situation wherein their forces could be beaten by the IDF. My guess is they would decide on direct intervention only if they felt very confident that that intervention would be successful. Under any circumstances we can envisage, there would be very little room for that kind of confidence on their part.

Do you believe that the Soviet Union has the need to test new weapon systems in a war against Israel in order to rectify the damage done to them in past wars where their weapon systems didn't stand up against those used by Israel?

No. I believe the Soviet leadership has a reasonably realistic estimate of the quality of their weaponry. They are probably aware that their weaponry in most areas is not a match for Western weaponry. Therefore, another conflict would serve only as further proof of this inferiority.

How influential is the Soviet Union in its relationship with Syria, and how is it affecting Syrian policy—domestic and foreign?

There is a large Soviet presence in Syria, and there is a vast program of Soviet military assistance to Syria. But I would not say that the Syrians are vassals of the Soviet Union. The Syrian relationship with the Soviet Union is not similar to that of Bulgaria, East Germany, or Poland. The Syrian dictator, Assad, has retained a very significant degree of independence, and it doesn't appear that Syria takes her orders from the Soviet Union. Of course, being so dependent on the Soviet Union means Assad gives very significant consideration to what the Soviet Union does and does not want. If Assad weighs a military option, I'm sure one of his major considerations as to whether or not that option should be exercised is what the position of the Soviet Union would be vis-à-vis that option.

Do you believe that in the near future it could be in the best interest of the Soviet Union to encourage Syria to go to war with Israel?

No. I'm sure it's a war that the Syrians would lose. Therefore, in the final result, it would not benefit Soviet interests even as they are viewed from the Kremlin.

In supporting Syria, how influential has the Soviet Union been in affecting events in Lebanon?

Quite influential in the past. The Soviet Union has been and continues to be a very strong supporter of the PLO and various other terrorist organizations either affiliated with, or dissident from, the PLO. The vast stockpile of arms that the IDF uncovered in Lebanon during the Lebanese operation was almost totally of Soviet manufacture and supplied by the Soviet Union. When Katyusha rockets fall on the northern part of Israel, as has happened just recently, they are Katyushas manufactured in the Soviet Union.

The PLO had training camps in the Soviet Union—maybe still does at the present time. Documentation uncovered during the Lebanese operation provided evidence of training received by PLO terrorists in the Soviet Union. And, of course, the Soviet Union supplied and backed the Syrians in Lebanon.

How effective, how important, and how dangerous are the Soviet arms relationships with countries like Libya, South Yemen, and Algeria?

A Soviet arms relationship is dangerous in all cases—whether it is Algeria, Libya, Syria, South Yemen, or Egypt. The Soviets produce vast quantities of arms. They have an arms production capacity far larger than the Western world, and they produce advanced weaponry. Fortunately, most of it is not as advanced as the most advanced American or Israeli weaponry. They put large quantities of advanced weaponry into the hands of dictators who have no compunctions about the use of violence or the use of this weaponry. It is very dangerous for the entire world.

Do you believe that the Soviet Union could establish strong military ties with any other Arab country beside Syria?

Yes, of course. The Soviet Union has strong military ties with South Yemen— The Peoples Democratic Republic of Yemen, as it is called. The Soviet Union also has ties with Iraq, even if they're not that strong at the present time. And that is not necessarily the end of the list. The Soviet Union had very strong ties with Egypt in the past.

We know none of the Arab countries are ideologically in the Western camp. If they have a Western orientation, it's not because they are believers in democracy, freedom, or equality. Similarly, the Arab countries that have their ties with the Soviet Union are not necessarily tied to the Soviet Union because they are ideologically Communists.

It is important to recall that there is a very strong trend of radicalism in the Arab world. Today the most pronounced trends in all the Arab countries are Moslem fundamentalism on the one hand and Marxist radicalism on the other. A country like Iraq is a Marxist radical state. In a country like Syria, the ruling Baath party is a Marxist party. As we can tell by the name they have chosen for themselves, The Peoples Democratic Republic of Yemen is also in that camp. It is quite possible that other Arab countries could fall into the Soviet orbit in future years.

Do you believe there can be peace negotiations and a settlement between Israel and another Arab country without the Soviet Union's involvement, acquiescence, and/or approval?

Absolutely. As a matter of fact, it is very difficult to envisage the possibility of an accommodation between Israel and an Arab country with the Soviet Union's involvement. In the only case so far in which a peace treaty has been signed—the Israeli-Egyptian peace treaty, the treaty was achieved without Soviet involvement. It could not have been achieved had the Soviets been involved.

Other Eastern European Bloc Countries

After World War II, West Germany paid and is still paying reparation. East Germany has not. Do you foresee a time when East Germany, too, will make reparation?

No, not as long as East Germany is in the Eastern bloc. The West Germans felt the need to do it and wanted to rehabilitate themselves into the community of nations, which, in effect, meant to them the Western community of nations. East Germany does not feel the need to rehabilitate herself within the Eastern bloc. There is no focus on the part East Germany played in the Holocaust and the murder of 6 million Jews. Why, then, should they pay any kind of price for rehabilitation when they don't feel the need to do it?

Vast amounts of Jewish property were confiscated in Poland during World War II. Do you think that this property will ever be returned to the Jews?

Probably not. The Jews are gone. My own father was a very wealthy man in Latvia—not Poland, but not far removed. All of that's gone, and no one in the family has any anticipation that it will ever be returned.

Do you believe Israel and Poland can establish economic ties based on Poland's vast amount of natural resources, which Israel doesn't possess, in exchange for Israel's technology?

As I said before, once the Soviet Union establishes diplomatic relations with Israel, the Poles will follow suit. The Poles might even move in advance of the Soviets, if they become a little more independent than they have been in the past. It would be in Poland's interest to have relations with Israel. The economic ramifications of that relationship are just part of the overall picture. It would likewise be in Israel's interest, since the Polish market for Israeli products and technology would be significant.

The large Polish-Jewish population in Israel harbors bad feelings toward Poland because of her behavior toward Jews during, and in the decades prior to, the Holocaust. Under these circumstances, do you believe cultural ties can be established between Israel and Poland?

Yes. There is no parallel when it comes to Israelis' feelings about and terrible memories of Poland and their feelings and memories regarding Germany and Germans. Nevertheless, today we have not only diplomatic relations with the Federal Republic of Germany, but we also have some cultural ties. If and when we have diplomatic relations with Poland, we shall also have cultural ties, despite the behavior of many—not all—of the Poles during the Holocaust. Such behavior applied not only to the Poles but also to the Rumanians, the Ukrainians, the Lithuanians, the Latvians, and the Estonians. The peoples of Europe, with very few exceptions—the Danes and perhaps the Bulgarians—behaved in a most horrible manner toward the Jews during the Holocaust. In many cases, they actively participated in the murder of Jews.

After the 1967 War, all Eastern bloc countries, except Rumania, broke diplomatic relations with Israel. Since that time, Rumania has been Israel's "window" into the Eastern bloc countries, as well as sometimes into the Arab world. Do you see that role for Rumania continuing? Do you believe, if diplomatic relations or economic ties are established in the Eastern bloc, that it will come by way of contacts through Rumania?

As long as Rumania is the only Eastern bloc country that has diplomatic relations with Israel, it affords a channel of communication that doesn't exist through any other country in some specific areas. If and when diplomatic relations are established with the Soviet Union and other satellite countries, then, of course, Rumania will cease to fulfill this unique function.

Rumania is not the necessary avenue for the establishment of diplomatic relations with the Soviet Union or with other satellite countries. It's possible it can be done directly. Meetings have been held between representatives of Israel and of the Kremlin. On a number of occasions, I personally met with Mr. Dobrynin, the former Soviet ambassador in Washington. There is really no need for intermediaries or for a parallel channel. When the time comes, I'm sure it will be done directly.

Of all the Eastern bloc countries, the greatest number of Israeli tourists go to Rumania and to Yugoslavia. Do you see reciprocity in tourism whereby Rumanians will be able to come to Israel as tourists?

Today, Rumanians, in principle, can come to Israel as tourists. But Rumania, like all Soviet satellite countries, is relatively poor and very short of foreign exchange. As a result, she doesn't represent a very great source of tourism to

Israel or any other country. We probably have some tourists coming to Israel today from Eastern satellite countries such as Hungary. Because of the low standard of living, these satellite countries are not great potential sources of tourism, at least not in the immediate future.

Rumania was the contact point for the Sadat peace initiatives, as well as for many other false starts of initiatives for peace with the Arabs, especially Jordan. Do you believe that, in the future, any deal with Arab countries will come through a similar, third-party vehicle, using Rumania as the focal point?

It's possible but not necessary. You may remember that the contacts preceding Sadat's visit to Jerusalem were not only made in Rumania, they were also made in Morocco. To some extent, the United States played a role. When it's impossible to have direct contact with an Arab country that does not have diplomatic relations with Israel—and that's not always impossible—there are third-party countries, not hostile to Israel, that do have relationships both with Israel and with Arab countries. Not only Rumania, but also the United States and Egypt could fulfill that role. It could be any one of a number of countries.

Rumania still has a large residue of Jewish people who would like to emigrate to Israel, yet over the years there has been only a slight trickle of Rumanian Jews making aliyah. *Do you see any possibility that all Rumanian Jews would be permitted to emigrate to Israel, thus finalizing the* aliyah?

Yes. There has been a steady stream of Rumanian Jews coming to Israel over the years. As far as we can tell, barring any unforeseen change in the policy of the Rumanian government, that will continue until the time when everyone who wants to leave will have come to Israel.

Hungary has been the most successful country in the Eastern bloc in establishing small, capitalistic units. There are small enterprises, not owned by the state, in which lots of money is being made by individual entrepreneurs. Since Israel has a large community of Hungarian-speaking Jews who came from Hungary, do you see the possibility of commercial ties between Israeli and Hungarian enterprises? Do you foresee economic ties developing with Hungary through these small entrepreneurships?

If and when diplomatic relations between Israel and Hungary are established, I'm sure trade relationships will follow. It's even possible that we might develop some trade relationships in the absence of diplomatic relations. There is talk today about the possibility of an economic relationship developing with Poland, even before diplomatic relations are established. If that door is opened, then Israelis of Hungarian origin, who know the country and the language, certainly could be helpful in speeding the development of relationships. But, we're not there yet.

Hungary's success in establishing these small, private entrepreneurships has become known throughout the world. Do you think this activity will spread through the other Eastern bloc countries and undermine Soviet control?

Looking at the distant future, it's very difficult to conceive of the Communist regime and the Communist system maintaining itself unchanged over the years. Considering the demonstrated success of Western democracy and Western economic systems, inevitably, Soviet rule and Communist systems will gravitate in that direction. Whether this will happen as a result of revolutions, coups d'etat, or some sudden upheaval or whether we will have a gradual change like we see in Hungary today—where over a period of years the economy has been moving toward the free Western-style economy, there is no way of knowing. It may be that graduated change will prevent upheaval and will bring about a movement toward Western-style economy and democracy without any tremors. Perhaps some of the rulers of the Eastern countries realize that unless they allow this gradual change, they will experience upheaval.

The second-largest tourist activity between Israel and the Eastern bloc countries is to Hungary. Do you see any possibility that Hungarians will be allowed to come to Israel as tourists?

It has a great deal to do with Hungary's economic situation and whether their standard of living and the foreign currency balances are such as to permit that kind of traffic.

Given the relaxing of certain conditions in Hungary, a situation that doesn't exist in any other Communist country, do you think it is possible that she would establish diplomatic relations with Israel, like Rumania did, without Soviet approval?

It doesn't appear that it will happen. We've seen too long a period during which the Rumanians were the only ones who maintained diplomatic relations with Israel. None of the other Soviet satellites followed suit, and, to me, that is an indication that the Kremlin signaled very clearly that they did not want them to follow suit. It would take some change in the Kremlin for that situation to be altered. If there were to be a change in the Kremlin, it's my guess that there would be movement toward the resumption of diplomatic relations between the Soviet Union and Israel. This would, of course, immediately open the door for countries like Hungary, Bulgaria, and the others as well.

Bulgaria has always been good to her Jews, and there is a very large Bulgarian-Jewish community in Israel today. Even though Bulgaria severed diplomatic ties with Israel after the 1967 War, she never severed economic ties. Do you think Bulgaria would be the first Eastern bloc country to establish diplomatic relations after the Soviet Union?

After the Soviet Union, they will all establish diplomatic relations. It is difficult to predict who's going to be first and who will be second. It will just be a matter of chance.

In the early 1950s, the Bulgarian air force shot down an El Al civilian airplane. That it was known beforehand to be a civilian plane was obvious to everyone. What is your understanding of why it was done, and what the significance of it was?

I don't know, and I'm not even sure that I know everything that is known. I was in the United States at the time. I really can't tell you whether this was a mistake or whether it was a deliberate act intended to give some kind of signal. Whatever signal might have been intended is not comprehensible in our terms here in Israel—it's still not understood.

In the early days of the Jewish State, Israel was able to maintain very close ties with Yugoslavia. Israel had two chiefs of staff of Yugoslavian origin, and there have been ongoing economic ties with Yugoslavia. Many Israeli tourists go to Yugoslavia, and a trickle of Yugoslavs come to Israel. Do you see any possibility that Israel will be able to maintain existing or establish better ties with Yugoslavia in the future?

Even though Yugoslavia is not in the Soviet bloc, the answer, also, is a function of Soviet resumption of diplomatic ties with Israel. Countries like Yugoslavia, or like the Peoples Republic of China, are following the Soviet cue. They do not want to open themselves to charges that they have taken a line that is not consistent with the progressive revolutionary line as advocated by Communist countries throughout the world. Even though neither of these two countries is in the Soviet bloc, they are waiting for the Soviets to make the first move.

ISRAEL AND COMMUNIST CHINA

During the fifties, sixties, and seventies, why did Communist China take an even more extreme political stand in the United Nations and in other international forums in regard to the support of the PLO and the extremist factions of the PLO than did the Soviet Union?

Communist China saw herself then—and to some extent even sees herself today—as being in competition with the Soviet Union for the sympathy of Third World countries. It is her perception that the more extreme a position she takes in support of the PLO, the better she will look to the Third World countries. China assumes that the PLO has influence in the Third World, and it's true—the PLO has support in, and clearly some influence on, the countries of the Third World. That really explains it all. China feels she can engage in such competitive activity with the Soviet Union without really suffering any penalties.

How do you perceive Communist China's attitude toward Israel at the present time? Does she still support the PLO and the extremist factions of the PLO?

Considering the fact that China is a Communist country with a very strong ideological basis to her regime, she has a rather pragmatic attitude on internal matters, as well as on her external relationships. Because China considers her position in the Third World as important and competes against the Soviet Union for a position there, she has adopted a position of support for the PLO, which has influence in the Third World. With regard to the PLO and Israel, if China has any opinion on the Middle East conflict, I doubt that it's of any great importance to her.

Is the establishment of diplomatic relations with Communist China important to Israel, and why?

Again, Israel believes in the universality of diplomatic relations. In principle, we are interested in diplomatic relations with everyone and, certainly, with a country like China, the most populous country in the world. Our primary and immediate interest, of course, is commercial relations with China. With a population of 1 billion, she represents a vast market; even a small niche of her market could be of great importance to Israel's economy. We can have economic relationships without diplomatic relations, but it usually is better when they go together.

If Israel establishes, either openly or clandestinely, technical or economic relations with Communist China, will it infuriate the Soviets and cause a reaction which will be even more anti-Israel than the Soviet Union is today?

The attitude of the Soviet Union toward Israel has nothing to do with such Israeli actions. The question was raised in the past whether or not the establishment of strategic cooperation between Israel and the United States might infuriate the Soviet Union and cause them to take an even more anti-Israeli attitude. There's no connection at all. The Soviets have an anti-Israel attitude because that is consistent with their interests as they perceive them. They know that Israel is a country that's part of the Free World. Of course, as the Soviets know, nothing will change that; therefore, beyond that, whatever Israel does or doesn't do will not effect Soviet policy.

Soviet policy is motivated by trying to gain approval in the Arab world. If anything, the Soviets are impressed by Israeli strength and achievements. What might mitigate the Soviet attitude towards Israel would be Israel's becoming even stronger or her establishment of better relationships with Communist China—or any other country in the world. The stronger Israel looks to the Soviet Union, the better the chances are that the Soviets may try to placate Israel and take a softer line. The people in the Kremlin are also very pragmatic. We shouldn't think of them in terms of their being infuriated and in their anger taking a particular action. They don't operate that way.

What impact would the establishment of diplomatic relations with Communist China have on Taiwan?

Taiwan doesn't have diplomatic relations with Israel at the present time, so it will not have any effect at all.

If Israel were to establish any kind of relationship with Communist China, openly or clandestinely, on any level, whether it is economic, cultural, political, or military, do you think it would require prior approval by the United States?

No, I'm sure it would not. The United States has diplomatic relations with Communist China, so there's no reason why she would object to Israel's having diplomatic relations with China. Israel is not in the habit of asking the permission of any country—not even the United States, Israel's greatest friend—before she establishes diplomatic relations with a country. Certainly not in this case would Israel seek prior approval, since the United States has diplomatic relations with China.

Can you foresee open diplomatic relations with Communist China and Israel taking place? Do you see their starting with economic, cultural, political, or some sort of military relationship through the transfer of military technology to Communist China?

It's not impossible, but it doesn't look very promising at the present time. This is because China is competing for approval in the Third World against the Soviet Union. She is using her anti-Israeli, pro-PLO posture as a card in that competition, and she doesn't feel she's paying any price for playing that card. China feels she is in a position to gain whatever she can in trade relationships with Israel without abandoning her official anti-Israel position. As long as that's the situation, it's difficult to see why she would change her position.

As you remember, American relationships with Communist China started through an exchange of ping-pong matches between the Chinese and the Americans. In Jerusalem, there is a "China Chair" at the Hebrew University. Do you believe that this could be the core of the beginnings of some sort of cultural relationship between Communist China and Israel?

It could be, but it doesn't have to be. The way it looks right now, they will not want to have open diplomatic relations with us for the reasons that I've explained. Whatever else the Chinese want to do with us, they will find a way of doing. They are very pragmatic. They will not need the chair for Chinese studies at the Hebrew University. If it could serve their ends, they would use it, but if it weren't there, they would find another way.

Presently, Israel has been playing a role in helping to improve China's agriculture through the exchange of agricultural systems. Do you believe this will be expanded further?

Yes. If the Chinese feel they can assist themselves by working with us or by gaining knowledge or technology from us, they will do it.

In the early 1950s, Ben Gurion failed to recognize Communist China at a time when he had an opportunity to establish diplomatic relations with her. Do you believe he made a fundamental mistake? It is understood that he didn't do it because of fear of alienating the United States. Do you feel that this was a basic mistake?

I believe in the universality of diplomatic relations. I can't see any reason for turning down diplomatic relations. Although I wasn't involved in the decision at the time, that would have been my opinion; so in retrospect, it was a mistake.

That doesn't mean that had we recognized China at that time, the Chinese wouldn't have broken diplomatic relations with us between then and now. It might be an illusion to think we would still have diplomatic relations and a Chinese ambassador here if we had recognized China at that time. If we had, she probably would have recalled her ambassador at the same time the Soviets did.

If diplomatic relations were to be established between China and Israel, does Israel have the human resources who speak and understand Chinese to staff an embassy?

It's not essential to have Chinese speakers staff an embassy in China. The vast majority of embassies in Israel are not staffed by Hebrew-speaking personnel. I'm sure it would be advantageous to have people who speak Chinese, but it's not essential. Many of the embassies of other countries in China are not staffed by Chinese speakers. We do, however, have many people with linguistic abilities. If there were to be a need for Chinese speakers to staff positions in an Israeli embassy or consulate in China, it wouldn't take very long before we had them.

ISRAEL AND THE THIRD WORLD

India

India is not a Moslem country and has Moslem enemies, yet she has never established diplomatic relations with Israel. Can you explain why?

There are two reasons. First, although India is not a Moslem country in the sense that the majority of the population is not Moslem, she does have a large Moslem population. I don't doubt that has been a consideration in the policy that the Indian government has adopted toward Israel.

Secondly, over the years, India has vied for the position of leader of the Third World. Considering the attitude of most Third World countries toward the PLO, and considering the economic leverage that the Arab world has had on many Third World countries, the Indian government has found it wisest to take an anti-Israel position.

Why has India, since the establishment of the State of Israel, taken such an anti-Israel posture in all political forums, given that she is not a Moslem state and that her enemy, Pakistan, is a Moslem country?

Again, it's the Moslem population in India, and it's the role that India sees for herself as leader of the Third World. Additionally, in the conflict between India and Pakistan, it has turned out that Pakistan has been backed by the United States, and India has been backed by the Soviet Union. This is another dimension that has moved the Indians in the direction of taking positions consistent with, and not deviating too far from, those of the Soviets, such as an anti-Israel position.

Given India's insecurity based on the growing military strength of Pakistan, and Pakistan's alliance with the United States, do you see some sort of military cooperation taking place between India and Israel? Do you foresee a militarily related relationship between India and Israel developing based on commonality of national interests?

It's not impossible. With very few exceptions, all countries with a military or security problem do have the inclination to turn to Israel, because we are known to be a country with lots of military experience and a very advanced defense industry. When it comes to security problems, all other principles usually fall by the wayside if a country feels she can help herself and strengthen her security.

At some time, India, which has a security problem, could conceivably think her security interests might be served by turning to Israel. It may have to be surreptitiously or clandestinely that she develops her relationship with Israel and gets Israeli assistance. But the same might equally be true of Pakistan. As I've said, it's generally true of countries that have real security problems that such problems have an overriding importance as opposed to all other considerations.

Do you foresee any economic ties developing between India and Israel?

Again, it's not impossible. For Israel, India represents a very large market, with her population over ½ billion. But those ties are not there at the present time.

Do you foresee a thaw in the relationship between India and Israel and the establishment of diplomatic relations?

The basic consideration that speaks for improving relationships between India and Israel is that both countries are democratic countries. I am a firm believer that in the final analysis, common values and common ideals make for common strategic interests. Therefore, I see the Indian relationship with the Soviet Union as an aberration and not long-lasting. If India continues to be a democratic country, and we hope that she will—we see no indications to the contrary— sooner or later she will find herself in the Western camp of the Free World. Then she will find herself in the same camp as Israel.

Black Africa

All the Black African nations received their independence after World War II. They had been either French-, Italian-, or English-governed. Prior to the 1973 War, Israel had excellent economic and, in most cases, diplomatic relations with all of the Black African countries. These relations were broken by the African countries after the 1973 War. It was believed that after Camp David, ties with the Black African countries would be re-established. It hasn't really happened, except in a few exceptional cases. Why? Do you believe in the near future whatever the reasons that have blocked it will be eliminated, and there will be a re-establishment of diplomatic relations?

Once diplomatic relations with Israel are broken, they are not easy to re-establish, because the countries who consider re-establishing these relations weigh the penalties that they may have to pay and the sanctions that may be imposed upon them by the Arab world as a result. These penalties may decrease in magnitude with the drop in the price of oil, which is bound to decrease the leverage that the Arab world has on Third World and African countries. We may see some sign of that already in the few African countries that have decided to re-establish diplomatic relations with Israel—Liberia, the Ivory Coast, and Zaire. These are signs of the times, and I believe we'll have a lot more of that.

What will have to happen before Israel will be able to re-establish herself in Black Africa as the channel for agricultural and infrastructure technology transfer, as was the case prior to the 1973 Yom Kippur War?

First of all, we weren't the channel; we were the origin. It was Israeli know-how that was channeled to Black African countries. Israeli assistance was very much appreciated and considered important by all the Black African countries that enjoyed the benefits of it. But the Arab world's financial leverage—and maybe even blackmail—brought about a situation whereby Black African nations were ready to forego Israeli assistance in order not to forego the financial assistance that they were promised or offered by the Arab world. The leverage that the Arab world has had on Black African countries will decrease with the drop in the price of oil, and we will probably have a return of the degree of technical cooperation that existed in the past between Israel and African countries.

Prior to 1973, Israel had aid programs in most African countries, financed mainly by the United States. They covered agricultural as well as military training. Do you believe it is possible that these aid programs can be re-established? Is this not in the interests of both the United States and the Black nations?

Yes. Israel has very specific capabilities that can be of assistance to countries in Africa. She has the technology and the know-how, and Israelis are motivated to transfer that know-how and technology. This is why Israel had such good relationships with African countries before the Six-Day War. I'm sure what serves today as an incentive to African countries to re-establish diplomatic relations with Israel

are the advantages they believe they will gain by re-establishing such relations—
Israeli know-how, technology, and assistance.

*How do you foresee the development of future ties between Israel and
Black African countries taking place?*

Arab leverage on Black Africa stems primarily from Arab economic capability;
therefore, the Arab world has had the ability to use an economic stick to promise
assistance to Black Africa. It has been able to condition the Black African nations
to maintain no relationship with Israel and has threatened that whatever economic
assistance was being given would be cut off if a relationship were to be established with Israel. But as the economic power of the Arab world decreases with
the drop in the price of oil, Arab economic assistance and leverage on Third
World countries will decrease. As the leverage that the Arab world has over
African countries drops, we will see an increasing tendency on the part of those
countries to establish or re-establish relationships with Israel. We have already
seen the beginning of that, and I believe it will continue.

*In Black Africa, Ethiopia is, militarily, the most powerful non-Moslem
nation. For the last few years, she has been waging war with Somalia, a
member nation of the Arab League. For thousands of years, there has
existed in Ethiopia a not insignificant Jewish community referred to as
the Falashas. Yet, Israel and Ethiopia have not maintained diplomatic
relations since the fall of Haile Selassie. Can you explain what conditions
would have to prevail for there to be a renormalization of such diplomatic
relations?*

At the present time, Israel is ready to have diplomatic relations with every
country on the globe, including Ethiopia. If Ethiopia and Israel do not have
diplomatic relations, it is only the fault of the Ethiopians. The Ethiopian government is a Marxist government, largely under the influence of the Soviet Union,
which takes a pro-Soviet and pro-Arab line. That explains it all. That's the reason
they don't want diplomatic relations with Israel. If the time comes when the
Ethiopian government changes its position, or there's a different Ethiopian government, then we will see relationships between Ethiopia and Israel.

Burma and Nigeria

When U Nu was the Prime Minister of Burma, Israel had good relations with this country. Then, a dictatorship developed. What has happened to these relations?

Today, Burma sees herself as an integral part of the Third World; therefore, she tries to take positions consistent with those of other Third World countries, especially with those Third World countries that claim to be in positions of leadership.

The most populous country in Black Africa is Nigeria, and it is Moslem. Israel had good relations with Nigeria until the Yom Kippur War in 1973. Do you believe the drop in oil prices and Nigeria's need for all kinds of technological assistance will provide an opportunity for the re-establishment of those relations?

It will certainly enhance the possibility that we will have a resumption or an improvement of those relations. Nigeria, although a large oil exporter, was also under pressure from the Arab world to break her relationships with Israel. Although we don't have diplomatic relationships at the present time, there are many commercial relationships between Israel and Nigeria. I can't predict the full impact of the drop in the price of oil on Nigeria, but it creates a problem for her because she was accustomed to obtaining a very large part of her income from the sale of oil. In spite of this, Israeli-Nigerian relations are likely to improve.

ISRAEL AND THE NON-ARAB MOSLEM WORLD

Iran

It has been reported in the American press that the United States is interested in Israel selling special weapons to Iraq. If Israel were to do this, couldn't it have future detrimental effects on any possible good relations between Israel and Iran, especially the Iranian military?

Israel is not interested in selling special or non-special weapons either to Iraq or Iran. Both of these countries under their present leaderships, Saddam Hussein in Iraq and Khomieni in Iran, are deadly enemies of Israel. And that tells it all.

What can Israel do to prepare for the post-Khomieni period in Iran to attempt to get back to the same kind of relations that existed under the Shah?

We don't need any spiritual preparation for that sort of thing. As a matter of fact, that applies to any of the countries that today are on terms of hostility with Israel or consider themselves to be in a state of war with Israel. We don't have to prepare ourselves for a change in their positions vis-á-vis Israel. We will welcome it when it comes. That includes Iran.

For the sake of the Iranian people, we would like to see a change in the government of Iran. We'd like to see Iran become a modern, civilized, democratic, Western country—a country with Western values, Western attitudes, a regard for human life, and a desire for peaceful relations with all countries, including Israel. When that day comes, as I'm sure it will, Israel will be ready.

Do you foresee the possibility of the Iraqi-Iranian War coming to a conclusion sometime in the near future? If you do, what do you believe the outcome will be?

I don't believe that either country has the ability to score a decisive victory over the other. The Iraqis certainly cannot go on to capture Teheran; that's completely out of the question. Although the Iranians have a somewhat better chance of going on to Baghdad because the distance from Baghdad to the Iraqi-Iranian border is much shorter, that's a very unlikely occurrence, as well. So I don't foresee a decisive military victory by either side. If the war goes on, they simply continue in this crazy slugging match they're engaged in.

There's little question that the continuation of this war is not in the interests of either country and certainly not in the interests of the people of either Iraq or Iran. Hundreds of thousands of people have already been killed in this slaughter. What we've seen so far is that the dictators who run these countries, Saddam Hussein and Khomieni, are simply incapable of winding that war down. I believe they would like to do so, but they can't—they have become the prisoners of their own rhetoric and past actions.

The most likely circumstances that might lead to a winding down of this war—an end to the slaughter cycle—would be if one of these leaders were to leave this world, and that's possible. Khomieni is an elderly gentleman, and although he seems to have the attributes of longevity in his genes, one of these days he won't be around any more. That may be an opportunity for a wind-down, but who knows how long that will take? Iraq is a volatile dictatorial regime where leaders have been assassinated in the past, and it could happen to Saddam Hussein. But he's been in power now for a good number of years, and who knows how much longer he will remain in power? Under the present circumstances, a winding down of the war is unlikely and, unfortunately, as long as these two gentlemen run their respective countries, it's not very probable.

Can you comment on Iranian terrorist activity and how it can be controlled?

Iran is a supporter of terrorist activity. By the way, so is Iraq, even though these two countries are at war with each other. Our contact with Iranian-supported terrorist activity has been, primarily, in Lebanon where the Iranians have been encouraging, promoting, financing, directing, and generally supporting terrorist activity by the extremist Shiite organizations—primarily, the Hezbala. Almost daily they attempt to carry out terrorist activities against the population and the IDF in the security zone in Southern Lebanon. Much of this activity is carried out by the Hezbala, which we know is directed and financed by Iran.

There are sizable Kurdish populations in both Iraq and Iran, and there is a sizable territory that straddles both Iraq and Iran called Kurdistan. It is inhabited almost exclusively by Kurds. Israel previously supported the Kurdish insurrection movement in Iraq. Should Israel attempt to help the Kurds establish their own nation now that Iraq and Iran are involved in an all-out war? Would it not serve Israel's interests if a Kurdish nation would arise carved out of both Iraq and Iran?

The Kurds are one of the national minorities in the Middle East that have suffered a great deal. They have not been able to attain national independence or even autonomy, although they have sacrificed a great deal for that aim. They have fought for many years against the Iraqi and Iranian governments in order to assert their independence. With the attraction that the PLO has managed to arouse, it is interesting that there has not been a similar movement in the world in support of Kurdish national aspirations which, in my view, have far greater legitimacy. There is far more justice attached to their claims and to their grievances.

Israel, in principle, has supported, and will continue in the future to support, the rectification of the grievances of the Kurdish people. In the past, Israel has assisted Kurdish fighters who fought against Iraq in hope of attaining Kurdish independence. What Israel's reaction in the future would be will, first and foremost, be determined by just what approaches or requests were to be made by the people who speak for the Kurds. It's not something that Israel would initiate. To the best of my knowledge, in recent years there has not been any attempt on the part of the Kurdish people to make any contact with Israel.

Pakistan

Given the fact that Pakistan will soon join the nuclear weapons club (financed by Libya and partially by Saudi Arabia), do you believe she will pose a new threat to Israel?

Any proliferation of nuclear weaponry in the world poses a threat for everyone and, therefore, also for Israel. In that sense, if Pakistan becomes a nuclear nation, it will not be good for anyone, including Israel. I doubt that it poses a specific threat for Israel. Pakistan is rather far removed from Israel, and she has not, in recent years, been moving in circles of Moslem extremism or been associated with Arabic extremism. It would take some change in Pakistan—which is not impossible—before we would say that the capability she might acquire could serve as a specific threat to Israel.

The Soviet Union perceives Pakistan and Israel as the two forces blocking her free access to Asia. Do you believe a common alliance or military relationship can develop between Pakistan and Israel based on their having the Soviet Union as a common enemy?

No, that doesn't serve as a common denominator; the countries are simply too far apart for that. Pakistan views herself as a Western-oriented country and is viewed as such by the Western world, including the United States. The fact that Israel is an integral part of the Western world tends to dull some of the native animosity that might exist in Pakistan toward Israel.

Pakistan is a Sunni Moslem country. In a sense, both real and implied, she is threatened by Iran because Iran wants to establish a Shiite Moslem world. At this point in time, do you see any shared interests between Israel and Pakistan because Iran is a common enemy?

No. With Iran tied down in the war with Iraq, she doesn't represent an immediate threat to Pakistanis. Pakistan sees her most imminent threat as coming from India, and she sees that threat as being real. As I said before, countries that are faced by real security threats sometimes consider trying to obtain some assistance from Israel. I wouldn't count that out.

Do you see any economic ties developing between Israel and Pakistan, whether openly or clandestinely, based on Pakistan's technological base, industrialization, and possession of large amounts of raw materials—

economic ties as those that existed between Israel and Iran during the days of the Shah?

It's not impossible, but we don't see any signs of that right now. With regard to Iran, we have to remember that under the Shah, she was a Moslem country but not a Moslem republic. I'm not sure if it's correct to refer to her then as a secular country, but she was not then a country placing total emphasis on her Moslem nature. She felt then that in certain areas she could get assistance from Israel—perhaps under better terms than she could get from elsewhere.

There are some obvious hindrances to the development of such relations between Pakistan and Israel because Pakistan is not only a Moslem country, but she is also a Moslem republic. There is great emphasis put on her Moslem nature and the Moslem religion is the law of the land. Quite naturally, she would probably prefer to obtain from other places whatever assistance she could conceivably get from Israel.

Do you foresee any possibility that Pakistan, under the influence of her strong economic ties with Libya and Saudi Arabia, would join the Arab countries in any future war against Israel?

Again, it's not outside the realm of possibility, but it's not very likely. Pakistan is far removed and has problems of her own. My guess is that Pakistan would be hesitant about taking on the risks that such involvement would bring with it.

Indonesia and Malaysia

Even though Indonesia and Malaysia are Moslem countries, do you see any possibility for the development of technological or economic ties with Israel?

When we look at Moslem countries, the farther they are from Israel, the better the possibilites for establishing relationships, and the lesser the possibility that they become an integral part of an Arab or Moslem war front against Israel.

Do you foresee Israel sharing her agricultural expertise with Indonesia and Malaysia?

If Indonesia and Malaysia were to request agricultural assistance from Israel, we certainly would consider providing it.

ISRAEL AND THE ARAB WORLD

Egypt

What were the rewards for Israel from the Camp David Accords with Egypt?

On the positive side of the ledger, it is a peace treaty with a country with which we had fought five wars during a thirty-year period of belligerence. Those five wars, in one way or another, were initiated by Egypt. Just what weight we attach to the positive side of the ledger depends on whether we feel that the alternative to the treaty would have been war.

If we feel the alternative to signing that treaty would have been war, that is, that in that intervening seven years, we would have had at least one war with Egypt, and maybe even more, then we'd be likely to assign a lot of weight to that treaty as having been an instrument for preventing war—war that we would have won but which inevitably would have cost the lives of thousands in Israel. If we were to postulate that there would not have been a war in any case because the relationship of non-active belligerence that existed between October of 1973 (the end of the Yom Kippur War) and 1977 (when Sadat came to Jerusalem) would have simply continued, even without a peace treaty being signed, then we would assign relatively little weight to the positive side of the ledger. All we would see is the price we paid for the treaty without substantial benefits.

There is no one who can say with certainty whether we would or would not have had a war in the absence of a peace treaty between Israel and Egypt. Personally, I think it's very unlikely that we would have had a war, because the Yom Kippur War demonstrated to the Egyptians that they had no military option. They started a war under the best possible initial circumstances—hitting Israel by surprise simultaneously from the north and the south—and yet within three weeks, the Israeli army was standing 100 kilometers from Cairo.

The whole peace initiative on the part of Sadat stemmed from a fatigue with war—a realization that it was leading nowhere and that Egypt had to find some kind of accommodation with Israel. If that's really true, then it means that (1) we weren't facing another war with Egypt, and, perhaps most important and most painful to us, (2) we could have achieved a peace treaty under much better terms.

Can you define whether the Egyptians have violated or not lived up to the Camp David Accords? Do you believe that, in the future, the Egyptians will keep that portion of the agreement which talks about demilitarization of the Sinai?

Although there is not total violation of the peace treaty between Israel and Egypt, there are very significant violations of different aspects of the treaty. There are violations of the treaty that the Egyptians claim do not represent violations. Some Egyptians say there are similar violations on the part of Israel—that there's a symmetry in terms of violations—but that's not the case.

In the demilitarization annex of the peace treaty—a very important part of the treaty for Israel and her security, the deployment of Egyptian troops in the Sinai is limited; Egypt is restricted in the number of tanks and artillery that she can maintain east of the Suez Canal. This area is called Zone A of the Sinai Peninsula, and there's been no violation of that restriction. To the best of my knowledge, the Egyptians have never exceeded the equipment they are allowed to maintain. At the present time, the Egyptians probably have fewer tanks and artillery in the area than they are permitted to have by that demilitarization annex. However, they have built an infrastructure of fortifications and facilities for armed units far larger than the treaty indicates they are allowed to maintain in the area.

According to the treaty, they are allowed to maintain one armored division in the area, yet they have built up facilities and fortifications for even more than an army-sized military establishment. In that, I see a clear violation of the treaty. Although it is true that the military annex does not deal specifically with fortifications and infrastructure, such a buildup certainly is a violation of the spirit of the treaty. In effect, it is there in order to permit the rapid introduction of large armed forces into the area. This is something that they are not allowed to do under the treaty, and we have let the Egyptians know that we see in this a violation of the treaty. The multinational force that is stationed in the Sinai has taken a somewhat ambiguous position. Although they have tried to get the Egyptians to discontinue the building of this infrastructure, they have not been ready to take an unequivocal stand by stating that it is a violation of the treaty and demanding that the Egyptians disassemble whatever they have built there.

Until very recently, the outstanding violation of the treaty was the absence of an Egyptian ambassador in Israel. This was a specific commitment that Egypt undertook in the peace treaty—that a resident ambassador would be maintained in Israel. It was over five years ago that the ambassador was recalled for "consultation." For over four years that consultation continued, without the ambassador having been returned. That was a violation of the treaty.

Under the various provisions of the treaty, we negotiated agreements with the Egyptians to establish trade relations, cultural exchanges, and tourist exchanges. The Egyptians have not implemented any of that. They committed themselves to negotiate with Israel for autonomy in Gaza, Judea, and Samaria. The Egyptians broke off these negotiations, and there haven't been any for over four years. So, there are several significant violations of the treaty by the Egyptians.

Egyptians, as a result of the Camp David Accords or the 1973 War, have gone from a Russian system—Russian arms and Russian tactics—to an all-Western system—based primarily on American weapon systems. They are building a very large military system and army—probably one of the largest in the Middle East. Who are they preparing to fight? Who is their enemy?

When asked that question by the United States, the Egyptians will generally point to Libya. Although Libya could be a danger, and Qadaffi is one of the Middle East's crazy quartet—Qadaffi, Assad, Khomeini, and Saddam Hussein—the Libyan army is no match for the Egyptian army. There is no justification at all for Egypt's continuing to expand the size of her forces if the cause for this expansion is claimed to be Libya. The Egyptian army, as it is today, or even as it was two years ago, is much more than a match for Libya. It's difficult to understand why Egypt wants to expend scarce economic resources for a continuous arms buildup when she is a country in dire economic straits.

In the absence of Libya's being a serious threat, or one that requires the expansion of Egypt's armed forces, the answer as to why this expansion is continuing could be a self-sustaining momentum—a desire by Egypt to have a large army and to be able to show that she is a military power. It may be important for internal reasons. I'm sure there is a very significant bureaucratic battle going on with people in the military continuing to demand allocation of additional resources—better, newer, and more modern equipment. Since Egypt is a totalitarian state, the military class represents a very significant pressure group and, to some extent, explains the reason why Egypt continues to allocate resources to expanding her military base.

But, we can't discount the possibility that the Egyptians are looking at a contingency—maybe some kind of a confrontation with Israel at some future date, and they feel they need a large military force for such a contingency.

Do you think that Egypt is involved in supporting terrorism against Israel?

No, I don't believe that is the case. At the present time, we need to remember that the Egyptian government and President Mubarak are maintaining cordial—maybe even more than cordial—relationships with Mr. Arafat and the PLO, a terrorist organization. But I wouldn't go so far as to say that they are supporting or encouraging the terrorist activity of that organization.

On what country do you think the Egyptian government or politicians and military will focus their attention and animosity and against whom will they prepare their defenses—Israel, Libya, or Sudan?

Sudan represents no threat of significance to Egypt. Libya could be a threat, but, again, the Egyptian army is much more than a match for the Libyan army. In that sense, if the Egyptians are thinking of contingencies and perhaps in the future being pulled into some grand Arab alliance—if not joining it—then it's difficult to conceive that the military planners in Egypt are not looking at Israel, perhaps primarily at Israel.

Do you believe the Taba issue is a pretext to Egypt's living up to certain agreements of the peace treaty, or is it a focal issue? If we can solve the Taba issue, then cultural ties between Israel and Egypt will be restored and expanded, tourism will flourish, and all the agreements of the Camp David Accords, which have to do with normalization, will be lived up to. In other words, is Taba what blocks the real peace?

We have to assume that there is some degree of rationale behind the positions that leaders of countries take. But there is no rationale whatsoever for making Taba a crucial issue in Israeli-Egyptian relationships. Taba is an area the size of ten square kilometers. To Egypt, it is nothing more than another ten square kilometers of sand and desert—over and above the entire Sinai which Israel has already turned over to her. There can be no rationale on Egypt's part for saying control or sovereignty over that ten square kilometers will make the difference between peace and war with Israel or make the difference between a normal, friendly relationship and a cold war relationship between the two countries.

That being the case, there must be something else behind that view, behind the stand that Egypt has taken on the Taba issue—playing it up as being crucial to the very relationship between Israel and Egypt, rather than down playing it as a minor affair. Therefore, I'm convinced that it is not, as sometimes claimed, the stumbling block, or the last remaining stumbling block, to real, permanent, and true peaceful relationships between Israel and Egypt. It is a pretext for keeping relationships at their present level, which is very far from the expectations of those who attended the signing of the peace treaty between the two countries, and very far from what is called for by the text of the treaty.

Given the fact that both Israel and Egypt want to contain Russia in the Middle East, do you believe that there can be some limited political military strategic alliance with Egypt?

There could be, but there isn't at the present time. And it really doesn't seem very likely because Egypt, just as some other countries that are Western-oriented, looks to others for blocking the Soviet Union. She doesn't feel that she should assume any great obligations or accept any particular penalties in order to do that. If the United States and Israel are determined to block Soviet penetration, why should Egypt have to pay any kind of price for joining that kind of entente? Clearly, Egypt doesn't want to, and she doesn't.

Do you see economic ties or trade with Egypt expanding in the future based on Egypt's need for Israel's agricultural expertise?

Egypt can use that expertise very badly, but over eight years have gone by since the Israeli-Egyptian peace treaty was signed, and Egypt has not made use of that expertise. Clearly, the system of incentives as viewed from Cairo is such that the disadvantages of using that expertise outweigh the advantages.

Martial law has been maintained in Egypt since the assassination of Sadat by Sunni Fundamentalist Moslems. There have been rumors of a number of threats on the life of Mubarak by Sunni Fundamentalists. There have been fundamentalist riots in Egypt; universities have been closed; and there has been a call for Sharia law by large sections of the population. Do you believe that the Egyptian government is under a real viable threat to become a Sunni Fundamentalist state?

Egypt is a country that has the seeds of great instability. It starts from the squalid economic situation that Egypt is in—the country is in a terrible state of poverty. The GNP per-capita in Egypt is about $500 or $600 a year. She is overpopulated and has tremendous social and urban problems. One just has to visit Cairo to see the magnitude of the problems that Egypt faces. In many ways, she's a country just barely holding her head above water.

There's no doubt that there's such a tremendous reservoir of discontent and bitterness among the population with their lot that anything can happen at any time. The discontent and opposition in Egypt has traditionally taken two paths: (1) the path of Moslem Fundamentalists, who feel the answer lies in turning Egypt into a Moslem republic governed by Moslem law, and (2) the path of radical leftist organizations. The threat to the present regime comes from either of them, or conceivably even from both of them, because those factions can walk together as they have done in other Arab countries on occasion.

Given the real threat to Sudan, which is of vital interest to Egypt, and the ongoing animosity with Libya, do you believe that it's in the best interest of Egypt to maintain secure and quiet borders with Israel and that Egypt will understand that it is in her best interest to maintain these secure and quiet borders?

I'm convinced that it's in Egypt's interest to have a quiet and friendly border with Israel, regardless of any other considerations. What possible interests could Egypt have in maintaining belligerency on her border with Israel? What possible interest could Egypt have in a war with Israel, given that Israel has proven she is perfectly capable of defending herself and defeating the Egyptian army, or defeating the combined Arab armies, if it came to that? As we have seen, Egyptian leaders, like Nasser and Sadat, who engineered the Yom Kippur War, have worked against the best interests of Egypt, which totalitarian rulers do time and again.

Do you believe that the vast amount of American financial and military aid to Egypt will serve as a brake on any future attempt by her even to "coll off" relations with Israel?

I wish it were true, but I don't think so. The United States could use that leverage and should signal to Egypt that violating the terms of the peace treaty with Israel will prejudice relationships with the United States as well as the scope of U.S. aid to Egypt. That may halt the slide in Israeli-Egyptian relationships, but the buildup of Egyptian armed forces harbors the potential for belligerence and hostility in the area.

Egypt could be dragged into another war by other Arab countries simply because she has such a large armed force—simply because the argument that would be advanced is that her force is large enough to make the difference; therefore, she should join another attack on Israel. It's difficult for me to see anything good coming from increasing the very large military establishment that Egypt already has.

Syria

Syria is a country run by an Alawii minority, in concert with Christians and Druse, against a majority of Sunni Moslems. Do you believe that the present power structure can survive in the long run? If there is a change, how will it effect Syria's relationship with Israel?

Generally, totalitarian governments will not survive in the long run, but the short run can be very long, as we see in the Soviet Union or even in the case of Assad in Syria, who has been in power since 1970. In the long run, I see these dictatorial regimes as anachronistic—running against the tide of modern times; eventually, they will be replaced by Western-type democracies.

Given the massive military buildup of modern Russian weapon systems since the Syrian-Israeli confrontation in Lebanon several years ago, when do you think the Assad regime will feel that there is a strategic military balance between Syria and Israel?

It cannot be expressed only in dimensions of numbers or quality of weaponry. Assad certainly has a very large army under his control at the present time. He has 1/2 million men under arms, 4,000 tanks, 600 fighter aircraft, and a very advanced array of surface-to-air missle systems. It's clear that he wants more and feels he needs more. The important thing here is that strategic parity is just a word that he's using. He's looking to create the kind of conditions that will permit him to go to war against Israel. The very fact that he's not at war with Israel right now means that he doesn't feel he's arrived at that situation as yet.

The other part of the equation that I'm sure he's weighing is the Israeli capability. If he sees Israel cutting her defense budget, he may feel things are moving in his favor and figure that that's the equivalent of additional arms he might be obtaining. I doubt anyone can say when he'll feel he's had enough or when he'll be in a position to go to war. It includes other elements. Does he feel he can hit Israel by surprise? Does he feel he can repeat another Yom Kippur War, where Israel will suffer the disadvantages of being hit first? On our end, we will, of course, do everything possible to make sure he will never enjoy that advantage again.

When this military balance is achieved in the perception of Assad, do you believe it will trigger war against Israel?

Yes. Assad has demonstrated time and again that he has no hesitations about the use of violence and about going to war. Clearly, therefore, his only calculation is whether he will achieve his political objectives. He's not concerned about the cost in Syrian lives and certainly not in Israeli lives. He has one consideration only—will he achieve his objectives? And that, by the way, is almost totally analogous to the thinking of Saddam Hussein, the dictator of Iraq, who started his war against Iran based on a simple calculation—which turned out to be a miscalculation—that he had the military capability to achieve his objectives. To him, the costs were really of no consequence. He had no hesitations or reticence about using violence.

What will Israel's response be if Syria were to invade Jordan militarily?

Israel would not permit so drastic a change in the strategic situation as would be involved by Syrian occupation of Jordan or by the stationing of Syrian troops on the Jordan River. That is something that we would not agree to, and clearly, therefore, it is something that we would not allow to happen.

On the other hand, what would Israel's response be if Syria were to undermine successfully the Hussein regime, assassinate the king, bring down the government, and replace it with a government that is sympathetic to and aligned with Syria?

We can have a Jordanian government sympathetic and aligned to Syria even without Syrian subversion. Jordan joined the Six-Day War in 1967, together with Egypt and Syria. King Hussein could make up with Syria tomorrow and create a Jordanian-Syrian alliance. We don't have control and don't insist on control of the internal affairs of Jordan, although we may be more favorably disposed toward a particular development. Such an alliance is one thing, but the stationing of Syrian troops in Jordan is another.

What will Israel's response be if Syria were really to take over control of Lebanon—totally occupy her and control the government?

Again, the dominant issue for Israel would be the deployment of Syrian troops. We will not permit the movement of Syrian troops southward toward the Israeli border. We would not stand for a situation in which we would find the Syrian army deployed on Israel's northern border, and the Syrians know that.

Do you believe there is any possibility, as long as an Alawite regime is in power, for Israel and Syria to have some sort of settlement over some basic issues? If the Alawite regime is replaced by a Sunni regime, do you believe, in the longer term, it is possible for peace or some sort of settlement with Syria, like the settlement that was achieved with Egypt?

It doesn't have anything to do with whether the regime is controlled by Alawis, Sunni, Christians, or Druse. If anything, the minority population in Syria, like the Alawis, might even feel a need under certain circumstances to cooperate with other minorities in a region like Israel. We've heard that tune as well from some Alawis. A basic change will come in Syria's attitude toward Israel when the regime in Syria changes—when Syria moves from totalitarianism toward democracy, with all of the constraints that that implies about the use of weapons and war.

Jordan

How long do you think the Hussein regime can survive? How long do you think he can personally survive? How long can his kingdom survive? How long before the Palestinians actually take over the country and make it a Palestinian state?

Jordan is a Palestinian state in the sense that its entire population is Palestinian. Some people in the West tend to apply the terminology of nineteenth and twentieth century European nation-states to the Middle East, and, generally, that is a misapplication. The countries in the Middle East are there as a result of lines drawn on a map by Mr. Sykes and Messieur Picot toward the end of World War I, when the British and French, between them, divided the Middle East. That's when the borders of Palestine were drawn.

All of the residents of Jordan are the people—or descendents of the people— who lived within the borders of Palestine as they were drawn then. It was at that time, also, that the borders of other countries in the Middle East were drawn, like Lebanon, Syria, and Iraq. There's no clear answer to the question of whether there is a Saudi nation or not. There certainly was no Saudi nation before World War I. Thirty years ago, many people would have replied positively to the question as to whether there is a Lebanese nation. But when the question is asked today, most people are somewhat perplexed and say there is no such thing as a Lebanese nation. They look at what's going on within the borders of the country that's called Lebanon and see that there is no national cohesion at all.

Of course, there is no Palestinian nation in the sense that there's a French nation or an Italian nation. But, to the extent to which some degree of national cohesion connects people who lived—or the descendents of those who lived—within the mandated territory of Palestine as it was defined after World War I, all of the people living in Jordan, which represents 75 percent of the mandated territory of Palestine, are Palestinians.

There are those who insist on differentiating between East Palestinians—Palestinians from the east bank of the Jordan, which is Jordan, and West Palestinians—Palestinians from the west bank of Jordan, which is Gaza, Judea, Samaria, and the State of Israel proper. To them, we point out that today, 60 percent of Jordan's population originally came from the west bank or are descendents of people who came from the west bank. So, it's a Palestinian state and that can be said without any qualifications.

The fact that King Hussein and his family are not Palestinians—not the descendents of people who lived in the mandated territory of Palestine—should really come as no surprise. Hussein is one of the last absolute monarchs left in the world, and absolute monarchs, by tradition, were imported from other countries or from other royal families. His family, the Hashemite family, wasn't really royal; they were imported by the British from what is today Saudi Arabia. His grandfather, Abdullah, was enthroned first as the Emir and, finally, as the King of Jordan, and the country was established by Great Britain in a betrayal of the trust that was given to her by the League of Nations. Jordan (or Transjordan) was supposed to be an integral part of the territory in which a Jewish state was going to be established.

If there were to be free and democratic elections in Jordan, and King Hussein were to drop his title and run for the prime ministership, he might not be elected. It may be that if Mr. Arafat or one of the other people from the PLO ran against him, the PLO would be elected. Nobody knows just how popular a man like Hussein is today, because he runs Jordan in an absolute and autocratic manner.

How long will Jordan continue to be an absolute monarchy? As I said, Hussein is one of the last absolute monarchs left in the world. Saudi Arabia is still an absolute monarchy, but I don't know of any other place in the world, except for some of the African countries, where we can still find absolute monarchs. They are on the way out, so it's just a question of time.

It's true that Hussein has been on the throne of Jordan ever since the assassination of his grandfather, or shortly thereafter—probably thirty-five years now—which is a good length of time. Considering his grandfather was assassinated, many people thought it was only a question of time before he, too, would be assassinated. I'm sure he's on the "hit list." He came very close to being overthrown and even assassinated in September of 1970, in "Black September," when the PLO tried to take over Jordan. There is no reason to believe that 100 years from now Jordan will still be an absolute kingdom ruled by one of King Hussein's descendents. He's on his way out, but no one can tell how long it will take.

Do you believe there can be peace with Jordan without territorial compromise? If so, what kind of peace will it be? Does it pay to make peace with Jordan believing that the regime and kingdom of Hussein is being threatened and is in a long-term state of instability?

First of all, there is peace with Jordan. It's not a formal peace, and we don't have an exchange of diplomats, but the Israeli-Jordanian border is quiet and has been quiet now for over fifteen years. Although formally Jordan insists she is in a state of war with Israel, in actuality there is no war between Israel and Jordan. There is certainly no immediate danger of such a war breaking out.

If a danger like that exists, it exists only because Jordan might be pulled into the vortex of a grand Arab coalition that might be formed in order to attack Israel again. But if that were to happen, it would happen even if Jordan had signed a peace treaty with Israel. That's the danger that exists in the Arab world as long as it maintains its present configuration. That's the danger that exists even in Egypt, which has signed a peace treaty with Israel. We can't rule out the possibility that she might get pulled into another war that perhaps Syria would initiate against Israel.

That is not to say that we in Israel are not interested in signing a peace treaty with Jordan and establishing formal relations between our two countries. Certainly, there is a limit—and a relatively low limit—to the price we are ready to pay for that, because the actual change in the situation wouldn't be radical. I'm not of the opinion that we should be ready to make any territorial concessions in such negotiations. That would be counterproductive and make Israel weaker. It might serve as an invitation to hostility—to war and the dragging of Jordan into an Arab coalition that would fight against Israel thereafter. If the time comes when Jordan is ready to sign a formal peace treaty with Israel that doesn't involve territorial concessions—I don't believe that territories are or should be the major dimension in the relationships between countries—King Hussein will find Israel happy and eager to sign an agreement.

Given the kind of relations that really exist between Jordan and Israel— one where the border for commerce and goods is open and money is flowing back and forth to the Jordanian citizens in Judea and Samaria, what would the value of a formal peace treaty with Jordan be?

It's value would be similar to the value in raising the level of diplomatic representation with a country. If we have diplomatic representation with a country at the level of minister or councilor, we would like to see it improve to the level of ambassador. We would like to have full diplomatic relations, because it means that the channels of communication are just that much more open and the chances for improving our relationship that much better. If an improved relationship involves friendship, trade, cultural exchange, and economic cooperation—and there's really no reason why not, then a formal peace treaty will be an important step in that direction. In that sense, of course, Israel will be eager to arrive at a peace treaty with Jordan.

If by some internal means, the Palestinians take over the Hashemite kingdom of Jordan, remove the Bedouins from the power structure, and actually control the country, do you believe there could be peace?

There is no inherent reason why any Arab country cannot sign a peace treaty with Israel. Basically, there is no difference between the difficulties that were involved in signing the Israeli-Egyptian peace treaty and the difficulties that would be involved in a peace treaty with Syria or Jordan.

In the final analysis, it would depend on the rulers of the countries involved. We don't have a peace treaty with Syria—and it doesn't look like it's anywhere in the foreseeable future—because Assad doesn't want a peace treaty. He says it quite openly. If the leadership of Jordan, whether it's King Hussein today or somebody else tomorrow, wants a peace treaty, then it's possible to have a peace treaty.

Given the fact that Jordan is aligned with the United States and the West, do you believe the United States should be a major arms supplier of Jordan, modernizing her air defense systems and air force, and maintaining her at a high level of air force and air defense readiness?

Selling advanced weaponry to any of the Arab countries is a destabilizing function in the area. This is most certainly the case with countries like Jordan that insist they are in a state of war with Israel. The likelihood that this weaponry would be used against Israel is far higher than the likelihood that it might be used in some positive manner in terms of Western interests, e.g., in the defense of the Middle East against Soviet penetration.

This is not theory; it's been done before. The United States sold tanks to Jordan in the early sixties on the provision that those tanks would never cross the Jordan River. Despite the commitment that King Hussein undertook at the time the tanks were purchased, those American-supplied tanks crossed the Jordan River and were used in the Six-Day War in 1967 against Israel.

Additionally, the sale of advanced weaponry to Jordan means an immediate economic burden for Israel. It means we will have to make additional acquisitions of weaponry in order to balance those sales. It definitely increases the danger of war in the area. That's not good for Israel, and it's not good for U.S. interests, at least as I perceive them.

In the basic charter that was written by the British in the establishment of Transjordan back in 1923, it was stated that no Jew was allowed to settle, do commerce, reside, or own property in Transjordan. The modern kingdom of Jordan has kept that in her constitution and, as of today, Jordan is more Judenrein than Hilter had ever perceived Judenrein. Can Israel enter a peace arrangement with a country that has such discriminatory laws? Do you believe that in any settlement with Jordan, Israel must take a position that demands that Jordan change in its constitution that no Jew be allowed to make commerce or own land in Jordan?

Jordan is not the only Arab country that has discriminatory regulations against Jews. It is true for many, if not most, Arab countries. The very extreme discrimination that exists in Jordan, which provides the death penalty for any person who sells land to a Jew, of course, is obscene and revolting. It's difficult to reconcile the continuation of that kind of discrimination with peace between Israel and Jordan. If and when negotiations get started, Israel will certainly raise these issues and seek the removal of such discriminatory laws.

After the initial revolution in Lebanon in 1976, as the process of deterioration of the state of Lebanon came about, the financial center for the Arab world shifted from Lebanon over to Jordan and Aman. They became the financial centers for the Arab world especially because of the huge amounts of money that were accumulated due to the wealth of oil surplus. Now that these countries are becoming negative-balance-of-payment countries, what do you foresee happening to Aman as a financial center of the Arab world? As Jordan becomes more threatened by Syria, do you believe that the Arab money will flee and look for another Arab center?

Beirut, which had many attributes for the position of financial center for the Arab world, of course, has ceased to be such because of the anarchic conditions that prevail in Lebanon. I really don't know enough about Arab economics to be able to say whether or not Aman is a good location for Arab money. I wouldn't venture to make any suggestions to Arab financiers or Arab millionaires as to where they should put their money. My guess is that today a good part of Arab money is in the Western world because that's probably the safest place to put it. The trend will probably continue in that direction.

Lebanon

As the Lebanon situation unfolds, it is obvious (as of now) that Syria's influence in Lebanese internal affairs is fairly limited. What do you foresee as the outcome in the next few years—a Lebanon controlled by a Shiite majority or a Lebanon controlled by the Syrians? Who will the Christians be aligned with? Who will the Sunni Moslems be aligned with? Who will the Druse be aligned with?

We have all learned that forecasting future events in Lebanon is a very uncertain game. I don't presume to be in a position where I can foretell what Lebanon's future is going to be. Unfortunately, it sure looks like it's going to be more of the same—a continuation of that terrible tragedy that's taking a daily toll of tens of lives and driving a good part of the population living in Lebanon out of the country to seek refuge in other parts of the world.

There doesn't seem to be such a thing as a Lebanese nation—there doesn't seem to be that kind of cohesiveness among the various religious and ethnic groups. The Lebanese government is not capable of exercising jurisdiction in Lebanon, and she continues to be in a total state of anarchy. The power centers in Lebanon are not in the central government but rather in the various militias that are organized on ethnic or religious lines. Even there, in many of the cases, each ethnic or religious group does not necessarily have a single militia that represents its interests; rather, there frequently are a number of militias that vie for leadership of the ethnic community. It's difficult to see any kind of accommodation among the Christians, the Druse, the Shia, and the Sunni.

Today, approximately one-half of Lebanon is parceled up and under the control of one or the other of the militias. The Druse control the mountainous area—the Shouf, including the coastal area that borders on the Shouf. The Christians control the area north of Beirut around Juniyah. The Shia control a good part of Southern Lebanon. The Southern Lebanese Army (SLA), under General Lahad's leadership and with Israel's support, controls that part of Southern Lebanon that borders on Israel.

It's difficult to see that any of that will change radically in future years. The different ethnic groups and militias will seek help from almost any quarter. I don't think many of them have any particular ideological affinity or commitment to anybody else. In most cases, they see themselves as fighting for their lives and their existence, and they are ready to make deals with whomever it seems profitable at the moment.

Just what kind of Lebanon do you foresee—a cantonized nation with

many different little areas and different armies or a strong central govern-
ment? If it is a Lebanon that is a series of cantonized states, what will
Israel's relations be? What will be the economic, political, and military
alignments? On the other hand, if it is a strong central government,
organized as any other nation in the world, what will its relationship with
Israel be?

In the normal sense of the word, Lebanon doesn't exist as a state at the present time; it hasn't for the past fifteen years or so. It's a non-state, and it's not at all clear that in the foreseeable future it will become a state again, in the normal sense of the word. We certainly don't see the foundations or the beginnings of it. We don't see the cohesion that it would require among the different religious and ethnic groups. We don't see the central government's achieving the degree of authority that this would require. We don't see any movement in that direction at all. That's why, within the risk of prediction, it's going to be more of the same in the future.

It will continue with different militias exercising control over different parts of Lebanon and continuing to fight each other. Many people—surely everyone in Lebanon —are searching for a way to put an end to that constant slaughter. At the present time, there is no end in sight. We can't usefully discuss the relationships between Israel and Lebanon as we see her today; unfortunately, it seems that it's going to continue that way tomorrow.

Israel has good relationships with the population in the part of Southern Lebanon that's under control of the SLA, led by General Lahad. There is commonality of interests in many ways. That's probably the quietest and safest area of Lebanon, but, again, it's not as quiet and safe as we would like and that we consider to be a norm in any civilized country.

Iraq

Is it in Israel's best interest to see Iran defeat Iraq to the point where a
Shiite government sits in Baghdad as a result of the defeat? If not, and if
it seemed that Iraq would need some sort of assistance from Israel—
material, not men—would Israel in any way assist Iraq, given the history
of Saddam Hussein and Iraq's animosity towards Israel?

It's not in Israel's interest—nor do I believe it's in the interest of the Western world—that either Iraq or Iran become victors in that conflict. I don't think there's much of a danger of that. Neither of these countries has the military capability to defeat totally her opponent. There's no doubt, however, given the character of Khomeini in Iran or Saddam Hussein in Iraq—both ruthless dictators, each in his own way—that if one of them were to be victorious, he would shortly thereafter begin to direct his attention to other targets and other objectives. Israel would very likely be one of them but not the only one.

During the first few months of the war, when it looked like the Iraqis might be winning, the entire Persian Gulf began to tremble because they realized they were going to be next on Saddam Hussein's "hit list." In recent months, following Iranian victories, again the shock waves could be seen going through the Persian Gulf countries like Kuwait and Saudi Arabia, in fear that they were going to be next on the list.

Earlier you mentioned Iraqi terrorist activity. Where are they active?

Iraqi terrorist activity, in recent years, has been directed primarily against other Arabs and other Arab countries like Syria. In many cases, it has been against members of Arab terrorist organizations but only those that are opposed by the Iraqi government. And, of course, there has been terrorism directed against Israelis that was supported, or is supported, by the Iraqis. The most notable case was the murder of the Israeli ambassador, Sholmo Argov, in London. That was carried out by the Abu Nidal faction, and that faction—certainly at that time— was supported by Iraq.

In the long run, do you believe a Sunni government in Iraq can survive a situation where the majority population of Shiites and a large minority of Kurds are in opposition to the state? In the long term, could such a government survive?

In the long term, countries in the Middle East will inevitably become democratic, pluralistic societies. If we take a giant step and ask ourselves what will Iraq look like a hundred years from now, we can see that it's not going to be a Sunni government, and it's not going to be a Shiite government. If Iraq continues to exist, it will be an Iraqi government that will be representative of the different nationalities, ethnic groups, and religious groups that live in Iraq. And that goes for other Arab countries, as well. A hundred years from now, the government of Syria is not going to be an Alawite government, a Druse government, or a government that is identified solely with a particular religious community. It will be a government that is representative of the people who live in the country. Given the very slow current rate of progress in that direction—in effect, a zero rate—in most Arab countries, the next decade is probably going to be more of the same.

If a Shiite government comes to power in Iraq, would Jordan and Israel join forces against the regime in Iraq in some political, economic, or military way?

First of all, the likelihood of that happening is very small. The Shiite population of Iraq—which Khomeini for a while thought he was going to be able to mobilize in his favor—doesn't seem to have come out against the Iraqi government or even against the Iraqi war effort. To my knowledge, there are no known cases of sabotage by Shiite underground members directed against the present Iraqi government. Although I don't consider myself to be an expert on Iraq, I don't know of any Middle Eastern observer or people who know Iraq well who foresee at all the possibility of a Shiite takeover in Iraq.

Saddam Hussein may be pushed from power. Iraq has had a succession of coups d'etat and a succession of assassinations. He is a totalitarian dictator, and he is said to have murdered a number of people in Iraq with his own hands, including generals and others in leading positions. I'm sure that there are lots of people in Iraq who would like to put him out of the way, and that quite possibly will happen, but those people who want to do that are not necessarily Shiites.

Even though it's a remote possibility, there is a chance that Iran could topple the Iraqi government, control defense in Iraq, and be Iraqi-Shiite dominated. If that were to happen, however remote, what effect do you think it would have on the integrity of the Gulf States and Saudi Arabia, and what kind of response do you think would come from the United States?

It's very unlikely that it would happen. As I've said before, the victory of either party in this crazy conflict—Iraq or Iran—would be a source of very great concern to the countries of the Persian Gulf. Whether it's Iraq or Iran that would win, she would direct her attention and her ambitions to the Persian Gulf.

Saudi Arabia

A few years ago, the Islamic Fundamentalists in Saudi Arabia had control of the mosque and almost brought down the Saudi regime. There have been many reports that there have been a number of attempts of revolt in Saudi Arabia and a possible takeover of the country. In the long term or medium term, how viable is this regime run by princes and kings?

Saudi Arabia is a medieval state, and, clearly, in the long run, it will not continue to exist in its present form. It is completely out of tune with the times—it's an anachronism on the map of the world today. But, here again, whereas with confidence we can state that in the long run it cannot continue to exist in its present form, nobody can tell how long it will last—one more day, one more year, or ten more years.

If such a system in which a few thousand men control the whole country is not viable and can't survive in the long run, then what are the alternatives within Saudi Arabia, given that it isn't a democratic system, has never developed a strong middle class, has never had a political party system, and has never had any other power centers other than military?

I've never been to Saudi Arabia, but there is no question in my mind that over the past few decades, there's been a movement toward westernization there. Even if not directed by the government, it's a movement that came about quite naturally, considering the large degree of Western influence, the very large amounts of money that flowed into the country, and the number of Saudis who have studied abroad.

Eventually, even that part of the world, with its oil and with its sand, will be run more or less on the Western model. What does that mean? It means people being elected to office. Sooner or later it will come to Saudi Arabia, as well; whether it's going to take five years or fifty years, I don't think anybody knows.

After the Yom Kippur War and the rise in oil prices, Saudi Arabia became a center of power in the Middle East for American foreign policy. Saudi Arabia used her influence in Washington to undermine Israel and those things that were important to Israel. Does Saudi Arabia have the same power in Washington today that she did then? Since that time, even though oil prices and her oil income are down, Saudi Arabia has invested large amounts of money in the United States and has accumulated lots of good will from the people she has hired. Will this have a long-term effect?

Saudi Arabia is a country which still commands considerable income—although it is rapidly declining with the decline in the price of oil. She has very large financial assets as well as very significant investments in the Western world, particularly the United States. She represents a very sizable market for U.S. manufacturers and that, of course, gives her a great deal of leverage and influence.

There is a correlation between the price of oil and the influence that Saudi Arabia has. Her influence grew with the rise in the price of oil. She has been looked upon as a country of great importance in recent years by people in Washington and by the government of the United States, directly as a result of her enrichment. As the price of oil falls, some of that will diminish. Saudi Arabia will continue to be an economic power for many years to come and will, therefore, maintain the influence that goes with that kind of power.

Is the buildup in military power in Saudi Arabia a military threat to the State of Israel?

Eventually, of course, it could be a military threat. The Saudi Arabians have a vast armory of very high quality weapons—the best that the United States and Western Europe have to offer. Today, the Saudi Arabian air force has ninety F15 aircraft. There is probably not another air force in the world, next to the U.S. Air Force, that has that number of F15s, one of the finest airplanes in existence. They have not only the F15s but also have now acquired Tornado aircraft from Western Europe.

Some people say the Saudis won't be able to use their weapons, and I hope that's true, but there's no way of being sure. If you have money, you can buy not only equipment but also people who can use and maintain that equipment. Saudi Arabia has money, and in all likelihood can buy people to fly and maintain her aircraft. Therefore, we certainly can't discount the possibility that this high-quality equipment which exists in Saudi Arabia in very significant quantities could be used against Israel.

In every major Arab war with Israel, the Saudi Arabians contributed through involvement of troops. In each case, Israel did not respond directly against Saudi Arabia—just against the troops. In the future, do you foresee a war in which Israel would strike out and punish Saudi Arabia if she involved her troops on a local level?

It would depend on the circumstances, and there would be no sense in signaling Arab countries or saying ahead of time exactly what we would do. If Saudi Arabia becomes a belligerent in a war against Israel, there's no question that she will take upon herself all the risks that this entails.

The American public is constantly being told that the PLO represents the Palestinian people and has the support of all the Arab countries. Does Saudi Arabia support the PLO because it believes in its cause or because the princes themselves are personally intimidated and afraid for their lives?

Primarily, Saudi support for the PLO and for PLO terrorism —and the Saudis are the major source of financial support for the PLO and its terrorism—is in the realm of protection money. As rich as they are, the Saudis are afraid of their own shadows, and they are particularly afraid of the PLO, a terrorist organization that could reach out and hit Saudi princes and the Saudi royal family in the centers of power in Saudi Arabia. There is no question in my mind that, in return for very large financial contributions, the Saudis are getting a commitment from the PLO that they will leave the Saudi ruling class untouched.

Libya

Due to Libya's support of all radical forces in the Middle East against Israel, do you foresee a time when Israel will feel justified to strike at Libya directly to destroy her support of these radical forces?

Again, if Libya takes an active, belligerent position against Israel, she cannot expect to retain any kind of immunity. Israel has shown in the past that we are ready to do and will do whatever we feel is necessary to protect ourselves and to assure our security. That will continue to be our policy in future years, as well.

Libya and Egypt have been natural enemies since Sadat. Libya has intimidated and intended to undermine the Sadat and Mubarak regimes. Do you foresee a time when Egypt and Israel may coordinate in some way to destroy the Libyan regime?

It's really not part of the norms of the Western world in this day and age for countries to go out and destroy other regimes. That has not been—and I don't really foresee in the future that it would be—an objective of Israeli policy. Israel does not get herself involved in the internal politics of another country, whether near to or distant from Israel, in an attempt to destroy that regime. Israel will continue to defend herself and continue to protect her interests. In the final analysis, the nature of the regimes in any of the Arab countries will be determined by the people who live in those countries.

What effect do you think the American raid against Libya has had and will have on terrorism against Israel?

It will serve to decrease the level and scope of terrorist activity. Primarily, it serves as a warning to countries that have supported terrorism in the past—particularly, in this case, Libya, where terrorist bases were hit. Syria, also, has realized that she might very well be the next target. If that turns out to be the case, then, of course, it's going to have an even greater effect on decreasing terrorist activity against Israel, since some of the terrorist activity against Israel was supported by the Libyans and, much of it, by the Syrians.

We must be careful not to assume that the American raid —important as it was—is going to put an end to terrorism. But if it turns out to be that that is an indication of a consistent policy to be followed by Western countries, then, in time, it will lead to the suppression of terrorism throughout the world.

Do you foresee Libya becoming more Western-oriented after Qadaffi's regime?

Libya has been in the throes of "Mad Dog Qadaffi"—as Ronald Reagan called him—for a number of years. The fact that a country can be ruled by such an eccentric and irrational personality and the fact that Qadaffi can engender the kind of enthusiasm that he engenders among the Libyan population are indications of the state of Libyan society. It's very difficult to be optimistic about Libya's becoming a modern democratic Western country after Qadaffi goes. We would like to see that come about, but it's not really to be expected in the near future.

Morocco

Morocco is the only Arab country, other than Egypt, that allows Israeli tourists. She has shown many signs of receptivity to some sort of political overtures (clandestine anyway) with Israel. Do you believe that these relations can develop in the future? Do you believe that Morocco will be the place in which an expansion of peace between Israel and her Arab neighbors will take place? Remember, of course, that there is a very large Moroccan-Jewish population here who are able to go back and forth to Morocco as tourists.

Morocco is another case where there is an absolute monarchy—Hassan, and absolute monarchs tend to do what they consider to be good for themselves. Any questions that may surround the policies followed by the King of Morocco are answered by considering them from his vantage point and realizing that he doesn't want to take any risks upon himself. Morocco, formally, is also a country that is in a state of war with Israel, and, from King Hassan's vantage point, he has no particular incentive to make peace with Israel.

Also, he probably feels he would be taking certain risks upon himself if he were to negotiate a treaty with Israel or if he were to take an active role in Middle East politicking. So, we see that he's not taking an active role in Middle East politicking—he's trying to stay away. And he's adopting the standard extremist Arab positions. Whether he believes in them personally or not is questionable; clearly, he considers that to be healthy for himself and for his regime.

How significant was the Ifrane Summit meeting between King Hassan and Shimon Peres? Will it have a long-term impact on peace in the Middle East?

Any time an Arab leader meets with an Israeli leader, it is a step forward in the peace process. This was only the third time since the establishment of the State of Israel that an Arab leader met publicly with an Israeli prime minister. It was a significant move on the part of Hassan, but it is difficult to tell now what effect it will have on peace in this area in the future.

Algeria and Tunisia

Of all the Arab states, except for Syria and Libya, Algeria is the most radical and the most anti-Israel. Can you explain why it is, and why it's different from Tunisia and Morocco?

First of all, add Iraq to Libya and Syria when you talk about fanatic anti-Israel Arab states. Why do the Algerians take that position? It probably goes together with the fact that the Algerian regime is a radical Marxist regime. Leftist radical movements throughout the Middle East—not only in Algeria but also in Syria, Iraq, and Egypt in the past—have generally taken an anti-Israel line. It all goes together—Marxism, pro-Soviet position, and an anti-Israel position.

Do you foresee a major conflict between Algeria and Morocco or Algeria and Tunisia on issues, such as a sub-Sahara and future control over Tunisia, which could have an affect on Israel?

The Arab world is a very unstable and volatile world with a long tradition of intolerance, fanaticism, and brutality; therefore, hostility between Arab countries is the norm rather than the exception. Belligerency and the breakout of fighting between Arab countries is something we see frequently in the Middle East. In the area that you're referring to, there has been continuous fighting. It's the former area of Spanish Morocco, where the Polisario have been fighting the Moroccans for close to twenty years. The Algerians are obviously involved in that fighting on the side of the Polisario or at least in their support.

There has been hostility at various times between Algeria and Tunisia and between Tunisia and Libya. It would not be totally improbable that we will see a renewal or an intensification of hostilities between these countries. How would that effect Israel? The countries are rather far removed from here, and there shouldn't be any direct effect on Israel. But they are still close enough—and this world is small enough—that when fighting breaks out anywhere, it could conceivably effect Israel.

The President of Tunisia, Bourguiba, who has been in power for thirty or forty years, is dying. What do you see as the future for Tunisia should the equivalent monarchy fall? Will she remain a moderate Arab state or will the influence of Libya radicalize her?

Although I've been to Tunisia and traveled through the country extensively in 1948, I'm not an expert on Tunisia today. I don't know enough about the current internal politics in Tunisia to be able to make what I'd call an accurate prediction as to what will happen after Bourguiba leaves. From a distance, however, I would expect that there is a significant difference between Tunisia and Libya in the sense that Tunisia has had a stable and reasonably moderate government for a number of years. I assume that's a reflection of the state of Tunisian society, although knowing the Arab world, it's not to be discounted that there could be a deterioration after Bourguiba leaves. If that should happen, some Marxist radical or Moslem Fundamentalist group could come into power.

Yemen

North Yemen is a moderate Arab state similar in policies towards Israel and the West to those of Saudi Arabia and the Gulf States. South Yemen is the only truly Marxist Arab country and radical in her attitude towards Israel similar to Algeria, Iraq, Libya, and Syria. Do you foresee South and North Yemen continuing as viable independent states, or is a takeover inevitable by one or the other? There's been a war there recently.

First of all, North Yemen and Saudi Arabia are not moderate Arab states. They are Arab countries that have extremely hostile, fanatical, anti-Israel positions. The exact state of affairs in Yemen today is not really known to anyone, except the people in Yemen. They've had Marxist radicals there who are in power, out of power, or somewhere in between, and, at the present time, no one really knows just what the situation is.

The hostility between South Yemen and North Yemen is characteristic of what occurs in the Arab world. Can these two countries continue to exist as independent states? The only observation that might be worthwhile making is that international boundaries seem to have very considerable life spans.

Since the end of World War II, we can think of very few cases where countries have ceased to exist—somehow they succeed in perpetuating themselves. Even a noncountry like Lebanon still continues to exist in its own peculiar way. In the Middle East and in the Arab world—with all the hostilities, all of the countries that existed or came into existence at the end of World War II continue to exist to this very day. My projection is that it will continue to be the case with North Yemen and South Yemen.

South Yemen is strategically situated at the mouth of the Bab el Mandeb Straits. Israel went to war when Egypt sealed the Straits of Tiran. Do you foresee South Yemen trying to seal off the Bab el Mandeb Straits from Israeli entrance to the Red Sea and the Port of Elat? What would Israel do in such a case?

It's theoretically possible considering the geography, but it's not very likely. The South Yemenis know that Israel would not stand for it and that she would use the means at her disposal to break that kind of blockade or to make life very uncomfortable for anyone who tried to impose such a blockade. There are other countries that use the Bab el Mandeb Straits—first and foremost being Egypt—so a blockade would influence them as well.

Sudan, Oman, Kuwait, and the Arab Gulf States

There has been an ongoing revolution within the Arab-dominated Sudan with the Blacks that occupy the south trying to secede from the Arabs of the North. Given Egypt's view of Sudan and the Nile River, what do you think Egypt might do if the Blacks were to succeed in establishing independence in the south? In what way would this affect Israel?

During the last six months—since Gaafar al-Nimeiry was removed from power in Sudan, the Egyptians have been losing their influence in Sudan. I doubt they have the capability of doing anything, regardless of what happens at the southern end of Sudan, which is over 1,000 miles from Cairo. I doubt anyone knows what's going to happen there. The Black population in southern Sudan has been in a state of discontent for many years, and, during some of those years, they were in a state of active revolt. As yet, it has not produced any definitive results nor a separation of the Black areas of Sudan from Sudan, and I don't believe that's likely in the near future.

Oman, Kuwait, and the Arab Gulf States are all sparsely populated countries with huge oil reserves and a huge drop in income from what they've enjoyed for the past twelve years. These low-population countries have no military establishment to speak of. How do you think these countries will be internally effected by the great drop in income?

These are very rich countries that have among the highest GNPs per capita in the world. They should have very significant reserves, and, if they've managed their finances at all reasonably, should be able to ride out a wave of low oil prices over the next few years. If they have squandered their resources and not managed their finances wisely, they will have trouble riding out that kind of a period. If they do, it can lead to all kinds of instability in these areas—which are not stable to begin with.

Do you foresee Shiite revolution occurring in places like Bahrain and Kuwait, which have high percentages of Shiites within their populations, giving rise to the collapse of their existing monarchies?

We see the very dynamic behavior of the Shiite population in Lebanon, which in large measure is engineered and manipulated from Teheran, Iran. There is a real process of reawakening among the Shiite population in Lebanon, which is of direct concern to Israel because a good part of that population is in southern Lebanon—right next to Israel's borders. We haven't seen the end of it yet. There are Shia militias; there are all kinds of ultra-extremist Shia organizations; and there's much internal fighting among the Shia. In Lebanon they have managed to establish themselves as perhaps the dominant ethnic group there today. Twenty or thirty years ago, they were the most backward group—the hewers of wood and carriers of water.

Based on what's been happening in Lebanon, it would seem that the same sort of thing could happen in other countries in which the Shias represent a significant part of the population. This is especially so if those countries are in the Gulf closer to Iran because they could be easily incited and manipulated by the Iranians. That forecast of Shia activism and rebellion becomes even more likely if the Iranians continue to have successes in their war with Iraq.

If there were to be a collapse in the monarchies and these nations were to be radicalized, what effect would this have on Israel?

All these states have very strong anti-Israel positions. These are not states that have any tremendous military potential and don't represent any real danger to Israel. They have contributed their vast resources to the armament of Arab states that are in the state of war with Israel, and I don't suppose that would change if they were taken over by radical regimes.

ISRAEL AND LATIN AMERICA

Mexico, Central America, and Cuba

Israel has a special relationship with Mexico in that Mexico is her major supplier of oil. In the past, Mexico has purchased Israel's small transport planes for her police force and probably has bought other weapon systems. How do you see the further development of the relationship between Mexico and Israel?

In the present oil market, Israel is relatively free to buy her oil wherever she considers it to be convenient, opportune, or in her best interests. It is likely that Mexico will continue to supply Israel with oil, but I'm not sure she is or will be "the" major oil supplier. Israel, of course, is interested in a good relationship with Mexico, and these relations could be developed to the mutual advantage of the two countries. In very general terms, there's room for optimism for further strengthening of the relationship between Mexico and Israel.

Costa Rica, El Salvador, Guatemala, Honduras, Nicaragua, and Panama are Central American countries in which the United States has a vital interest in keeping out the Soviet and Cuban influences. As reported in the American press, Israel has been a major arms supplier to these nations. What should Israel's attitude be toward supplying arms to these nations or to the Contras fighting the leftist Nicaraguan regime? In other words, what should her attitude be toward those countries that are supporting the United States?

As I've said before, Israel is a member of the democratic community of nations of which the United States is the leader. When it comes to the selling of Israeli manufactured military equipment, our natural inclination is to sell—if there is a demand for this equipment—to countries or forces that are aligned with the West.

Fidel Castro's Cuba is a mortal enemy of the United States and has been since his emergence to power in 1960. Yet, Castro's Cuba and Israel maintained cordial diplomatic and economic relations until the Yom Kippur War. Given the present struggle between the United States and Cuba, should Israel seek to develop a line of communication with Cuba in order to try to re-establish the kind of relationship they had prior to the 1973 War?

Because Israel has a long-standing policy of universality of diplomatic relations, I doubt we would turn down Cuba if she wanted to establish diplomatic relations with us today. If we were to respond positively to such a request, it would not be an indication that Israel in any way supports Fidel Castro or his regime. Israel does not support these kinds of totalitarian regimes. It would simply be an indication that Israel believes in the universality of diplomatic relations. But I see no reason why Israel should pursue Cuba to try to re-establish these relationships. It was the Cubans who broke off the relationships, and it's the Cubans who would have to take the initiative to re-establish them. Israel isn't suffering any kind of penalty by the absence of these relationships, so it's a situation for the Cubans to correct, if they want to.

South America

It has been commonly recognized that if a nation has a population in excess of 100 million people and an industrial technological base, then that nation has the capability of becoming a great power and even developing to the point of doing basic research in components and materials. Brazil possesses these characteristics. It is anticipated within the next two decades that Brazil will be a great power—one of the great powers of the world. How do you foresee the relationship between Brazil and Israel developing over the next decade?

At the present time, Brazil is the tenth or eleventh country in terms of gross national product ranking. So, in many ways, you might consider her to be a power even now. She has very great potential in the future of going up in the scale of major industrial countries in the world.

Israel, being a country that has and will continue to have a very high level of technology, will be a leader in science, in technology, and in their industrial applications. I expect, therefore, that Israel will have close and mutually beneficial relationships with the industrially advanced countries in the world. If Brazil is going to be an advanced industrial country—and I think that's very likely, I would expect that there would be close relationships between Brazil and Israel.

Israel supplied Argentina with weapons before and during the Falkland War. The war is now over. How is the military relationship between Argentina and Israel developing? What kind of relationship do you see developing in the future?

Israel sold weapons to Argentina before the Falkland War, as did Great Britain. Remember, the aircraft carrier that the Argentinians used in the war was one they purchased from Great Britain. Israel did not continue sending supplies during the Falkland fighting. We were asked by the United States not to do that, and we immediately ceased shipping any supplies during the fighting. Israel has a very advanced defense industry, and, as a result, she exports defense products. South America, including Argentina, has been in the past, and I suppose will be in the future, one of the markets for those products.

Argentina has the second largest Jewish population in the Western hemisphere—almost 500,000 Jews, and there is a large Argentinian-Jewish community in Israel. Do you anticipate or foresee a large aliyah from Argentina to Israel, considering that over the years that country has exhibited such anti-Semitism that Jews have felt threatened there?

I'm not sure that your statistics are right about the size of the Jewish community in Argentina. The estimates I've heard indicate that the size of the Argentinian-Jewish community is about 1/4 million, which would make it smaller than the Canadian-Jewish community. So, it may not even rank as the second largest Jewish community in the Western hemisphere. However, that's still a very sizable Jewish community.

Over the years, there has been aliyah from Argentina to Israel, and at the present time, Argentina is one of the sources of aliyah from Western countries to Israel. In fact, aliyah from Argentina is not much smaller than aliyah from the

United States, even though Argentina has a far smaller Jewish population than the United States. We would certainly expect, hope for, and work toward increasing the immigration of Argentinian Jews to Israel.

The situation in Argentina has certainly not been conducive to Jews wanting to continue to live there. The generally unstable situation, the dictatorial regimes in the past, and the brutality used by the military caste against people in Argentina—including members of the Jewish community and anti-Semitic excesses—are conditions that would make Argentinian-Jews want to come to Israel. Perhaps we will have a sizable immigration.

Over the years, it has been rumored that Israel has been supplying arms and military training to the Chilean army. Chile has an enemy in Latin America, namely Argentina. Since the United States has never supplied modern weapons to any country in Latin America, Chile has need for an external source, as does Argentina. Are these rumors true? If not, do you foresee a military relationship or commercial tie developing between Israel and Argentina or Chile?

We have a defense industry that is significant for a small country like Israel. That defense industry is essential for Israel's security. Maintaining such a defense industry requires markets that are larger than Israel herself can provide; therefore, our defense industries do export their products. South America is one of the markets for the products of Israel's defense industry. It has not been our policy in the past, and it will not be our policy in the future, to give an itemized list of the customers of Israel's defense industry. So, there wouldn't be any point in discussing in detail just where sales are being made—whether they are being made to Argentina, Chile, or any other country—and what the future is likely to hold.

Bolivia, Columbia, Ecuador, Paraguay, Peru, and Uruguay are small, impoverished countries with limited resources and masses of people living in abject poverty. Should Israel attempt to provide projects in agriculture and infrastructure, as she did in Black Africa prior to the 1973 War, in order to establish a better position in South America?

Israel is ready to provide assistance to almost all countries that are interested in receiving her assistance, unless they happen to be countries that are intrinsically hostile to Israel or the Free World. We have provided and will continue to provide, upon request, assistance to South American countries. We are particularly inclined to give this assistance to South American countries that are democratic. We are happy to see that there's a trend in South America today toward democracy. There are a number of countries there that have moved from a dictatorship to a democratic rule. Wherever possible and whenever we can find it within our means, we do extend assistance to these countries.

ISRAEL AND THE FIFTH WORLD

South Africa

You do, obviously, understand that there has been a lot of criticism of Israel for having certain kinds of ties with South Africa that have never been officially recognized by the Israeli government. What kind of economic, military, and industrial relations is Israel maintaining with South Africa today?

I know of this criticism, but I don't understand it. I don't think there's any foundation to it. Israel believes in the universality of diplomatic relations. She is not the only country that has diplomatic relations with South Africa. The United States has diplomatic relations with South Africa. Israel is not the only country that has trade relations with South Africa, although she is certainly far from being the major trading partner.

In looking at the relationship that is maintained between Israel and South Africa, we have to bear in mind that most of the Black African nations have severed their relationships with Israel. We are not interested in maintaining a position of splendid isolation in this part of the world. We're interested in establishing evolving relationships with the countries in Africa and in Asia. We are in a particularly difficult situation when it comes to Africa because of the fact that most African countries have severed their relationships with Israel.

So, those people who direct any kind of criticism against us for maintaining relations with South Africa would be more consistent if they: first, directed that criticism against countries far larger than Israel, like the United States or other Western countries, who maintain such a relationship; and, second, directed that criticism against the Black countries of Africa that insist on not having any relationships with Israel.

Taiwan

What kind of military and economic ties does Israel have with Taiwan today?

We don't have any ties in the literal sense of the word. There are no diplomatic relations. Taiwan does not officially recognize Israel. There have been some trade relations, but they're really minimal in scope.

Along what lines do you believe Israel will develop relations with Taiwan in the future? Economic? Military? Political?

I don't foresee any great developments in this area. I don't think Israel is going to make any special efforts as long as Taiwan insists on not having any formal diplomatic relations with us.

South Korea

Has Israel been successful in developing economic ties with South Korea on any basis?

We are only at the beginning there.

Do you foresee further development and in what way do you think it could develop?

There's room for increasing relationships, particularly trade, between Israel and South Korea to the mutual benefit of both countries. South Korea is rather far away, and that makes it difficult, but in time relationships will develop.

ISRAEL AND THE NATIONS OF THE PACIFIC

Singapore

In many ways, Israel and Singapore are similar. They are small, have small populations, are surrounded by enemies, and have a need for a large military establishment relative to their size. Are these similarities sufficient to encourage a relationship between Israel and Singapore?

Singapore and Israel already have a good relationship, recognized on both sides as being of mutual benefit to the two countries.

In the past, Israel has developed economic and military ties with Singapore by being a major supplier of weapon systems. How do you see this relationship developing?

Israel has a good trade relationship with Singapore, although I can't quote you facts and figures on what the volume of that trade is. As a matter of fact, the Singapore foreign minister was in Israel recently. As to whether or not Israel is a major supplier of weapon systems to Singapore, I repeat what I've said before. It is the policy of Israel, and to my knowledge, it's the policy of all countries whose defense industries engage in exports, not to detail or itemize the list of customers, for reasons that are obvious to everybody.

Japan

Can you explain why the Japanese have taken such an anti-Israel posture in the United Nations and in international forums? Can you foresee a time when this position will change?

That's a clear case of placing commercial interests above principle. Japan is a democratic country and a member of the Free-World community. She should have a natural affinity toward and a commonality of interests with Israel, not just a commonality of values and ideals. But in the past, she has clearly given her commercial interests priority over the values and ideals. Being possibly the largest, single purchaser of oil from Arab countries, the Japanese have decided to take a very anti-Israel attitude in international forums. It's their announced policy.

Israel and Japan have formal diplomatic relationships, with all that it implies, but that's almost where it stops. Most Japanese cars are not sold in Israel. It is Japanese policy not to sell their cars in Israel and not to allow Japanese manufacturers to sell their cars in Israel. We have some, but you don't see many of the cars that you see in the United States, like the Datsun and Toyota.

That's just one of many examples of the standoffish attitude that Japan has taken toward Israel. Now again, if I'm correct in stating that this is reflective of commercial interests, as the price of oil goes down and the oil market eases up, perhaps the Japanese will feel less compelled to take that kind of position.

It is understood by most economists in the world that Japan, in the future, will be, if not the biggest country economically, certainly the second largest country in the world from the standpoint of GNP and growth of GNP. What kind of relations do you see developing with Japan, given her importance and her size? What can Israel do to overcome whatever problems exist today and encourage better relations?

As far as GNP is concerned, Japan is the third largest country in the world. She may outrank the Soviet Union someday; it's not impossible. But it's really not important whether she's second, third, or fourth, Japan is obviously a country of very great importance economically; therefore, she is a country of very great importance.

We have certainly been unhappy about the fact that the Japanese have insisted on distancing themselves from Israel to such an extent as to, in effect, preclude a good trade relationship that would be beneficial to both countries. Japan can obviously live without Israel, and Israel can live without Japan, but both countries would benefit from economic cooperation. We hope the Japanese will come to that conclusion, because Israel is certainly interested.

For many years, we didn't have a defense attaché in Tokyo. When I was Minister of Defense, I appointed an Israeli defense attaché there. I made that appointment in full realization of the very great importance that Japan has for Israel and in the hope that in the areas of defense, we could find some subjects of common interest and room for cooperation.

Do you see in the future any national interests developing that are coincidental between Japan and Israel? Where could these areas of coincidence and interests be?

In this ideologically polarized world we live in, countries that are members of the Free World—which are democracies—have common strategic interests; therefore, Japan and Israel have common strategic interests. Being a member of the Free World, Japan, I'm sure, would like to forestall Soviet penetration of different parts of the world, including—and maybe even very importantly—the Middle East. This is also Israel's interest; therefore, it behooves the two countries to work in concert in the pursuance of these interests. Sooner or later that conclusion will become apparent to the Japanese, as well.

Being a center of scientific and technologic know-how, Israel has a great deal to offer any technologically advanced country, and Japan is such a country. If a proper relationship is established, Israel and Japan will find that there are many areas in which their capabilities are complimentary and in which it pays them to work together.

Over the years, there has developed, through the efforts of one Japanese professor, a conversion to Judaism of a group of Japanese. Do you see this as a possible basis for strengthening cultural or even economic ties between Japan and Israel?

I've never met this professor, but I'm sure that the Japanese who have adopted the Jewish religion—converted to Judaism—have a greater affinity and a greater interest in Israel than the Japanese who are not Jews. If I believe there is a commonality of interests between Israelis and Japanese generally, then I believe this must certainly be true for the Japanese of the Jewish religion.

Australia and New Zealand

Israel has concentrated her economic forays into various parts of the world. One part that has been neglected includes Australia and New Zealand. Is this only because of distance, given that these two countries are part of the Western world and are, basically, part of the Western alliance of nations?

It's basically because of distance. There is a limit to what Israel can do at any one time. But, quite naturally, economic relationships between Israel and countries throughout the world will increase as time goes by, particularly, our relationships with the Western countries that share common interests with us. That, of course, is true for Australia and New Zealand.

How are economic, political, or military ties with Australia and New

Zealand developing? What relationship do you see between Israel and these countries in the future?

There is great commonality among Australia, New Zealand, countries of Western Europe, and Japan. These are all Western countries and in time they will all be industrial countries. They will find that there is complimentarity between Israeli know-how and things they want to do. There should be room for investments from Australia and New Zealand in Israel, for exports from Israel to Australia and New Zealand, and for exports from those countries to Israel. We are just at the beginning of that activity.

Officially, Australia, NATO, and Western Europe all enjoy the equivalent status of strategic ally to the United States. New Zealand also held that status until recently when her position was downgraded because she refused port-of-call for American nuclear ships. Israel does not have such an official status. Do you foresee Israel receiving that most important status of being a strategic ally to the United States?

I don't know what that official status means, and I don't even know where and in what documents it is defined. Relationships between Israel and the United States are probably closer than the relationships between the United States and any other country, including, I would dare say, Australia and New Zealand. We might just look at the case of the Lavi. There is no other Western country in the world that is producing a fighter aircraft in cooperation with the United States. To me, that continues to be an indication of the level of relationship that exist between Israel and the United States—a relationship, for the most part, unrivaled by that between the United States and any other country.

Epilogue

Recently, the American public's attitudes and perceptions of Israel, Arabs, and the Middle East have been buffeted by a number of dramatic, front-page news events. Many times it seems these events are so cataclysmic that they come to be the focus of American-Israeli relations and the relations between the United States and the Arab world. These events continue to bombard us at a dizzying pace. They seem to be the most convenient ammunition in the struggle for the hearts and minds of the American public, her elected officials, and the media.

Since I embarked on this project in June 1985, the following events have taken place: the growth in Arab terrorism against U.S. and Western targets, including the kidnapping and murder of American citizens and the bombings of cafes in Western European cities and airports; the highjacking of the ship Achilles Laura; the highjacking of the TWA jetliner; the Iran-Contra affair; the Pollard affair; Gorbachev's rise to power and his new policy of "liberalization"; the Vananu spy case; and the Syrian military occupation of West Beirut. These events certainly have had or will have their impact in the short term, but they are not issues that will determine the fundamental mutual strategic relationship between the United States and Israel. They only tend to cloud and detract from the real motivations behind American-Israeli cooperation, and the significance of these events will not make a lasting impression. For these reasons—and sometimes because of sensitivities to Israeli security—these seemingly important events have not found their way into this book.

The intent of this book is to touch upon fundamental issues that concern Israel and world Jewry, Israel and her infrastructure, and Israel and her relationship to other nations, so that it will not become out-of-date and will withstand the test of time. Most of the material in this book should be relevant for years to come— despite the radical changes which seem to occur almost daily in this troubled region. By the time this book reaches your hand, I am sure that several events will have occurred that will require clarification according to the fundamental issues which have been presented here.

Moshe Arens is confident that American-Israeli relations will continue to grow closer—regardless of the party in power or the person leading the party. I believe that, even though fundamental American policies may not change toward Israel and the Middle East, the quality of America's support for Israel will always depend on the orientation of the political party in power and its leadership.

What must not be forgotten is that nations do not have permanent allies, nor do they have permanent enemies; they have only permanent interests. Israel's problem, therefore, is not the fact that America has changed allies or enemies in the last forty years but that the interpretation of American interests has shifted in the past as new people and parties have ascended to power. These "changes of the guard" have often times caused the quality of American support for Israel to fluctuate. I have attempted to demonstrate in this book why it is in America's interest—regardless of which party is in power—for the mutual strategic relationship between the two countries to be of the highest quality.

Let this book be a testament to the fundamental interests that Israel, the Jews, and the Western world share, and let it be a beacon for clarifying the real issues we often muddle in the Middle East.

Index